EVERYDAY
Slow Cooker
& ONE DISH RECIPES

TASTE OF HOME BOOKS • RDA ENTHUSIAST BRANDS, LLC • MILWAUKEE, WI

ISBN:
D 978-1-61765-899-0
U 978-1-61765-900-3

Component Number:
D 119400049H
U 119400051H

LOCC: 1944-6382

Deputy Editor: Mark Hagen
Senior Art Director: Raeann Thompson
Editor: Christine Rukavena
Senior Designer: Courtney Lovetere
Designer: Jazmin Delgado
Copy Editor: Amy Rabideau Silvers
Food Editor: Rashanda Cobbins

Cover Photography:
Photographer: Dan Roberts
Set Stylist: Stacey Genaw
Food Stylist: Josh Rink

Pictured on front cover:
Grampa's German-Style Pot Roast, p. 16
Pictured on title page:
Shredded Lamb Sliders, p. 90
Pictured on back cover:
Hamburger Dip, p. 82; Parmesan-Crusted
Tilapia, p. 147; Double Jack Mac, p. 206

Printed in USA
1 3 5 7 9 10 8 6 4 2

**SLOW-COOKER
STRAWBERRY
SODA CAKE
PAGE 90**

Contents

More ways to connect with us:

SHOPTASTEOFHOME.COM

Family favorites are at your fingertips!

Discover 337 cherished dishes that home cooks love to serve their families. Find great recipes for the slow cooker, stovetop and oven in this three-in-one cookbook.

Flip through these pages and you'll discover hundreds of piping-hot dishes your family is sure to love—and that you will love cooking! These simple recipes are easy to prepare, reader-shared and Test Kitchen-approved. From comforting enchiladas to gooey slow-cooked pudding cake, this book is brimming with irresistible dishes you'll want in your repertoire. Hundreds of new favorites are just waiting to be discovered. Go ahead, find a new idea for dinner today!

HANDY ICONS IN THIS BOOK

🍎 Recipes are lower in calories, fat and/or sodium, as determined by a registered dietitian nutritionist.

❄ These fix-ahead dishes include directions for freezing and reheating.

BLACK BEAN & CHICKEN ENCHILADA LASAGNA
PAGE 183

77

40

Slow-Cook with Confidence

Follow these tips for slow-cooking success every time.

PLAN AHEAD TO PREP AND GO.
In most cases, you can prepare and load ingredients into the slow-cooker insert beforehand and store it in the refrigerator overnight. But an insert can crack if exposed to rapid temperature changes. Let the insert sit out just long enough to reach room temperature before placing in the slow cooker.

USE THAWED INGREDIENTS.
Although throwing frozen chicken breasts into the slow cooker may seem easy, it's not a smart shortcut. Thawing foods in a slow cooker can create the ideal environment for bacteria to grow, so thaw frozen meat and veggies ahead of time. The exception: If using a prepackaged slow-cooker meal kit, follow instructions as written.

LINE THE CROCK FOR EASE OF USE.
Some recipes in this book call for a **foil collar** or **sling.** Here's why:

▶ A **foil collar** prevents scorching of rich, saucy dishes near the slow-cooker's heating element. To make a collar, fold two 18-in.-long pieces of foil into strips 4 in. wide. Line the crock's perimeter with the strips; spray with cooking spray.

▶ A **sling** helps you lift layered foods out of the crock without much fuss. To make, fold one or more pieces of heavy-duty foil into strips. Place on bottom and up sides of the slow cooker; coat with cooking spray.

TAKE THE TIME TO BROWN.
Give yourself a few extra minutes to brown your meat in a skillet before placing in the slow cooker. Doing so will add rich color and more flavor to the finished dish.

KEEP THE LID CLOSED.
Don't peek! While it's tempting to lift the lid and check on your meal's progress, resist the urge. Every time you open the lid, you'll have to add about 30 minutes to the total cooking time.

ADJUST COOK TIME AS NEEDED.
Live at a high altitude? Slow cooking will take longer. Add about 30 minutes for each hour of cooking the recipe calls for; legumes will take about twice as long.

Want your food done sooner? Cooking one hour on high is roughly equal to two hours on low, so adjust the recipe to suit your schedule.

Stovetop Suppers Are Super Convenient

Stovetop cooking is quick and easy. In fact, many of the stovetop meals in this book need just one pot, making cleanup a breeze. Haul out your favorite skillet and let's get cooking!

CHOOSE THE RIGHT PAN FOR THE JOB.

The right cookware can simplify meal preparation when cooking on the stovetop. The basic skillets every kitchen needs include a 10- or 12-in. skillet with lid and an 8- or 9-in. saute/omelet pan.

Good quality cookware conducts heat quickly and cooks food evenly. The type of metal and thickness of the pan affect performance. Consider there pros and cons for each of the most common cookware metals:

Copper does conduct heat the best, but it is expensive, tarnishes (and usually requires periodic polishing) and reacts with acidic ingredients, which is why the interior of a copper pan is usually lined with tin or stainless steel.

109

Aluminum is a good conductor of heat and is less expensive than copper. However, aluminum reacts with acidic ingredients.

Anodized aluminum has the same positive qualities as aluminum, but the surface is electrochemically treated so it will not react to acidic ingredients. The surface is resistant to scratches and is nonstick.

Cast iron conducts heat very well. It is usually heavy. Cast iron also needs regular seasoning to prevent sticking and rusting.

122

Nonstick is especially preferred for cooking delicate foods, such as eggs, pancakes or thin fish fillets. It won't scorch foods if you're cooking batches. It can be scratched easily and has maximum temperature limitations.

Stainless steel is durable and retains its new look for years. It isn't a good conductor of heat, which is why it often has an aluminum or copper core or bottom.

152

MASTER THESE COMMON STOVETOP COOKING TECHNIQUES.

Sauteeing Add a small amount of oil to a hot skillet and heat over medium-high heat. For best results, cut food into uniform pieces before adding. Don't overcrowd in pan. Stir frequently while cooking.

Frying Pour ¼-½ in. oil into a skillet. Heat over medium-high heat until hot. The oil is ready when it shimmers (gives off visible waves of heat). Never leave the pan unattended, and don't overheat the oil or it will smoke. Pat food dry before frying and, if desired, dip in batter or coat it with crumbs. Fry, uncovered, until food is golden brown and cooked through.

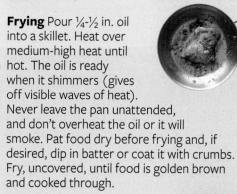

Braising Season meat; coat with flour if recipe directs. In Dutch oven, brown meat in oil in batches. To ensure nice browning, do not crowd. Set meat aside; cook vegetables, adding flour if recipe directs. Add broth gradually, stirring to deglaze pan and to keep lumps from forming. Return meat to pan and stir until mixture comes to a boil.

Steaming Place a steamer basket or bamboo steamer in a pan with water. Bring water to a boil (boiling water shouldn't touch the steamer) and place food in the basket; cover and steam. Add more boiling water to pan as necessary, making sure pan does not run dry.

202

219

Oven Entrees Bake Hands-Free

You can't beat a meal-in-one specialty for convenience and comfort. Review these hints while the oven preheats.

CHOOSE THE RIGHT BAKEWARE.

Metal baking pans Excellent conductors of heat, these create nice browning on rolls, coffee cakes and other baked goods. Metal is a safe, smart choice for under the broiler. It may react with acidic foods such as tomato sauce or cranberries and create a metallic taste or discoloration.

Glass baking dishes Glass provides slower, more even baking for egg dishes, custards and casseroles. It takes longer to heat than metal, but once heated, the dish holds the heat longer. This is undesirable for many desserts, as sugary batters may overbrown in glass. If you wish to bake in a glass dish even though the recipe calls for a metal pan, decrease the oven temperature by 25°.

Other baking dishes Ceramic or stoneware baking dishes generally perform much like glass but are more attractive. They may be safe for higher temperatures than glass; refer to the manufacturer's instructions.

CONFIRM THE OVEN'S TEMPERATURE.

Use an oven thermometer to check. Preheat oven to the desired temperature; place an oven thermometer on the center rack. Close the oven door and leave the oven on at the set temperature. Keep thermometer in the oven for 15 minutes before reading. Adjust the oven temperature accordingly to ensure best baking results.

NEGATE HOT OR COOL SPOTS.

To test your oven for uneven temperatures, try the bread test. Heat the oven to 350° while arranging six to nine slices of white bread on a large cookie sheet. Place in oven for 5-10 minutes; check if the slices are starting to brown or burn. If some slices are noticeably darker or lighter than others, the oven may have hot or cool spots. To negate this, rotate pans while baking.

ELIMINATE SPILLS—THE SMART WAY.

Line a rimmed baking sheet with foil and place it on the bottom oven rack directly below the baking dish. Any drips or spills from the recipe will fall onto the foil-lined pan instead of the oven bottom.

We don't recommend lining the bottom of your oven with aluminum foil or other liners, as there's a chance that they could melt and stick to the oven, causing damage.

Want to clean up a drip while it's still hot? Grab your oven mitt, a pair of tongs and a damp dishcloth. Use the tongs to move the cloth and help prevent burns.

199

GRAMPA'S
GERMAN-STYLE
POT ROAST
PAGE 16

74

53

35

80

Slow Cooker

Looking for crowd-pleasing party fare that's easy to keep warm? How about yummy cake to treat the family, minus the heat and hassle of baking? You'll find plenty of set-and-forget delights that everybody will love right here. We've packed in 113 amazing slow-cooked dishes, from family breakfasts and sensational sammies to exciting twists on beloved classics.

Beef & Ground Beef

PEPPERED MEAT LOAF

PEPPERED MEAT LOAF

I came up with this easy dinner one day while experimenting in the kitchen. Everyone who tries it, loves it!
—*Laura Burgess, Mount Vernon, SD*

- -

PREP: 30 min. • **COOK:** 6 hours
MAKES: 12 servings

    3 large baking potatoes, peeled
       and quartered lengthwise
    2 large eggs, lightly beaten
    1 large onion, chopped
    1 can (8 oz.) tomato sauce
    ¾ cup crushed saltines
    ½ cup ketchup
    3 garlic cloves, minced
    2 tsp. Worcestershire sauce
    ½ tsp. seasoned salt
    ½ tsp. seasoned pepper
    3 lbs. ground beef
    1 lb. spicy bulk pork sausage
SAUCE
    1 cup ketchup
    ⅓ cup packed brown sugar
   1½ tsp. ground mustard
    ½ tsp. ground nutmeg

1. Cut three 25x3-in. strips of heavy-duty foil; crisscross so they resemble spokes of a wheel. Place strips on bottom and up sides of a 6- or 7-qt. slow cooker. Coat strips with cooking spray. Top with potatoes.
2. In a large bowl, combine eggs, onion, tomato sauce, saltines, ketchup, garlic, Worcestershire sauce, seasoned salt and seasoned pepper. Add beef and sausage; mix lightly but thoroughly. Shape into a loaf; transfer to slow cooker. Combine sauce ingredients; pour over top.
3. Cook, covered, on low until a thermometer inserted into meat loaf reads at least 160° and potatoes are tender, 6-6½ hours. Using the foil strips as handles, remove meat loaf to a platter.

1 PIECE MEAT LOAF WITH 1 POTATO WEDGE: 489 cal., 25g fat (9g sat. fat), 127mg chol., 951mg sod., 37g carb. (16g sugars, 3g fiber), 29g pro.

MOO SHU LETTUCE CUPS

BEEF IN MUSHROOM GRAVY
This is one of the best and easiest meals I've ever made. It has only four ingredients, and they all go into the pot at once. The meat is nicely seasoned and makes its own gravy. It tastes wonderful over mashed potatoes.
—*Margery Bryan, Moses Lake, WA*

PREP: 10 min. • **COOK:** 7 hours
MAKES: 6 servings

- 2 to 2½ lbs. boneless beef round steak
- 1 to 2 envelopes onion soup mix
- 1 can (10¾ oz.) condensed cream of mushroom soup, undiluted
- ½ cup water
  Mashed potatoes, optional

Cut steak into 6 pieces; place in a 3-qt. slow cooker. Combine the soup mix, soup and water; pour over beef. Cover and cook on low for 7-8 hours or until meat is tender. If desired, serve with mashed potatoes.
FREEZE OPTION: Place beef in freezer containers; top with gravy. Cool and freeze. To use, partially thaw in refrigerator overnight. Heat through in a covered saucepan, gently stirring and adding a little water if necessary.
1 SERVING: 241 cal., 7g fat (2g sat. fat), 87mg chol., 810mg sod., 7g carb. (1g sugars, 1g fiber), 35g pro.

"This was delicious, inexpensive and oh-so-easy! Everyone enjoyed the tender, flavorful beef. I'm sure you could use any cut of steak you liked, but the round steak cooked up nicely in my slow cooker."
—A642483, TASTEOFHOME.COM

MOO SHU LETTUCE CUPS
I turned ordinary ground beef into a new classic. Sweet and savory flavors make this dish a dinnertime favorite. We love the meat mixture served in flour tortillas, too!
—*Christine Keating, Norwalk, CA*

PREP: 25 min. • **COOK:** 3 hours
MAKES: 4 servings

- ¼ cup apricot preserves
- 3 Tbsp. hoisin sauce
- 2 Tbsp. soy sauce
- 1 Tbsp. honey
- ½ tsp. sesame oil
- ¼ tsp. crushed red pepper flakes, optional
- 1 lb. lean ground beef (90% lean)
- ½ cup chopped onion
- 3 garlic cloves, minced
- 1 tsp. minced fresh gingerroot
- 1 cup sliced fresh mushrooms
- 1 medium carrot, diced
- 1 celery rib, diced
- ½ cup chopped sweet red pepper
- 12 Bibb lettuce leaves
  Sliced green onions

1. Mix first 5 ingredients and, if desired, pepper flakes. In a large skillet, cook and crumble beef with onion, garlic and ginger over medium heat until meat is no longer pink, 5-7 minutes. Transfer to a 3- or 4-qt. slow cooker. Add mushrooms, carrot, celery and pepper; stir in sauce mixture.
2. Cook, covered, on low until vegetables are tender and flavors are blended, 3-4 hours. Serve in lettuce leaves; sprinkle with sliced green onions.
3 FILLED LETTUCE CUPS: 311 cal., 11g fat (4g sat. fat), 71mg chol., 744mg sod., 29g carb. (19g sugars, 2g fiber), 25g pro.

SLOW-COOKER GOLOMBKI

I modified my mom's classic Polish dish to fit my hectic life. Instead of boiling the cabbage and then filling it with beef, I just toss the ingredients in the slow cooker. It's much easier and tastes just as good.
—Mary Walker, Clermont, FL

- -

PREP: 25 min. • **COOK:** 6 hours
MAKES: 8 servings

- 1   lb. ground beef
- 1   small onion, chopped
- 1   cup uncooked converted rice
- ¾   tsp. salt
- ¼   tsp. pepper
- 1   jar (24 oz.) meatless spaghetti sauce
- 2   cans (10¾ oz. each) condensed tomato soup, undiluted
- 1   cup water
- ½   tsp. sugar
- 1   medium head cabbage, chopped

1. In a large skillet, cook beef and onion over medium heat until meat is no longer pink; drain. Stir in the rice, salt and pepper. In a large bowl, combine the spaghetti sauce, soup, water and sugar.

2. In a 5-qt. slow cooker, layer one third of the sauce, half of the beef mixture and one third of the cabbage. Repeat layers; top with remaining sauce and cabbage.

3. Cook, covered, on low until cabbage and rice are tender, 6-8 hours.

1¼ CUPS: 307 cal., 7g fat (3g sat. fat), 35mg chol., 1166mg sod., 45g carb. (15g sugars, 6g fiber), 16g pro.

SPICY QUINOA STUFFED PEPPERS

Banana peppers can be tricky: Sometimes they are hot and sometimes they are not. If you want to be on the safe side, I recommend using Bianca peppers instead, which are a more sweet type of pepper.
—Danielle Lee, Sewickley, PA

- -

PREP: 45 min. • **COOK:** 3½ hours
MAKES: 4 servings

- 6   Tbsp. water
- 3   Tbsp. uncooked red or white quinoa, rinsed
- ½   lb. bulk spicy Italian sausage
- ½   lb. lean ground beef (90% lean)
- ½   cup tomato sauce

- 2   green onions, chopped
- 2   garlic cloves, minced
- 1½ tsp. Sriracha chili sauce
- ½   tsp. chili powder
- ¼   tsp. salt
- ⅛   tsp. pepper
- 16 mild banana peppers
- 2   cups reduced-sodium spicy V8 juice

1. In a small saucepan, bring water to a boil. Add quinoa. Reduce heat; simmer, covered, until liquid is absorbed, 12-15 minutes. Remove from heat; fluff with a fork.

2. In a large bowl, combine sausage, beef, tomato sauce, green onions, garlic, chili sauce, chili powder, salt, pepper and cooked quinoa. Cut and discard tops from banana peppers; remove seeds. Fill peppers with meat mixture.

3. Stand peppers upright in a 4-qt. slow cooker. Pour V8 juice over top. Cook, covered, on low until peppers are tender, 3½-4½ hours.

FREEZE OPTION: Freeze cooled stuffed peppers and sauce in freezer containers. To use, partially thaw in refrigerator overnight. Place in a microwave-safe dish, cover and microwave on high until heated through.

4 STUFFED PEPPERS: 412 cal., 22g fat (7g sat. fat), 74mg chol., 965mg sod., 29g carb. (11g sugars, 13g fiber), 26g pro.

TEST KITCHEN TIP

If you have leftover quinoa, feel free to substitute ½ cup of cooked quinoa in the filling. If you can't find banana peppers, try Bianca peppers or regular bell peppers.

SPICY QUINOA STUFFED PEPPERS

SLOW-COOKER MEATBALL STEW

HEALTHY SLOW-COOKED MEAT LOAF

What could be easier than this recipe for an Italian-inspired meat loaf made in the slow cooker? No fuss, easy cleanup and great taste; it's all right here!
—*Sharon Delaney-Chronis, South Milwaukee, WI*

- -

PREP: 15 min. • **COOK:** 3 hours
MAKES: 8 servings

- 1 **cup soft bread crumbs**
- 1½ **cups spaghetti sauce, divided**
- 1 **large egg, lightly beaten**
- 2 **Tbsp. dried minced onion**
- 1 **tsp. salt**
- ½ **tsp. garlic powder**
- ½ **tsp. Italian seasoning**
- ¼ **tsp. pepper**
- 2 **lbs. lean ground beef (90% lean)**

1. Cut four 20x3-in. strips of heavy-duty foil and crisscross so they resemble spokes of a wheel. Place strips on the bottom and up the sides of a 3-qt. slow cooker. Coat strips with cooking spray.
2. In a large bowl, combine bread crumbs, 1 cup spaghetti sauce, egg, onion, and seasonings. Crumble beef over mixture and mix well. Shape into a loaf; place in the center of the strips.
3. Spoon remaining the spaghetti sauce over meat loaf. Cover and cook on low for 3-4 hours or until a thermometer reads 160°. Using foil strips as handles, remove meat loaf to a platter.

1 SLICE: 243 cal., 12g fat (4g sat. fat), 98mg chol., 635mg sod., 8g carb. (4g sugars, 1g fiber), 24g pro. **DIABETIC EXCHANGES:** 3 lean meat, 1 fat, ½ starch.

TEST KITCHEN TIP

If you don't have Italian seasoning, you can mix up your own with equal amounts of basil, thyme, rosemary and oregano. You can also add parsley flakes, marjoram, sage, savory or garlic powder.

SLOW-COOKER MEATBALL STEW

This recipe was a lifesaver when I worked full time and needed a dinner the kids would enjoy when we got home. It is perfect to let your young ones help prepare. They can chop, peel, mix and pour. It doesn't matter if the veggies are all different sizes—your children will still devour this fun and tasty stew.
—*Kallee Krong-Mccreery, Escondido, CA*

- -

PREP: 20 min. • **COOK:** 6 hours
MAKES: 8 servings

- 4 **peeled medium potatoes, cut into ½-in. cubes**
- 4 **medium carrots, cut into ½-in. cubes**
- 2 **celery ribs, cut into ½-in. cubes**
- 1 **medium onion, diced**
- ¼ **cup frozen corn (if your elephant likes corn; optional if not)**
- 1 **pkg. (28 to 32 oz.) frozen fully cooked home-style meatballs**
- 1½ **cups ketchup**
- 1½ **cups water**
- 1 **Tbsp. white vinegar**
- 1 **tsp. dried basil**
   Biscuits or dinner rolls, optional

In a 5-qt. slow cooker, combine potatoes, carrots, celery and onion; add corn if desired. Add meatballs. In a bowl, mix ketchup, water, vinegar and basil; pour over meatballs. Cook, covered, on low until meatballs are cooked through, 6-8 hours. If desired, serve with biscuits or dinner rolls.

1 CUP: 449 cal., 26g fat (12g sat. fat), 41mg chol., 1322mg sod., 40g carb. (17g sugars, 4g fiber), 16g pro.

MEATBALL
TORTELLINI

MEATBALL TORTELLINI

I combined some favorite staples from our freezer and pantry to come up with this easy dish. It uses just a few ingredients and requires little preparation.
—Tracie Bergeron, Chauvin, LA

PREP: 10 min. • **COOK:** 3 hours
MAKES: 6 servings

- 1 pkg. frozen fully cooked Italian meatballs (12 oz.), thawed
- 2 cups uncooked dried cheese tortellini
- 2 cans (10¾ oz. each) condensed cream of mushroom soup, undiluted
- 2¼ cups water
- 1 tsp. Creole seasoning
- 1 pkg. (16 oz.) frozen California-blend vegetables, thawed

1. In a 3-qt. slow cooker, combine meatballs and tortellini. In a large bowl, whisk soup, water and Creole seasoning. Pour over meatball mixture; stir well.

2. Cook, covered, on low until tortellini are tender, 3-4 hours. Add vegetables during last half-hour of cooking.

NOTE: The following spices may be substituted for 1 tsp. Creole seasoning: ¼ tsp. each salt, garlic powder and paprika; and a pinch each of dried thyme, ground cumin and cayenne pepper.

1 CUP: 408 cal., 23g fat (10g sat. fat), 55mg chol., 1592mg sod., 35g carb. (3g sugars, 6g fiber), 16g pro.

"Loved how easy this was to make, with items I normally keep on hand in the freezer or pantry until ready to use. Tasted quite yummy also!"
—LIBBIPEACH, TASTEOFHOME.COM

CARIBBEAN BEEF SHORT RIBS

CARIBBEAN BEEF SHORT RIBS

This is a fantastic change of pace from a typical slow-cooker beef dish. Its combination of flavors—short ribs, rum and fruit—make it feel like an exotic Caribbean treat.
—Loanne Chiu, Fort Worth, TX

PREP: 30 min. • **COOK:** 5½ hours
MAKES: 8 servings

- 3 lbs. boneless beef short ribs, cut into 1½-in. pieces
- ¼ cup olive oil
- ⅔ cup thawed pineapple juice concentrate
- ⅔ cup reduced-sodium soy sauce
- ½ cup water
- ⅓ cup rum
- ⅓ cup honey
- 2 Tbsp. minced fresh gingerroot
- 6 garlic cloves, minced
- 2 tsp. pepper
- 1 tsp. ground allspice
- ½ tsp. salt
- 2 large sweet red peppers, chopped
- 2 cups cubed fresh pineapple
- 2 cups cubed peeled mango
- 6 green onions, cut into 1-in. pieces
- 2 Tbsp. cornstarch
- 2 Tbsp. cold water
- Lettuce leaves

1. In a large skillet, brown ribs in oil in batches on all sides. Transfer to a 4-qt. slow cooker.

2. Add the pineapple juice concentrate, soy sauce, water, rum, honey, ginger, garlic, pepper, allspice and salt to the skillet. Bring to a boil; reduce heat and simmer for 5 minutes. Pour over ribs.

3. Cover and cook on low for 5-6 hours or until meat is tender. Stir in red peppers. Top with the pineapple, mango and onions (do not stir). Cover and cook 30 minutes longer or until heated through.

4. Remove beef mixture to a large bowl; keep warm. Transfer cooking juices to a small saucepan. Combine cornstarch and cold water until smooth; gradually stir into pan. Bring to a boil; cook and stir for 2 minutes or until thickened. Serve beef mixture on lettuce; drizzle with sauce.

1 CUP BEEF MIXTURE WITH ⅓ CUP SAUCE: 450 cal., 20g fat (7g sat. fat), 68mg chol., 1004mg sod., 42g carb. (34g sugars, 3g fiber), 26g pro.

CABBAGE ROLL STEW

A head of cabbage seems like it never ends. Here's a delicious way to use it up. My husband is this stew's biggest fan.
—*Pamela Kennemer, Sand Springs, OK*

PREP: 25 min. • **COOK:** 5 hours
MAKES: 8 servings (3 qt.)

- 2 cans (14½ oz. each) petite diced tomatoes, drained
- 1 can (14½ oz.) reduced-sodium beef broth
- 1 can (8 oz.) tomato sauce
- 1 Tbsp. cider vinegar
- 1 Tbsp. Worcestershire sauce
- 1 tsp. garlic powder
- 1 tsp. Cajun seasoning
- ½ tsp. salt
- ½ tsp. pepper
- 1 medium head cabbage (about 2 lbs.), cut into 1½-in. pieces
- 1½ lbs. ground beef
- ½ lb. bulk Italian sausage
- 1 medium onion, chopped
- 3 garlic cloves, minced
  Hot cooked rice and chopped fresh parsley, optional

1. Mix first 9 ingredients. Place cabbage in a 5- or 6-qt. slow cooker.
2. In a large skillet, cook and crumble beef and sausage with onion and garlic over medium-high heat until no longer pink, 7-9 minutes; drain. Spoon over cabbage; top with tomato mixture.
3. Cook, covered, on low until cabbage is tender and flavors are blended, 5-6 hours. If desired, serve with hot rice and sprinkle with chopped parsley.
FREEZE OPTION: Freeze the cooled meat mixture in freezer containers. To use, partially thaw in refrigerator overnight. Heat through in a saucepan, stirring occasionally.
1½ CUPS CABBAGE MIXTURE: 195 cal., 11g fat (4g sat. fat), 46mg chol., 564mg sod., 11g carb. (6g sugars, 4g fiber), 14g pro.

GRAMPA'S
GERMAN-STYLE
POT ROAST

GRAMPA'S GERMAN-STYLE POT ROAST

Grampa was of German heritage and loved the Old Country recipes given to him by his mother. I made a few changes to give this recipe an updated flavor and to use my slow cooker instead of the oven.
—*Nancy Heishman, Las Vegas, NV*

PREP: 20 min. • **COOK:** 6 hours
MAKES: 8 servings

- 4 thick-sliced bacon strips
- 1 lb. baby Yukon Gold potatoes
- 4 medium carrots, sliced
- 1 can (14 oz.) sauerkraut, rinsed and well drained
- ¾ cup chopped dill pickles
- 1 tsp. smoked paprika
- 1 tsp. ground allspice
- ½ tsp. kosher salt
- ½ tsp. pepper
- 1 boneless beef chuck roast (3 lbs.)
- 2 pkg. (14.4 oz. each) frozen pearl onions, thawed
- 4 garlic cloves, minced
- ½ cup stout beer or beef broth
- ⅓ cup Dusseldorf mustard
- ½ cup sour cream
- ½ cup minced fresh parsley

1. In a large skillet, cook bacon over medium heat until crisp. Remove to paper towels to drain.
2. Meanwhile, place the potatoes, carrots, sauerkraut and pickles in a 7-qt. slow cooker. Mix paprika, allspice, salt and pepper; rub over roast. Brown roast in drippings over medium heat. Transfer to slow cooker. Add onions and garlic to drippings; cook and stir 1 minute. Stir in beer and mustard; pour over meat. Crumble bacon; add to slow cooker.
3. Cook, covered, on low until meat and vegetables are tender, 6-8 hours. Remove roast; let stand 10 minutes before slicing. Strain cooking juices. Reserve vegetables and juices; skim fat. Return reserved vegetables and cooking juices to slow cooker. Stir in sour cream; heat through. Serve with the roast; sprinkle with parsley.
1 SERVING: 552 cal., 31g fat (12g sat. fat), 127mg chol., 926mg sod., 28g carb. (9g sugars, 6g fiber), 39g pro.

SLOW-COOKER BEEF BARBACOA

I love this beef barbacoa because the meat is fall-apart tender and the sauce is smoky, slightly spicy and so flavorful. It's an amazing alternative to ground beef tacos or even pulled pork carnitas. It's also versatile. You can have a soft taco bar and let people make their own—or offer mouthwatering Mexican pizzas or rice bowls.
—Holly Sander, Lake Mary, FL

- -

PREP: 20 min. • **COOK:** 6 hours
MAKES: 8 servings

- 1 beef rump or bottom round roast (3 lbs.)
- ½ cup minced fresh cilantro
- ⅓ cup tomato paste
- 8 garlic cloves, minced
- 2 Tbsp. chipotle peppers in adobo sauce, plus 1 Tbsp. sauce
- 2 Tbsp. cider vinegar
- 4 tsp. ground cumin
- 1 Tbsp. brown sugar
- 1½ tsp. salt
- 1 tsp. pepper
- 1 cup beef stock
- 1 cup beer or additional stock
- 16 corn tortillas (6 in.)
  Pico de gallo
  Optional toppings: Lime wedges, queso and additional cilantro

1. Cut roast in half. Mix next 9 ingredients; rub over roast. Place in a 5-qt. slow cooker. Add stock and beer. Cook, covered, until meat is tender, 6-8 hours.

2. Remove the roast; shred with 2 forks. Reserve 3 cups cooking juices; discard remaining juices. Skim fat from reserved juices. Return beef and reserved juices to slow cooker; heat through.

3. Serve with tortillas and pico de gallo. If desired, serve with lime wedges, queso fresco and additional cilantro.

FREEZE OPTION: Place shredded beef in freezer containers. Cool and freeze. To use, partially thaw in refrigerator overnight. Heat through in a covered saucepan, stirring gently. Add a little broth if necessary.

2 FILLED TORTILLAS: 361 cal., 10g fat (3g sat. fat), 101mg chol., 652mg sod., 28g carb. (4g sugars, 4g fiber), 38g pro. **DIABETIC EXCHANGES:** 5 lean meat, 2 starch.

SWEDISH MEATBALLS ALFREDO

I'm a big fan of this potluck-perfect dish. It takes much less time than many other slow-cooker recipes. Plus, it's easy. I'm all for the easy!
—Carole Bess White, Portland, OR

- -

PREP: 10 min. • **COOK:** 2 hours
MAKES: 10 servings

- 2 jars (15 oz. each) roasted garlic Alfredo sauce
- 2 cups heavy whipping cream
- 2 cups sour cream
- ¾ tsp. hot pepper sauce
- ½ tsp. garlic powder
- ½ tsp. dill weed
- ⅛ tsp. pepper
- 1 pkg. (32 oz.) frozen fully cooked Swedish meatballs, thawed
  Paprika
  Hot cooked egg noodles

1. In a 5-qt. slow cooker, combine the first 7 ingredients. Stir in meatballs. Cook, covered, on low until meatballs are heated through, 2-3 hours.

2. Sprinkle with paprika. Serve with noodles.
1 CUP: 766 cal., 67g fat (38g sat. fat), 238mg chol., 1357mg sod., 16g carb. (7g sugars, 2g fiber), 21g pro.

SLOW-COOKER
BEEF BARBACOA

FAVORITE BEEF ROAST DINNER

TEXAS CHILI FRIES

The delicious chili goes together in minutes and then cooks while you run errands. The only way to make it even better is to pour it over crisp french fries and sprinkle with cheese.

—*Joan Hallford, North Richland Hills, TX*

- -

PREP: 20 min. • **COOK:** 6 hours
MAKES: 16 servings

- 1 medium onion, chopped
- 1 medium carrot, finely chopped
- 2 lbs. beef stew meat (cut into ½-in. pieces)
- 3 Tbsp. all-purpose flour, divided
- 2 Tbsp. canola oil
- 1 can (14½ oz.) Mexican diced tomatoes
- 1 envelope (1.25 oz.) chili seasoning mix
- 1 can (15 oz.) pinto beans, rinsed and drained
- 1 medium green pepper, chopped
- 1 jalapeno pepper, seeded and finely chopped
- 2 pkg. (32 oz. each) frozen french-fried potatoes
- 2 cups shredded sharp cheddar cheese
  Optional toppings: Sour cream and sliced jalapeno peppers

1. Place onion and carrot in a 5-qt. slow cooker. Toss beef with 2 Tbsp. flour. In a Dutch oven, heat oil over medium heat; brown beef in batches. Transfer meat to slow cooker.
2. Drain tomatoes; reserving liquid. In a small bowl, whisk drained tomato liquid, chili seasoning and remaining flour until blended; pour over beef. Stir in tomatoes, beans and peppers. Cook, covered, on low until meat is tender, about 6 hours.
3. Prepare fries according to the package directions. Serve chili over fries; sprinkle with cheese. If desired, top with sour cream and jalapeno slices.
1 SERVING: 374 cal., 16g fat (6g sat. fat), 49mg chol., 824mg sod., 32g carb. (4g sugars, 5g fiber), 19g pro.

FAVORITE BEEF ROAST DINNER

This is our family's favorite slow-cooked beef. My two children love it and always want seconds. I love putting together new flavor combos in the kitchen.

—*Sheryl Padilla, Peyton, CO*

- -

PREP: 15 min. • **COOK:** 6 hours
MAKES: 8 servings

- 4 medium potatoes, peeled and quartered
- ½ lb. fresh baby carrots
- 1 boneless beef chuck roast (3 to 4 lbs.)
- 4½ tsp. dried minced onion
- 3 garlic cloves, minced
- 1 Tbsp. Worcestershire sauce
- 1 tsp. garlic salt
- 1 tsp. celery seed
- 1 tsp. dried oregano
- 1 tsp. dried thyme
- 1 tsp. pepper

1. Place the potatoes, carrots and roast in a 6-qt. slow cooker. Sprinkle with remaining ingredients. Cover and cook on low 6-8 hours or until meat and vegetables are tender.
2. Skim fat from cooking juices; serve with roast and vegetables.
5 OZ. COOKED BEEF WITH ¾ CUP VEGETABLES AND 3 TBSP. COOKING JUICES: 368 cal., 16g fat (6g sat. fat), 111mg chol., 342mg sod., 19g carb. (3g sugars, 2g fiber), 35g pro. **DIABETIC EXCHANGES:** 5 lean meat, 1 starch.

DID YOU KNOW?

Worcestershire sauce was originally considered a mistake. In 1835, an English lord commissioned two chemists to duplicate a sauce he had tried in India. The pungent batch was disappointing and wound up in their cellar. When the pair stumbled upon the aged concoction two years later, they were pleasantly surprised by its unique taste.

TEXAS CHILI FRIES

SLOW-COOKED GREEN CHILI BEEF BURRITOS

This recipe gets rave reviews every time I make it. The shredded beef has a luscious slow-cooked flavor that you can't get anywhere else.
—*Jenny Flake, Newport Beach, CA*

PREP: 30 min. • **COOK:** 9 hours
MAKES: 12 servings

- 1 boneless beef chuck roast (3 lbs.)
- 1 can (14½ oz.) beef broth
- 2 cups green enchilada sauce
- 1 can (4 oz.) chopped green chilies
- ½ cup Mexican-style hot tomato sauce
- ½ tsp. salt
- ½ tsp. garlic powder
- ½ tsp. pepper.
- 12 flour tortillas (12 in.)
  Optional toppings: shredded lettuce, chopped tomatoes, shredded cheddar cheese and sour cream

1. Cut roast in half and place in a 3- or 4-qt. slow cooker. Add broth. Cover and cook on low for 8-9 hours or until meat is tender.
2. Remove beef. When cool enough to handle, shred meat with 2 forks. Skim fat from cooking liquid; reserve ½ cup liquid. Return shredded beef and reserved liquid to the slow cooker. Stir in the enchilada sauce, green chilies, tomato sauce, salt, garlic powder and pepper.
3. Cover and cook on low for 1 hour or until heated through. Spoon beef mixture down the center of tortillas; add toppings of your choice. Roll up.
NOTE: This recipe was tested with El Pato brand Mexican-style hot tomato sauce. If you cannot find Mexican-style hot tomato sauce, you may substitute ½ cup tomato sauce, 1 tsp. hot pepper sauce, ⅛ tsp. onion powder and ⅛ tsp. chili powder.
1 SERVING: 419 cal., 17g fat (6g sat. fat), 74mg chol., 1175mg sod., 36g carb. (2g sugars, 5g fiber), 29g pro.

CHILI MACARONI & CHEESE

CHILI MACARONI & CHEESE

What could be tastier on a cold winter day than chili or mac and cheese? Put them together and you have a terrific dish that warms you up and fills you up as well!
—*Nancy Foust, Stoneboro, PA*

PREP: 25 min. • **COOK:** 5 hours
MAKES: 12 servings (4½ qt.)

- 2½ lbs. lean ground beef (90% lean)
- 1 medium onion, chopped
- 1 medium green pepper, chopped
- 1 banana pepper, finely chopped
- 2 cans (28 oz. each) diced tomatoes, undrained
- 2 cans (16 oz. each) kidney beans, rinsed and drained
- 2½ tsp. chili powder
- 2 tsp. ground cumin

- 2 cups uncooked elbow macaroni
- 4 cups (16 oz.) shredded cheddar cheese
  Optional toppings: Sour cream and additional shredded cheddar cheese

1. In a Dutch oven, cook beef, onion and peppers over medium-high heat until beef is no longer pink and vegetables are tender, breaking up beef into crumbles, 8-10 minutes; drain. Transfer to a 7-qt. slow cooker. Stir in tomatoes, beans, chili powder and cumin. Cook, covered, on low until flavors are blended, 5-6 hours.
2. Meanwhile, cook macaroni according to the package directions; drain. Add to slow cooker. Stir in cheese until melted. If desired, serve with sour cream and additional cheese.
1½ CUPS: 447 cal., 21g fat (10g sat. fat), 96mg chol., 646mg sod., 30g carb. (7g sugars, 7g fiber), 35g pro.

SLOW-COOKER SALSA ROAST

This is so easy and fast to put together on your way out the door in the morning—and so good when you come home! Try it with rice or on soft tacos, or pile it on hamburger buns.

—*LaVonne Peden, Olympia, WA*

- -

PREP: 15 min. • **COOK:** 6 hours + standing
MAKES: 8 servings (2 cups gravy)

- ¼ tsp. garlic salt
- ¼ tsp. pepper
- 1 boneless beef chuck roast (3½ to 4 lbs.)
- 1 Tbsp. canola oil
- 1 jar (24 oz.) salsa
- 1 cup water
- 1 small onion, chopped
- 1 jalapeno pepper, seeded and finely chopped
- 1 envelope taco seasoning
- 1 Tbsp. cornstarch
- 1 Tbsp. cold water

1. Sprinkle roast with garlic salt and pepper. In a large skillet, heat oil over medium heat; brown roast on all sides. Transfer meat to a 5-qt. slow cooker. In a small bowl, combine salsa, water, onion, jalapeno and taco seasoning; pour over roast. Cook, covered, on low until meat is tender, 6-7 hours.

2. Remove the roast from slow cooker; tent with foil. Let stand 15 minutes before slicing. Reserve 2 cups cooking juices from slow cooker; discard remaining juices. Skim fat from reserved juices.

3. Transfer to a small saucepan; bring to a boil. In a small bowl, mix cornstarch and water until smooth; stir into salsa mixture. Return to a boil, stirring constantly; cook and stir until thickened, 1-2 minutes. Serve with roast.

NOTE: Wear disposable gloves when cutting hot peppers; the oils can burn skin. Avoid touching your face.

5 OZ. COOKED BEEF WITH ¼ CUP SAUCE: 402 cal., 21g fat (7g sat. fat), 129mg chol., 884mg sod., 11g carb. (3g sugars, 0 fiber), 39g pro.

SEASONED SHORT RIBS

These juicy barbecue-style short ribs are sure to be a hit with your family. Line the broiler pan with foil for easy cleanup.

—*Taste of Home Test Kitchen*

- -

PREP: 25 min. • **COOK:** 6 hours
MAKES: 4 servings

- 1½ cups tomato juice
- ½ cup maple syrup
- ¼ cup chopped onion
- 3 Tbsp. cider vinegar
- 1 Tbsp. Worcestershire sauce
- 1 Tbsp. Dijon mustard
- 2 tsp. minced garlic
- ¼ tsp. ground cinnamon
- ¼ tsp. ground cloves
- 4 lbs. bone-in beef short ribs
- 1 tsp. pepper
- 1 Tbsp. cornstarch
- 2 Tbsp. cold water

1. In a small bowl, combine first 9 ingredients; set aside. Cut ribs into serving pieces; place on a broiler pan. Sprinkle with pepper. Broil 4-6 in. from the heat for 3-5 minutes on each side or until browned; drain on paper towels.

2. Place ribs in a 5-qt. slow cooker; top with tomato juice mixture. Cover and cook on low for 6-7 hours or until meat is tender.

3. In a small bowl, combine cornstarch and cold water until smooth. Pour 1 cup cooking liquid into a small saucepan; skim off fat. Bring to a boil; stir in cornstarch mixture. Return to a boil; cook and stir for 2 minutes or until thickened. Serve over ribs.

1 SERVING: 1169 cal., 92g fat (39g sat. fat), 206mg chol., 538mg sod., 34g carb. (29g sugars, 1g fiber), 48g pro.

"This recipe turned out so good! These are the best ribs I have ever had. I forgot the last step of thickening the sauce with cornstarch, and it was still delicious. Highly recommend this recipe."

— SUGARBUSCH, TASTEOFHOME.COM

SLOW-COOKER SALSA ROAST

Poultry

**BOURBON BARBECUE
CHICKEN TACOS**

BOURBON BARBECUE CHICKEN TACOS

I wanted to try a different take on taco night and decided on barbecue for the theme. Even my father enjoyed this taco, and he doesn't care for tacos.
—LaDale Hymer, Cleveland, OK

PREP: 30 min. • **COOK:** 3 hours
MAKES: 8 servings

- 1 cup ketchup
- 1 small red onion, finely chopped
- ¼ cup packed brown sugar
- 2 Tbsp. Worcestershire sauce
- 2 Tbsp. maple syrup
- 2 Tbsp. cider vinegar
- 1 Tbsp. chopped fresh parsley
- 2 garlic cloves, minced
- ¼ tsp. pepper
- 3 Tbsp. bourbon, divided
- 1½ lbs. boneless skinless chicken breasts

SALSA

- 2 cups fresh or thawed frozen corn
- 1 cup chopped sweet red pepper
- ½ cup finely chopped red onion
- 2 medium limes, zested and juiced
- ⅛ tsp. hot pepper sauce
- ½ tsp. salt
- ¼ tsp. pepper
- 8 flour tortillas (8 in.)
  Minced cilantro, optional

1. In a 3-qt. slow cooker, combine the first 9 ingredients and 2 Tbsp. bourbon. Add chicken; turn to coat. Cook, covered, on low until a thermometer reads 165°, 3-4 hours. Remove chicken; shred with 2 forks. Return to slow cooker; stir in remaining bourbon. Heat through.
2. Meanwhile, for salsa, combine corn, red pepper, onion, lime juice, lime zest, hot sauce, salt, and pepper in a bowl. Serve shredded chicken in tortillas with salsa. If desired, top with cilantro.
1 TACO: 387 cal., 6g fat (2g sat. fat), 47mg chol., 855mg sod., 58g carb. (22g sugars, 4g fiber), 23g pro.

SLOW-COOKER ORANGE CHICKEN

BEST ITALIAN CHICKEN

A friend gave me this easy recipe years ago, and I've adjusted the spices over time to suit my family's tastes. They ask me to make it at least twice a month.
—*Judi Guizado, Rancho Cucamonga, CA*

PREP: 20 min. • **COOK:** 3 hours
MAKES: 6 servings

- 6 boneless skinless chicken breast halves
- 1 can (14½ oz.) Italian stewed tomatoes
- ¾ cup plus 3 Tbsp. water, divided
- 2 Tbsp. dried minced onion
- 2 tsp. chicken bouillon granules
- 2 tsp. chili powder
- ½ tsp. dried tarragon
- ½ tsp. Italian seasoning
- ¼ tsp. garlic powder
- 3 Tbsp. cornstarch
  Hot cooked rice

1. Place chicken in a 5-qt. slow cooker. In a small bowl, combine the tomatoes, ¾ cup water, onion, bouillon and seasonings; pour over chicken. Cover and cook on low for 3-4 hours or until a thermometer reads 170°.
2. Transfer chicken to a serving platter; keep warm. Transfer cooking juices to a small saucepan; bring to a boil. Combine cornstarch and remaining water until smooth. Gradually stir into the pan. Bring to a boil; cook and stir for 2 minutes or until thickened. Serve with chicken and rice.
1 SERVING: 285 cal., 5g fat (2g sat. fat), 125mg chol., 627mg sod., 10g carb. (4g sugars, 2g fiber), 47g pro.

"I thought this was great. However, I used chicken broth in place of the water and bouillon granules. I've never liked the strong taste of bouillon. Otherwise perfect!"
—TSUOP, TASTEOFHOME.COM

SLOW-COOKER ORANGE CHICKEN

This is a family-friendly recipe that even the kids will like. It's simple to prepare and flavorful enough to share with dinner guests.
—*Sherry Kozlowski, Morgantown, WV*

PREP: 20 min. • **COOK:** 3½ hours
MAKES: 6 servings

- 1 cup chicken broth
- 1 cup orange juice
- ½ cup honey
- ½ cup packed brown sugar
- 1 to 2 tsp. crushed red pepper flakes
- 2 Tbsp. rice vinegar
- 1 Tbsp. soy sauce
- 1 Tbsp. sesame oil
- 2 garlic cloves, minced
- ¼ tsp. ground ginger
- 6 boneless skinless chicken breast halves (about 6 oz. each)
- 3 Tbsp. cornstarch
- ¼ cup water
- 4 oz. uncooked rice noodles
  Chopped green onions

1. Combine first 10 ingredients until well mixed. Place chicken in a 4- or 5-qt. slow cooker; add broth mixture. Cook, covered, on low until tender, 3-4 hours. Remove chicken; when cool enough to handle, coarsely shred meat with 2 forks. Set aside.
2. In a small bowl, mix cornstarch and water until smooth; stir into cooking juices. Return chicken to slow cooker; add noodles. Cook, covered, on low for 15 minutes. Stir noodles; cook until thickened and noodles are tender, 15 minutes longer. Serve with green onions.
1 SERVING: 473 cal., 6g fat (1g sat. fat), 95mg chol., 520mg sod., 67g carb. (46g sugars, 1g fiber), 36g pro.

**FIERY SWEET
CHICKEN THIGHS**

FIERY SWEET CHICKEN THIGHS

This zesty chicken dish combines my love of spicy hot Thai food with a sweet, almost barbecuelike sauce.
—*Eve Gray, Marietta, GA*

- -

PREP: 15 min. • **COOK:** 4 hours
MAKES: 8 servings

- 2　Tbsp. peanut oil
- 4　lbs. boneless skinless chicken thighs
- 3　poblano peppers, chopped
- 1　medium onion, finely chopped
- 4　garlic cloves, minced
- ¾　cup apricot brandy or chicken broth
- ½　to 1 cup chili garlic sauce
- 2　to 3 Tbsp. Thai red chili paste

1. In a large skillet, heat oil over medium-high heat. Brown chicken in batches. Transfer to a 4- or 5-qt. slow cooker. Add the poblanos and onion to drippings; cook and stir until crisp-tender, 4-5 minutes. Add the garlic; cook 1 minute longer.
2. Remove from heat; add brandy. Cook over medium-high heat, stirring to loosen browned bits from pan. Stir in chili garlic sauce and chili paste; pour over chicken.
3. Cook, covered, on low until a meat thermometer inserted into chicken reads 165°, 4-5 hours.
1 SERVING: 421 cal., 21g fat (5g sat. fat), 152mg chol., 611mg sod., 8g carb. (5g sugars, 1g fiber), 43g pro.

TEST KITCHEN TIP
If you don't have apricot brandy but want a bit of the sweetness and complexity it would lend this dish, use chicken broth and 1-2 Tbsp. of apricot jam or orange marmalade.

SLOW-COOKER CHICKEN STROGANOFF

SLOW-COOKER CHICKEN STROGANOFF

This recipe is creamy, warm, satisfying and fairly inexpensive—and needs just a few ingredients! Who could ask for more on a cold winter evening? I will admit, though, that I have been known to make it during the summer, too.
—*Jason Kretzer, Grants Pass, OR*

- -

PREP: 15 min. • **COOK:** 4½ hours
MAKES: 8 servings

- 3　lbs. boneless skinless chicken thighs, cut into 1-in. pieces
- 2　cans (10½ oz. each) condensed cream of chicken with herbs soup, undiluted
- ½　cup dry white wine or chicken broth
- ½　lb. sliced baby portobello mushrooms
- 2　cups sour cream
- ¾　tsp. salt
　　Hot cooked egg noodles
　　Pepper
　　Chopped fresh parsley, optional

1. Place chicken, soup and wine in a 5- or 6-qt. slow cooker. Cook, covered, on high until a thermometer inserted into chicken reads at least 165°, about 3 hours. Cut chicken into bite-sized pieces; return to slow cooker.
2. Add sliced mushrooms. Cook, covered, on high until mushrooms are tender, 1½-2 hours longer. Stir in sour cream and salt. Serve with egg noodles; sprinkle with pepper and, if desired, parsley.
1⅓ CUPS: 447 cal., 29g fat (12g sat. fat), 133mg chol., 877mg sod., 9g carb. (3g sugars, 2g fiber), 36g pro.

ROSEMARY MUSHROOM CHICKEN

A delicate hint of rosemary lightly seasons the rich, creamy mushroom gravy in this savory dish. Cooking the chicken and gravy together cuts so much time during the dinner rush. Add noodles or rice for a complete supper.
—*Genny Monchamp, Redding, CA*

PREP: 30 min. • **COOK:** 7 hours
MAKES: 6 servings

- 6 chicken leg quarters, skin removed
- 2 cups sliced fresh mushrooms
- 2 cans (10¾ oz. each) condensed cream of mushroom soup, undiluted
- ½ cup white wine or chicken broth
- 1 tsp. garlic salt
- 1 tsp. dried rosemary, crushed
- ½ tsp. paprika
- ⅛ tsp. pepper
  Hot cooked egg noodles

Place chicken quarters in a 5- or 6-qt. slow cooker coated with cooking spray; top with mushrooms. Combine the soup, wine, garlic salt, rosemary, paprika and pepper; pour over top. Cover and cook on low for 7-9 hours or until chicken is tender. Serve with noodles.

1 SERVING: 294 cal., 14g fat (3g sat. fat), 94mg chol., 1107mg sod., 9 g carb. (1g sugars, 1g fiber), 28g pro.

"I've used virtually the same recipe for years—but on the stovetop. Mine suggests browning the chicken (and I use either skinless chicken breasts or thighs) in a deep frying pan, then adding the other ingredients and simmering with the lid on for about 45 minutes. I'm a little more generous with the rosemary and pepper. My family loves this! While it's cooking I get the veggies, salad and potatoes ready. I'll have to try it in my slow cooker now that I've seen this."
—REGI M, TASTEOFHOME.COM

BBQ CHICKEN & SMOKED SAUSAGE

BBQ CHICKEN & SMOKED SAUSAGE

My party-ready barbecue recipe works for weeknights, too. With just a few minutes of prep time, you still get that low-and-slow flavor everybody craves. (Thanks, slow cooker!) Throw in some minced jalapenos for extra oomph.
—*Kimberly Young, Mesquite, TX*

PREP: 30 min. • **COOK:** 4 hours
MAKES: 8 servings

- 1 medium onion, chopped
- 1 large sweet red pepper, cut into 1-in. pieces
- 4 bone-in chicken thighs, skin removed
- 4 chicken drumsticks, skin removed
- 1 pkg. (12 oz.) smoked sausage links, cut into 1-in. pieces
- 1 cup barbecue sauce
  Sliced seeded jalapeno pepper, optional

1. Place first 5 ingredients in a 4- or 5-qt. slow cooker; top with barbecue sauce. Cook, covered, on low until chicken is tender and a thermometer inserted in chicken reads at least 170°-175°, 4-5 hours.

2. Remove the chicken, sausage and vegetables from slow cooker; keep warm. Transfer cooking juices to a saucepan; bring to a boil. Reduce the heat; simmer, uncovered, until thickened, 15-20 minutes, stirring occasionally.

3. Serve chicken, sausage and vegetables with sauce. If desired, top with jalapeno.

1 SERVING: 331 cal., 18g fat (6g sat. fat), 91mg chol., 840mg sod., 17g carb. (13g sugars, 1g fiber), 24g pro.

CHUNKY CHICKEN CACCIATORE

This recipe is so versatile! Look in your fridge for anything else you want to throw in, such as red pepper, mushrooms, extra zucchini from the garden—you name it. And if you want a vegetarian dinner, go ahead and leave out the chicken.

—*Stephanie Loaiza, Layton, UT*

- -

PREP: 10 min. • **COOK:** 4 hours
MAKES: 6 servings

- 6 boneless skinless chicken thighs (about 1½ lbs.)
- 2 medium zucchini, cut into 1-in. slices
- 1 medium green pepper, cut into 1-in. pieces
- 1 large sweet onion, coarsely chopped
- ½ tsp. dried oregano
- 1 jar (24 oz.) garden-style spaghetti sauce
  Hot cooked spaghetti
  Sliced ripe olives and shredded Parmesan cheese, optional

1. Place chicken and vegetables in a 3-qt. slow cooker; sprinkle with oregano. Pour sauce over top. Cook, covered, on low 4-5 hours or until chicken is tender.
2. Remove chicken thighs; break up slightly with 2 forks. Return to slow cooker. Serve with spaghetti. If desired, top with olives and cheese.

FREEZE OPTION: Place the first 6 ingredients in a freezer container and freeze. To use, place container in refrigerator for 48 hours or until contents are completely thawed. Cook and serve as directed.

1 SERVING: 285 cal., 11g fat (2g sat. fat), 76mg chol., 507mg sod., 21g carb. (14g sugars, 3g fiber), 24g pro. **DIABETIC EXCHANGES:** 3 lean meat, 1½ starch.

CHICKEN MOLE OLE

You'll get a kick out of this full-flavored southwestern favorite that requires a bit of prep time but is well worth it.
—*Johnna Johnson, Scottsdale, AZ*

- -

PREP: 40 min. • **COOK:** 4 hours
MAKES: 6 servings

- 2 dried ancho chiles
- 1½ lbs. tomatillos, husks removed, halved
- 2 medium onions, sliced, divided
- 1 serrano pepper, halved and seeded
- 3 garlic cloves, peeled
- 3 lbs. bone-in chicken breast halves, skin removed
- 1 Tbsp. canola oil
- 2 tsp. ground cumin, divided
- 1½ tsp. chili powder
- 1 tsp. pepper
- ¼ tsp. ground cinnamon
- 2 whole cloves
- ½ cup almonds
- 1 oz. unsweetened chocolate, chopped
- 1 Tbsp. lime juice
- 1 tsp. salt
- 1½ cups shredded cheddar-Monterey Jack cheese
- ½ cup minced fresh cilantro

1. Place chiles in a small bowl. Cover with boiling water; let stand for 20 minutes. Drain. Remove stems and seeds. Coarsely chop; set aside. Place the tomatillos, 1 onion, serrano pepper and garlic in a greased 15x10x1-in. baking pan. Bake, uncovered, at 400° for 10-15 minutes or until tender, stirring once.
2. In a large skillet, brown chicken in oil. Transfer to a 4-qt. slow cooker. In the same skillet, saute remaining onion until tender. Add 1 tsp. cumin, chili powder, pepper, cinnamon, cloves and hydrated chiles; cook 1 minute longer. Discard cloves.
3. Place almonds in a food processor; cover and process until ground. Add spiced onion mixture and chocolate; cover and process until blended. Transfer to a small bowl.
4. Place the tomatillo mixture, lime juice, salt and remaining cumin in food processor; cover and process until chopped. Stir into almond mixture. Pour over chicken. Cook, covered, on low until the chicken is tender, 4-5 hours. Sprinkle with cheese and cilantro.

1 SERVING: 494 cal., 25g fat (10g sat. fat), 126mg chol., 671mg sod., 21g carb. (8g sugars, 7g fiber), 49g pro.

CHUNKY CHICKEN CACCIATORE

FREEZE OPTION: Place the cooled chicken mixture in freezer containers. To use, partially thaw in refrigerator overnight. Microwave, covered, on high in a microwave-safe dish until heated through, stirring gently; add a little broth or water if necessary.

1⅓ CUPS CHICKEN MIXTURE WITH ½ CUP COUSCOUS: 351 cal., 3g fat (1g sat. fat), 63mg chol., 699mg sod., 52g carb. (15g sugars, 7g fiber), 30g pro.

WEEKDAY CHICKEN CACCIATORE

Chicken cooked "cacciatore" means a dish prepared "hunter-style" with tomatoes, mushrooms, onions and seasonings. We add a touch of white wine to make ours northern Italian-style.
—*Lisa L. Bynum, Brandon, MS*

- -

PREP: 30 min. • **COOK:** 4 hours
MAKES: 4 servings

- 4   **chicken leg quarters**
- ½   **tsp. salt**
- ½   **tsp. pepper**
- 2   **Tbsp. olive oil**

SAUCE

- ½   **lb. sliced fresh mushrooms**
- 1   **medium onion, halved and thinly sliced**
- 1   **medium sweet red pepper, coarsely chopped**
- 2   **garlic cloves, minced**
- 1½   **tsp. minced fresh oregano or ½ tsp. dried oregano**
- ¼   **tsp. crushed red pepper flakes**
- ½   **tsp. salt**
- 1   **can (14½ oz.) diced tomatoes, undrained**
- ½   **cup white wine or chicken broth**
    Fresh oregano and grated Parmesan cheese, optional

1. Sprinkle chicken with salt and pepper. In a large skillet, heat oil over medium-high heat. Brown chicken on both sides.

2. In a 5-qt. slow cooker, combine sauce ingredients; arrange chicken over sauce. Cook, covered, on low until chicken and vegetables are tender, 4-6 hours. Top with fresh oregano and grated Parmesan cheese, if desired.

1 CHICKEN LEG QUARTER WITH 1⅓ CUPS SAUCE: 391 cal., 23g fat (5g sat. fat), 104mg chol., 849mg sod., 12g carb. (7g sugars, 3g fiber), 33g pro.

HARVESTTIME CHICKEN WITH COUSCOUS

HARVESTTIME CHICKEN WITH COUSCOUS

Even on busy days, I can start this chicken in a slow cooker and still get to work on time. When I come home, spinach salad and crescent rolls round out the menu.
—*Heidi Rudolph, Oregon, IL*

- -

PREP: 30 min. • **COOK:** 3 hours
MAKES: 6 servings

- 2   **medium sweet potatoes (about 1¼ lbs.), peeled and cut into ½-in. pieces**
- 1   **medium sweet red pepper, coarsely chopped**
- 1½   **lbs. boneless skinless chicken breasts**
- 1   **can (14½ oz.) stewed tomatoes, undrained**
- ½   **cup peach or mango salsa**
- ¼   **cup golden raisins**
- ½   **tsp. salt**
- ¼   **tsp. ground cumin**
- ¼   **tsp. ground cinnamon**
- ¼   **tsp. pepper**

COUSCOUS

- 1   **cup water**
- ½   **tsp. salt**
- 1   **cup uncooked whole wheat couscous**

1. In a 4-qt. slow cooker, layer the sweet potatoes, red pepper and chicken breasts. In a small bowl, mix tomatoes, salsa, raisins and seasonings; pour over chicken. Cook, covered, on low 3-4 hours or until sweet potatoes and chicken are tender.

2. About 10 minutes before serving, prepare couscous. In a small saucepan, bring water and salt to a boil. Stir in couscous. Remove from heat; let stand, covered, 5 minutes or until water is absorbed. Fluff with a fork.

3. Remove chicken from slow cooker; shred with 2 forks. Return to slow cooker, stirring gently to combine. Serve with couscous.

WEEKDAY CHICKEN CACCIATORE

GOLDEN CHICKEN & NOODLES

This tender chicken cooks up in a golden sauce that is nicely flavored with basil. It makes for a happy homecoming on those days when you don't have time to cook.
—*Charlotte McDaniel, Jacksonville, AL*

- -

PREP: 5 min. • **COOK:** 6 hours
MAKES: 6 servings

- 6 boneless skinless chicken breast halves (1½ lbs.)
- 2 cans (10½ oz. each) condensed broccoli cheese soup, undiluted
- 2 cups whole milk
- 1 small onion, chopped
- ½ to 1 tsp. salt, optional
- ½ to 1 tsp. dried basil
- ⅛ tsp. pepper
- Hot cooked noodles

Cut chicken pieces in half; place in a 5-qt. slow cooker. Combine the soup, milk, onion, salt if desired, basil and pepper; pour over chicken. Cover and cook on high for 1 hour. Reduce heat to low; cover and cook 5-6 hours longer or until chicken is tender. Serve over noodles.
1 CUP: 258 cal., 9g fat (4g sat. fat), 75mg chol., 762mg sod., 15g carb. (7g sugars, 0 fiber), 27g pro.

"Delicious! Cooks the chicken breast to a tender perfection and the sauce was wonderful. The whole family loved it!"
—TRACYLURA, TASTEOFHOME.COM

EASY SLOW-COOKER TAMALE DINNER

Here is a quick and easy dinner, which is very satisfying. No need to fool with corn husks here! My parents and friends often request this for dinner.
—*Laurel Lawshae, Round Rock, TX*

- -

PREP: 20 min. • **COOK:** 4 hours
MAKES: 4 servings

- 1 lb. ground turkey
- 1 large egg, lightly beaten
- 1½ cups 2% milk
- ¾ cup yellow cornmeal
- 1 can (14½ oz.) diced tomatoes, undrained
- 1 cup frozen corn, thawed
- 4 tsp. chili powder
- 2 tsp. ground cumin
- 1 tsp. salt
- 1 tsp. garlic powder
- 1 tsp. onion powder
- Shredded cheddar cheese, sour cream and salsa
- Chopped green onions, optional

1. In a small skillet, cook ground turkey over medium heat until no longer pink, 6-8 minutes, breaking into crumbles; drain. In a large bowl, combine the egg, milk and cornmeal until smooth. Add tomatoes, corn, seasonings and turkey.
2. Transfer to a greased 3-qt. slow cooker. Cook, covered, on low until the edges are browned, 4-5 hours. Serve with cheese, sour cream and salsa. If desired, top with onions.
1 SERVING: 402 cal., 13g fat (4g sat. fat), 129mg chol., 960mg sod., 43g carb. (9g sugars, 5g fiber), 31g pro.

EASY SLOW-COOKER TAMALE DINNER

SLOW-COOKED TURKEY WITH HERBED STUFFING

KING-SIZE DRUMSTICKS

Let your slow cooker do the work when these tender turkey legs are on the menu. Enchilada sauce, chiles and cumin give these king-size drummies a zesty treatment.
—Taste of Home *Test Kitchen*

- -

PREP: 15 min. • **COOK:** 8 hours
MAKES: 6 servings

- 1 can (10 oz.) enchilada sauce
- 1 can (4 oz.) chopped green chiles, drained
- 1 tsp. dried oregano
- ½ tsp. garlic salt
- ½ tsp. ground cumin
- 6 turkey drumsticks (12 oz. each), skin removed
- 3 Tbsp. cornstarch
- 3 Tbsp. cold water

1. In a large bowl, combine the enchilada sauce, chiles, oregano, garlic salt and cumin. Place the drumsticks in a 5-qt. slow cooker; top with sauce. Cook, covered, on low until a thermometer in turkey reads 180°, 8-10 hours.
2. Remove turkey to a serving platter; keep warm. Skim fat from cooking juices; transfer to a small saucepan. Bring liquid to a boil. Combine cornstarch and water until smooth. Gradually stir into the pan. Bring to a boil; cook and stir for 2 minutes or until thickened. Serve with turkey drumsticks.
1 DRUMSTICK: 306 cal., 7g fat (2g sat. fat), 202mg chol., 640mg sod., 7g carb. (1g sugars, 0 fiber), 51g pro.

SLOW-COOKED TURKEY WITH HERBED STUFFING

I'm all for turkey dinner, especially around the holidays. A whole turkey won't fit in my slow cooker, so thank goodness for turkey breast. I cook it with my grandma's easy stuffing recipe for a marvelous meal that doesn't require any hard work.
—Camille Beckstrand, Layton, UT

- -

PREP: 20 min. • **COOK:** 3 hours + standing
MAKES: 8 servings

- 1 boneless skinless turkey breast half (2 lbs.) or 2 lbs. turkey breast tenderloins
- 1 jar (12 oz.) turkey gravy, divided
- 1 can (10½ oz.) reduced-fat reduced-sodium condensed cream of mushroom soup, undiluted
- ½ tsp. salt
- ½ tsp. poultry seasoning
- ¼ tsp. pepper
- 1 medium Granny Smith apple, finely chopped
- 2 celery ribs, thinly sliced
- 1 small onion, finely chopped
- 1 cup sliced fresh mushrooms, optional
- 6 cups seasoned stuffing cubes

1. Place turkey in a 5- or 6-qt. slow cooker. Whisk ¼ cup gravy, condensed soup and seasonings. Cover and refrigerate remaining gravy. Stir apple, celery, onion and, if desired, mushrooms into the gravy mixture. Stir in stuffing cubes; spoon over turkey. Cook, covered, on low until a thermometer reads 170° and meat is tender, 3-4 hours.
2. Remove turkey from slow cooker; tent with foil. Let stand 10 minutes before slicing. Warm remaining gravy. Serve with turkey and stuffing.
4 OZ. COOKED TURKEY WITH ¾ CUP STUFFING AND 2 TBSP. GRAVY: 324 cal., 4g fat (1g sat. fat), 70mg chol., 1172mg sod., 38g carb. (5g sugars, 3g fiber), 32g pro.

BUSY-DAY CHICKEN FAJITAS

SLOW-COOKER CHICKEN ENCHILADA STUFFED PEPPERS

Utilize leftovers and clean out the fridge by making these super simple and tasty stuffed peppers! This is an ideal weekend meal or one you can put together quickly so you can run errands while it cooks.

—Katie Jasiewicz, Belle Isle, FL

- -

PREP: 20 min. • **COOK:** 3 hrs.
MAKES: 6 servings

- 2 **cups shredded cooked chicken**
- 1 **pkg. (8.8 oz.) ready-to-serve long grain rice**
- 1 **cup enchilada sauce**
- ¾ **cup shredded cheddar cheese, divided**
- 3 **Tbsp. minced red onion**
- ½ **tsp. ground cumin**
- ⅓ **cup water**
- 6 **medium bell peppers**
  Minced fresh cilantro, green onions and sour cream

1. In a bowl, combine chicken, rice, enchilada sauce, ½ cup cheese, red onion and cumin.
2. Pour water into a 6-qt. slow cooker. Cut and discard tops from peppers; remove seeds. Fill with chicken mixture; place in slow cooker. Cover the slow cooker with a double layer of white paper towels; place lid securely over towels. Cook on low, until tender, about 3-4 hours. During the last 20 minutes, discard paper towels; add the remaining cheese and cook, covered until melted. Serve with sour cream, cilantro and green onions.

1 STUFFED PEPPER: 267 cal., 10g fat (4g sat. fat), 56mg chol., 364mg sod., 23g carb. (6g sugars, 3g fiber), 20g pro. **DIABETIC EXCHANGES:** 3 lean meat, 1 starch, 1 vegetable, ½ fat.

TEST KITCHEN TIP
Lining the underside of the lid with paper towels helps collect some of the moisture and prevent the peppers from getting too wet. Mix and match your favorite enchilada ingredients in the filling.

BUSY-DAY CHICKEN FAJITAS

When I don't have much time to cook supper, chicken fajitas from the slow cooker are a flavorful way to keep my family satisfied. If you aren't cooking for youngsters, try spicing things up with medium or hot picante sauce.

—Michele Furry, Plains, MT

- -

PREP: 20 min. • **COOK:** 4 hours
MAKES: 6 servings

- 1 **lb. boneless skinless chicken breasts**
- 1 **can (15 oz.) black beans, rinsed and drained**
- 1 **medium green pepper, cut into strips**
- 1 **large onion, sliced**
- 1½ **cups picante sauce**
- ½ **tsp. garlic powder**
- ½ **tsp. ground cumin**
- 12 **flour tortillas (6 in.), warmed**
- 2 **cups shredded cheddar cheese**
  Optional toppings: Thinly sliced green onions, chopped tomatoes and sour cream, optional

1. Place chicken in a 4-qt. slow cooker; add black beans, pepper and onion. In a small bowl, mix picante sauce, garlic powder and cumin; pour over top. Cook, covered, on low until chicken is tender, 4-5 hours.
2. Remove chicken and cool slightly. Shred meat with 2 forks and return to slow cooker; heat through. Serve with tortillas, cheese and toppings of your choice.

2 FAJITAS: 508 cal., 20g fat (10g sat. fat), 79mg chol., 1192mg sod., 46g carb. (5g sugars, 6g fiber), 32g pro.

SLOW-COOKER
CHICKEN ENCHILADA
STUFFED PEPPERS

**COCONUT CHICKEN
& SWEET POTATO STEW**

COCONUT CHICKEN & SWEET POTATO STEW

This throw-together stew tastes like you spent hours in the kitchen. The flavors of coconut milk, sweet potato and coriander nicely complement the chicken. A garnish of cilantro and toasted coconut adds a bit of sophistication.

—*Nicole Filizetti, Stevens Point, WI*

PREP: 20 min. • **COOK:** 6 hours
MAKES: 8 servings (2½ qt.)

- 1½ lbs. boneless skinless chicken breasts, cubed
- 2 lbs. sweet potatoes (about 3 medium), peeled and cubed
- 3 cups canned coconut milk, divided
- 1 can (8 oz.) unsweetened pineapple tidbits, drained
- 1 small onion, chopped
- 1 tsp. ground coriander
- ½ tsp. salt
- ½ tsp. crushed red pepper flakes
- ¼ tsp. pepper
  Optional ingredients: Hot cooked basmati rice, toasted unsweetened shredded coconut, minced fresh cilantro and lime wedges

Combine the chicken, cubed sweet potatoes, 2 cups coconut milk, pineapple, onion and seasonings in a 4- or 5-qt. slow cooker. Cook, covered, on low until chicken and sweet potatoes are tender, 6-8 hours. Stir in remaining 1 cup coconut milk. If desired, serve with optional ingredients.

1¼ CUPS: 365 cal., 16g fat (14g sat. fat), 47mg chol., 223mg sod., 34g carb. (17g sugars, 4g fiber), 21g pro.3

DID YOU KNOW?

If you grow cilantro, you can also harvest its seeds, known as coriander. Let the seeds mature from green to brown, then cut heads with a few inches of stem and hang to dry. Gently loosen the seeds and store in a covered jar.

TANGY ORANGE CHICKEN THIGHS

TANGY ORANGE CHICKEN THIGHS

Here's a quick-prep recipe for tender, flavorful chicken in a tangy tomato-based sauce. You can easily be double or triple the recipe, depending on the size of your slow cooker.

—*Dahlia Abrams, Detroit, MI*

PREP: 20 min. • **COOK:** 5 hours
MAKES: 8 servings

- 2 cups sliced fresh carrots
- 1 can (14½ oz.) diced tomatoes, undrained
- 1 medium onion, chopped
- 1 can (6 oz.) tomato paste
- ½ cup orange juice
- 2 garlic cloves, minced
- 2 tsp. dried basil
- 1½ tsp. sugar
- ½ tsp. dried oregano
- ½ tsp. dried thyme
- ½ tsp. dried rosemary, crushed
- ½ tsp. pepper
- 2 tsp. grated orange zest, divided
- 8 boneless skinless chicken thighs (about 2 lbs.)
- 2 Tbsp. lemon juice
- 4 bacon strips, cooked and crumbled

1. In a 3-qt. slow cooker, combine the first 12 ingredients. Stir in 1 tsp. orange zest. Add chicken; spoon sauce over top. Cover and cook on low for 5-6 hours or until chicken is tender.

2. Remove to a serving platter. Stir lemon juice and remaining orange zest into sauce; pour over chicken. Sprinkle with bacon.

1 CHICKEN THIGH WITH ½ CUP SAUCE: 248 cal., 10g fat (3g sat. fat), 80mg chol., 236mg sod., 15g carb. (8g sugars, 3g fiber), 25g pro. **DIABETIC EXCHANGES:** 3 lean meat, 1 starch.

Other Entrees

**FRUITY
PORK ROAST**

FRUITY PORK ROAST

I like using the slow cooker because it gives me time for other preparations and frees the oven. Plus, it usually doesn't matter if you serve the food later than planned. This pork roast, which I created by adapting other recipes, gets a special flavor from the fruit.
—*Mary Jeppesen-Davis, St. Cloud, MN*

PREP: 25 min. • **COOK:** 5 hours + standing
MAKES: 8 servings

- ½   medium lemon, sliced
- ½   cup dried cranberries
- ⅓   cup golden raisins
- ⅓   cup unsweetened apple juice
- 3   Tbsp. sherry or additional unsweetened apple juice
- 1   tsp. minced garlic
- ½   tsp. ground mustard
- 1   boneless pork loin roast (3 lbs.)
- ½   tsp. salt
- ¼   tsp. pepper
- ⅛   to ¼ tsp. ground ginger
- 1   medium apple, peeled and sliced
- ½   cup packed fresh parsley sprigs

1. In a small bowl, combine first 7 ingredients; set aside. Cut roast in half; sprinkle with salt, pepper and ginger.
2. Transfer to a 5-qt. slow cooker. Pour fruit mixture over roast. Place apple and parsley around roast. Cover and cook on low until meat is tender, 5-6 hours.
3. Transfer meat to a serving platter. Let stand for 10-15 minutes before slicing.

5 OZ. COOKED PORK WITH ¼ CUP FRUIT MIXTURE: 272 cal., 8g fat (3g sat. fat), 85mg chol., 200mg sod., 15g carb. (12g sugars, 1g fiber), 33g pro. **DIABETIC EXCHANGES:** 5 lean meat, 1 fruit.

"This is a repeat request at home —so delicious. I shared it with my mom, and she has made it quite a few times as well."
—DEEFRAP, TASTEOFHOME.COM

BARBECUE PORK COBB SALAD

SQUASH & LENTIL LAMB STEW

My family lived in New Zealand many years ago. Every Sunday my mother made a lamb stew—it was Dad's favorite! I changed the recipe to suit my family, but it still tastes as exotic and Sunday-best as Mom's.
—*Nancy Heishman, Las Vegas, NV*

- -

PREP: 30 min. • **COOK:** 6 hours
MAKES: 8 servings (2½ qt.)

- 1   can (13.66 oz.) coconut milk
- ½   cup creamy peanut butter
- 2   Tbsp. red curry paste
- 1   Tbsp. hoisin sauce
- 1   tsp. salt
- ½   tsp. pepper
- 1   can (14½ oz.) chicken broth
- 3   tsp. olive oil, divided
- 1   lb. lamb or beef stew meat (1½-in. pieces)
- 2   small onions, chopped
- 1   Tbsp. minced fresh gingerroot
- 3   garlic cloves, minced
- 1   cup dried brown lentils, rinsed
- 4   cups cubed peeled butternut squash (about 1 lb.)
- 2   cups chopped fresh spinach
- ¼   cup minced fresh cilantro
- ¼   cup lime juice

1. In a 5- or 6-qt slow cooker, whisk together first 7 ingredients. In a large skillet, heat 2 tsp. oil over medium heat; brown lamb in batches. Add to slow cooker.
2. In the same skillet, saute chopped onions in remaining oil over medium heat until tender, 4-5 minutes. Add ginger and garlic; cook and stir 1 minute. Add to slow cooker. Stir in lentils and squash.
3. Cook, covered, on low until meat and lentils are tender, 6-8 hours. Stir in spinach until wilted. Stir in cilantro and lime juice.
FREEZE OPTION: Freeze cooled stew in freezer containers. To use, partially thaw in refrigerator overnight. Heat through in a saucepan, stirring occasionally and adding a little broth if necessary.
1¼ CUPS: 411 cal., 21g fat (11g sat. fat), 38mg chol., 777mg sod., 34g carb. (7g sugars, 6g fiber), 23g pro.

BARBECUE PORK COBB SALAD

My lunchtime salad gets way more interesting topped with barbecue pork, cheddar cheese and creamy avocado. It's as satisfying as it is scrumptious.
—*Shawn Carleton, San Diego, CA*

- -

PREP: 30 min. • **COOK:** 3 hours
MAKES: 6 servings

- 1¼   cups barbecue sauce
- ½   tsp. garlic powder
- ¼   tsp. paprika
- 1½   lbs. pork tenderloin
- 12   cups chopped romaine
- 3   plum tomatoes, chopped
- 2   avocados, peeled and chopped
- 2   small carrots, thinly sliced
- 1   medium sweet red or green pepper, chopped
- 3   hard-boiled large eggs, chopped
- 1½   cups shredded cheddar cheese
       Salad dressing of your choice

1. In a greased 3-qt. slow cooker, mix the barbecue sauce, garlic powder and paprika. Add pork; turn to coat. Cook, covered, on low 4-5 hours or until pork is tender.
2. Remove pork from slow cooker; shred into bite-sized pieces. In a bowl, toss pork with 1 cup barbecue sauce mixture. Place romaine on a large serving platter; arrange pork, vegetables, avocado, eggs, bacon and cheese over romaine. Drizzle with dressing.
FREEZE OPTION: Place shredded pork in freezer containers. Cool and freeze. To use, partially thaw in refrigerator overnight. Heat through in a covered saucepan, stirring gently. Add a little broth if necessary.
1 SERVING: 492 cal., 24g fat (9g sat. fat), 185mg chol., 868mg sod., 35g carb. (23g sugars, 7g fiber), 35g pro.

ITALIAN SAUSAGE
& QUINOA STEW

ITALIAN SAUSAGE & QUINOA STEW

I like how the sweetness of the orange and yellow peppers blend with the spiciness of the Italian sausage. If you have trouble finding quinoa, substitute rice or tiny pasta in this recipe.
—*Marietta Slater, Justin, TX*

PREP: 20 min. • **COOK:** 5 hours
MAKES: 8 servings

- 5 Italian sausage links (4 oz. each), casings removed
- ½ cup chopped onion
- 1 can (16 oz.) kidney beans, rinsed and drained
- 1 can (15¼ oz.) whole kernel corn, drained
- 1 each medium green, sweet orange and sweet yellow peppers, cut into ¾-in. pieces
- 1 cup quinoa, rinsed
- 1 medium zucchini, cut in half lengthwise and sliced into ¼-in. slices
- 3 garlic cloves, minced
- 1 tsp. ground cumin
- 1 tsp. dried oregano
- ¾ tsp. salt
- ½ tsp. crushed red pepper flakes
- ¼ tsp. pepper
- 1 can (14½ oz.) diced tomatoes, undrained
- 1 (14½ oz.) can beef broth
  Minced fresh cilantro

1. In a large skillet, cook the sausage and onion over medium heat until sausage is no longer pink, 5-7 minutes, breaking up sausage into large crumbles; drain.
2. Transfer sausage and onion to a 4- or 5-qt. slow cooker. Stir in the beans, corn, peppers, quinoa, zucchini, garlic, seasonings, tomatoes, and broth. Cook, covered, on low 5-6 hours or until vegetables and quinoa are tender. Sprinkle with cilantro.
1 SERVING: 363 cal., 17g fat (5g sat. fat), 38mg chol., 1188mg sod., 36g carb. (9g sugars, 8g fiber), 17g pro.

CRAZY DELICIOUS BABY BACK RIBS

CRAZY DELICIOUS BABY BACK RIBS

My husband craves baby back ribs, so we cook them multiple ways. This low and slow method with a tangy sauce is the best we've found.
—*Jan Whitworth, Roebuck, SC*

PREP: 15 min. • **COOK:** 5¼ hours
MAKES: 8 servings

- 2 Tbsp. smoked paprika
- 2 tsp. chili powder
- 2 tsp. garlic salt
- 1 tsp. onion powder
- 1 tsp. pepper
- ½ tsp. cayenne pepper
- 4 lbs. pork baby back ribs

SAUCE
- ½ cup Worcestershire sauce
- ½ cup mayonnaise
- ½ cup yellow mustard
- ¼ cup reduced-sodium soy sauce
- 3 Tbsp. hot pepper sauce

1. In a small bowl, combine first 6 ingredients. Cut ribs into serving-size pieces; rub with the seasoning mixture. Place ribs in a 6-qt. slow cooker. Cook, covered, on low until meat is tender, 5-6 hours.
2. Preheat oven to 375°. In a small bowl, whisk the sauce ingredients. Transfer ribs to a foil-lined 15x10x1-in. baking pan; brush with some of the sauce. Bake until browned, 15-20 minutes, turning once and brushing occasionally with sauce. Serve ribs with remaining sauce.
1 SERVING: 420 cal., 33g fat (9g sat. fat), 86mg chol., 1082mg sod., 6g carb. (2g sugars, 2g fiber), 24g pro.

SOUTHWESTERN BREAKFAST SLOW-COOKER CASSEROLE

I created this recipe as breakfast-for-dinner one day, and now it's become a favorite on chilly mornings. Such a wonderful aroma! Using extra-sharp cheddar cheese instead of the milder types allows you to use less, while giving you an extra boost of flavor.
—*Lisa Renshaw, KS City, MO*

PREP: 20 min. • **COOK:** 2½ hours + standing
MAKES: 8 servings

- 4 large eggs
- 8 large egg whites
- 1⅓ cups fat-free milk
- 3 tsp. chili powder
- ½ tsp. ground cumin
- ½ tsp. pepper
- ½ tsp. cayenne pepper
- 1 can (15 oz.) black beans, rinsed and drained
- 1 can (7 oz.) Mexicorn, drained
- 1 cup cubed fully cooked ham
- 1 cup shredded extra-sharp cheddar cheese
- 1 can (4 oz.) chopped green chiles, drained
- 6 slices whole wheat bread, lightly toasted and cubed
  Pico de gallo, optional

1. In a large bowl, whisk together the first 7 ingredients. Stir in the beans, corn, ham, cheese and chiles. Stir in bread to moisten. Transfer to a 5-qt. slow cooker coated with cooking spray.

2. Cook, covered, on low until a knife inserted in the center comes out clean, 2½-3½ hours. Let stand, uncovered, 10 minutes before serving. If desired, serve with pico de gallo.

1¼ CUPS: 270 cal., 9g fat (4g sat. fat), 119mg chol., 771mg sod., 25g carb. (5g sugars, 4g fiber), 21g pro. **DIABETIC EXCHANGES:** 3 lean meat, 1½ starch.

EASY POACHED SALMON

EASY POACHED SALMON

In 46 years of marriage, we had never tasted salmon until a friend told me about poaching it in a slow cooker. I tried it and got flaky, moist results with little fuss. I added some soy sauce for extra flavor.
—*Johnna Johnson, Scottsdale, AZ*

PREP: 45 min. • **COOK:** 1 hour
MAKES: 8 servings

- 6 cups water
- 1 medium onion, chopped
- 2 celery ribs, chopped
- 4 sprigs fresh parsley
- ½ cup dry white wine
- 1 Tbsp. soy sauce
- 8 whole peppercorns
- 1 bay leaf
- 1 salmon fillet (3 lbs.)
  Lemon slices and fresh dill

1. In a large saucepan, combine the first 8 ingredients. Bring to a boil; reduce heat. Simmer, covered, for 30 minutes. Strain; discarding vegetables and spices.

2. Cut three 20x3-in. strips of heavy-duty foil; crisscross so they resemble the spokes of a wheel. Place strips on bottom and up sides of a 7-qt. oval slow cooker. Pour poaching liquid into slow cooker. Carefully add salmon.

3. Cook, covered, on high 60-70 minutes or just until fish flakes easily with a fork (a thermometer inserted in fish should read at least 145°). Using foil strips as handles, remove salmon from cooking liquid. Serve warm or cold with lemon and dill.

4 OZ. COOKED SALMON: 266 cal., 16g fat (3g sat. fat), 85mg chol., 97mg sod., 0 carb. (0 sugars, 0 fiber), 29g pro. **DIABETIC EXCHANGES:** 4 lean meat.

HUNGARIAN TREASURE (SZEKELY GULYAS)

This combination of pork, sauerkraut, sour cream and paprika is heavenly served on buttery egg noodles with or without poppy seeds. Here's to great comfort food.
—Taste of Home *Test Kitchen*

- -

PREP: 25 min. • **COOK:** 3 hours
MAKES: 6 servings

1½ lbs. pork tenderloin, cubed
¼ tsp. salt
¼ tsp. pepper
1 Tbsp. olive oil
2 Tbsp. butter
1 large onion, chopped
6 garlic cloves, minced
½ tsp. smoked paprika
2 pkg. (1 lb. each) sauerkraut, rinsed and well drained
½ cup water
1½ cups sour cream
½ tsp. poppy seeds
   Hot cooked buttered egg noodles

1. Sprinkle pork with salt and pepper. In a large skillet, heat oil over medium-high heat; brown meat. Transfer meat to a 4- or 5-qt. slow cooker. In the same skillet, melt butter over medium-high heat. Add onion; cook and stir until tender, 6-8 minutes. Add garlic and paprika; cook 1 minute longer. Pour over meat. Add sauerkraut and water.
2. Cook, covered, on low until pork is tender, 3-4 hours. Stir in sour cream; sprinkle with poppy seeds. Serve with noodles.
1⅓ CUPS: 369 cal., 25g fat (12g sat. fat), 79mg chol., 1181mg sod., 12g carb. (6g sugars, 5g fiber), 26g pro.

SLOW-COOKED BIG BREAKFAST

We make this during holidays or on mornings when we know we're going to have a busy day. You can set this to cook overnight on low for an early breakfast, or for three hours on high for a leisurely brunch.
—Delisha Paris, Elizabeth City, NC

- -

PREP: 30 min. • **COOK:** 3 hours + standing
MAKES: 12 servings

1 lb. bulk pork sausage
2 lbs. potatoes (about 4 medium), peeled and cut into ½-in. cubes
¼ cup water
1 large onion, finely chopped
1 medium sweet red pepper, chopped
2 cups fresh spinach
1 cup chopped fresh mushrooms
1 lb. cubed deli ham
1 cup shredded cheddar cheese
12 large eggs
½ cup 2% milk
1 tsp. garlic powder
1 tsp. pepper
½ tsp. salt

1. In a large skillet, cook and crumble pork sausage over medium heat until no longer pink, 5-7 minutes; drain.
2. Meanwhile, place potatoes and water in a large microwave-safe dish. Microwave, covered, on high until potatoes are tender, 6 minutes, stirring halfway. Drain and add to sausage.
3. Stir in onion, sweet red pepper, spinach, mushrooms, ham and cheese. Transfer to a greased 6-qt. slow cooker.
4. Whisk together remaining ingredients until blended; pour over sausage mixture. Cook, covered, on low until eggs are set, 3-4 hours. Let stand, uncovered, 10 minutes before serving.
1 CUP: 303 cal., 18g fat (6g sat. fat), 236mg chol., 873mg sod., 14g carb. (3g sugars, 1g fiber), 21g pro.

HUNGARIAN TREASURE (SZEKELY GULYAS)

MAMA'S CARNITAS

FREEZE OPTION: Place shredded pork in freezer containers; top with juices. Cool and freeze. To use, partially thaw in refrigerator overnight. Heat through in a covered saucepan, stirring gently. Add a little broth if necessary.

NOTE: Wear disposable gloves when cutting hot peppers; the oils can burn skin. Avoid touching your face.

1 FILLED TORTILLA: 479 cal., 25g fat (11g sat. fat), 97mg chol., 776mg sod., 29g carb. (1g sugars, 0 fiber), 32g pro.

ASPARAGUS TUNA NOODLE CASSEROLE

I updated a traditional tuna casserole using fresh asparagus and asparagus soup. This is so different and so delicious. Use frozen asparagus when not in season.
—*Nancy Heishman, Las Vegas, NV*

PREP: 20 min. • **COOK:** 5 hours
MAKES: 8 servings

- 2 cups uncooked elbow macaroni
- 2 cans (10½ oz. each) condensed cream of asparagus soup, undiluted
- 2 cups sliced fresh mushrooms
- 1 medium sweet red pepper, chopped
- 1 small onion, chopped
- ¼ cup lemon juice
- 1 Tbsp. dried parsley flakes, divided
- 1½ tsp. smoked paprika, divided
- 1 tsp. garlic salt
- ½ tsp. pepper
- 2 lbs. fresh asparagus, cut into 1-in. pieces
- 2 pouches (6.4 oz. each) light tuna in water
- 1½ cups shredded Colby cheese
- 1 cup multigrain snack chips, crushed
- 4 bacon strips, cooked and crumbled

1. Cook macaroni according to package directions for al dente; drain. Transfer to a 4- or 5-qt. greased slow cooker. Stir in soup, mushrooms, red pepper, onion, lemon juice, 1½ tsp. parsley, 1 tsp. paprika, garlic salt and pepper. Cook, covered, on low 4 hours.
2. Stir in asparagus and tuna. Cook, covered, on low until asparagus is crisp-tender, 1 hour longer. Serve with cheese, crushed chips and bacon. Sprinkle with remaining 1½ tsp. parsley and ½ tsp. paprika.

1⅓ CUPS: 338 cal., 15g fat (6g sat. fat), 44mg chol., 1110mg sod., 30g carb. (5g sugars, 5g fiber), 22g pro.

MAMA'S CARNITAS

My husband loves to cook Mexican dishes. I'm more of an Italian-style cook, and the joke in our house is that I should leave all the Mexican cooking to him. HOWEVER, this dish of mine turned out so amazing my husband fell in love! It's all in the meat. If you can get an all-natural pork shoulder, it really makes a difference.
—*Chelsea Wickman, Painesville, OH*

PREP: 25 min. • **COOK:** 9 hours
MAKES: 16 servings

- 3 garlic cloves, minced
- 1 Tbsp. minced fresh cilantro
- ½ tsp. salt
- ½ tsp. dried oregano
- ½ tsp. chili powder
- ½ tsp. ground cumin
- ½ tsp. paprika
- ½ tsp. pepper
- ¼ tsp. cayenne pepper
- 1 bone-in pork shoulder roast (5 to 7 lbs.)
- ½ cup unsweetened pineapple juice
- ½ cup reduced-sodium soy sauce
- ½ cup beef stock
- ¼ cup lime juice
- 2 Anaheim peppers, seeded and diced
- 16 flour tortillas (8 in.)
- 1 cup creme fraiche or sour cream
- 2 cups shredded Monterey Jack cheese

1. In a small bowl, combine first 9 ingredients. Cut roast in half; rub all sides with the spice mixture. Place in a 5-qt. slow cooker coated with cooking spray. Combine pineapple juice, soy sauce, stock, lime juice and peppers; pour around meat.
2. Cover and cook on low for 9-11 hours or until meat is tender. Remove meat; skim fat. When cool enough to handle, remove meat from bones; discard bones. Shred meat and return to slow cooker; heat through.
3. With a slotted spoon, spoon ½ cup filling off center on each tortilla. Top with 1 Tbsp. creme fraiche and 2 Tbsp. cheese. Fold sides and ends over filling and roll up.

ASPARAGUS TUNA NOODLE CASSEROLE

SAUSAGE SAUERKRAUT SUPPER

With big, tender chunks of sausage, potatoes and carrots, this old-fashioned dinner will satisfy even the heartiest of appetites. It always disappears in a hurry whenever served at a family gathering or office potluck.
—Joalyce Graham, St. Petersburg, FL

PREP: 25 min. • **COOK:** 8 hours
MAKES: 10 servings

- 4 cups carrot chunks (2-in. pieces)
- 4 cups red potato chunks
- 2 cans (14 oz. each) sauerkraut, rinsed and drained
- 2½ lbs. fresh Polish sausage links
- 1 medium onion, thinly sliced
- 3 garlic cloves, minced
- 1½ cups dry white wine or chicken broth
- 1 tsp. pepper
- ½ tsp. caraway seeds

1. In a 5-qt. slow cooker, layer the carrots, potatoes and sauerkraut. In a large skillet, brown sausages. When cool enough to handle, cut into 3-in. pieces; transfer to slow cooker (slow cooker will be full). Reserve 1 Tbsp. drippings; saute onion and garlic in reserved drippings until tender.
2. Gradually add wine. Bring to a boil; stir to loosen browned bits. Stir in pepper and caraway. Pour over sausage. Cover and cook on low for 8-10 hours or until a thermometer inserted in the sausage reads 160°.
1 CUP: 517 cal., 37g fat (12g sat. fat), 72mg chol., 1442mg sod., 24g carb. (6g sugars, 5g fiber), 16g pro.

SLOW-COOKER BOURBON PORK CHOPS

My dad created a baked version of this recipe years ago. Delicious as it was, when I updated his recipe, I decided to try it in the slow cooker for even more moist and tender results. Bingo! Juicy, tasty and no fuss.
—Judy Batson, Tampa, FL

PREP: 20 min. • **COOK:** 3 hours
MAKES: 4 servings

- ¾ cup packed dark brown sugar
- ⅓ cup apple jelly
- 3 Tbsp. bourbon
- 3 Tbsp. reduced-sodium soy sauce
- 3 Tbsp. stone-ground mustard
- ½ tsp. coarsely ground pepper
- 1 Tbsp. olive oil
- 4 pork rib chops (1 in. thick and 8 oz. each)
- 2 Tbsp. water
- 1½ tsp. cornstarch

1. For the sauce, whisk together the first 6 ingredients. In a large skillet, heat oil over high heat. Brown pork chops; 2-3 minutes per side. Transfer to a 5-qt. slow cooker. Pour sauce over top.
2. Cook pork chops, covered, on low until thermometer inserted in pork reads at least 145°, 3-4 hours.
3. Remove chops from slow cooker; keep warm. Skim fat from cooking juices; transfer half of the cooking juices to a saucepan. Mix cornstarch and water until smooth; stir into saucepan. Bring to a boil; cook and stir until thickened, 1-2 minutes. Serve over chops.
1 PORK CHOP WITH 3 TBSP. SAUCE: 491 cal., 14g fat (4g sat. fat), 72mg chol., 715mg sod., 62g carb. (57g sugars, 1g fiber), 30g pro.

SLOW-COOKER BOURBON PORK CHOPS

SLAMMIN' LAMB

SLOW-COOKING SPAGHETTI SAUCE

This sauce gets a convenient head start from jarred spaghetti sauce. I simply add a few ingredients of my own. Most folks think it's homemade.
—*Margaret Shauers, Great Bend, KS*

- -

PREP: 20 min. • **COOK:** 3 hours
MAKES: 6 servings

  1 **lb. bulk Italian sausage**
  ¼ **tsp. cayenne pepper**
  1 **small onion, sliced**
  1 **medium green pepper, cut into strips**
  3½ **cups spaghetti sauce**
      Hot cooked spaghetti

1. In a large skillet, brown sausage and cayenne over medium heat until meat is no longer pink, 5-7 minutes, breaking into crumbles; drain.
2. Transfer to a 1½- or 2-qt. slow cooker. Add onion and green pepper. Pour spaghetti sauce on top. Cover and cook on high for 1 hour. Reduce heat to low and cook 2-3 hours longer. Serve with spaghetti.
¾ CUP: 241 cal., 15g fat (5g sat. fat), 33mg chol., 1018mg sod., 16g carb. (10g sugars, 3g fiber), 11g pro.

TEST KITCHEN TIP
Spaghetti-and-meatball pizza is a fun way to combine two Italian favorites. To make, toss leftover cooked spaghetti with some of the sauce, then layer it on a cheese pizza with chopped onion and frozen meatballs, thawed and cut in half. Bake until hot.

SLAMMIN' LAMB

This meat is easy, flavorful and best when marinated overnight. You can even mix it up and freeze it until you want to throw it in the crock! Make sure you have lots of pita bread on hand to soak up the juices.
—*Ruth Hartunian-Alumbaugh, Willimantic, CT*

- -

PREP: 20 min. + marinating
COOK: 4 hours • **MAKES:** 6 servings

  2 **small garlic bulbs**
  ¾ **cup plus 2 Tbsp. minced fresh mint, divided**
  ½ **cup balsamic vinegar**
  ¼ **cup olive oil**
  2 **lbs. boneless lamb, cut into 1-in. cubes**
      Hot cooked rice or warm pita breads, optional

1. Remove papery outer skin from garlic bulbs; cut off tops of bulbs, exposing the individual cloves. Peel and halve cloves. In a large dish, combine garlic, ¾ cup mint, vinegar and olive oil. Add lamb; turn to coat. Cover and refrigerate up to 24 hours.
2. Transfer lamb and marinade to a 3-qt. slow cooker. Cook, covered, on low until meat is tender, 4-5 hours. Sprinkle with remaining mint; if desired, serve with rice or pitas.
1 SERVING: 323 cal., 17g fat (4g sat. fat), 98mg chol., 102mg sod., 10g carb. (6g sugars, 1g fiber), 31g pro.

**SLOW-COOKER
JAMBALAYA RISOTTO**

SLOW-COOKER JAMBALAYA RISOTTO

I love risotto, but I don't always love the time and stirring it takes to get the creamy goodness. I found a slow-cooker risotto recipe and thought it was too good to be true. I decided to adapt a jambalaya recipe for this dish.
—*Angela Westra, Cambridge, MA*

PREP: 20 min. • **COOK:** 2 hours
MAKES: 6 servings

- 2½ cups chicken broth
- 1 can (14½ oz.) diced tomatoes, undrained
- 1½ cups tomato sauce
- 1¼ cups uncooked arborio rice
- 3 Tbsp. finely chopped onion
- 1 Tbsp. dried parsley flakes
- 1 Tbsp. olive oil
- ½ tsp. garlic powder
- ½ tsp. dried thyme
- ½ tsp. pepper
- ¼ tsp. salt
- ¼ tsp. cayenne pepper
- 1 bay leaf
- ½ lb. uncooked shrimp (31-40 per lb.), peeled and deveined and tails removed
- ½ lb. fully cooked andouille sausage links, sliced
- ⅔ cup shredded Parmesan cheese, optional

In a 4- or 5-qt. slow cooker, combine the first 13 ingredients. Cook, covered, on high for 1¾ hours. Stir in shrimp, sausage and, if desired, cheese. Cook until shrimp turn pink and rice is tender, 10-15 minutes longer. Remove bay leaf.

1½ CUPS: 335 cal., 11g fat (3g sat. fat), 97mg chol., 1276mg sod., 42g carb. (4g sugars, 3g fiber), 19g pro.

SLOW-COOKED PORK WITH ROOT VEGETABLES

SLOW-COOKED PORK WITH ROOT VEGETABLES

This awesome dish is truly a one-pot recipe. No need to brown the pork, as the rub gives it great color. As it cooks, the house fills with the amazing aroma of apples and pork. A perfect dinner for a chilly autumn day. Use cooking liquid as a sauce when ready to serve. If there is any leftover pork, it makes lovely pulled pork sandwiches.
—*Jackie Sharp, Suffolk, VA*

PREP: 25 min. • **COOK:** 3½ hours
MAKES: 10 servings

- 3 large sweet potatoes (about 2¼ lbs.)
- 2 medium turnips
- 1 tart medium apple
- ¼ cup water
- 1 medium onion, quartered
- 2 Tbsp. packed brown sugar
- 2 tsp. salt
- 1½ tsp. paprika
- ½ tsp. pepper
- 1 boneless pork loin roast (3 to 4 lbs.)
- ½ cup unsweetened apple juice
- 2 Tbsp. cider vinegar
- 1 Tbsp. Worcestershire sauce
- 1 tsp. salt
- 1 tsp. yellow mustard
- ¼ tsp. crushed red pepper flakes

1. Peel and cut sweet potatoes, turnips and apple into ¾-in. pieces. Microwave sweet potatoes, turnips and water, covered, on high until just slightly tender, 8-10 minutes. Drain; transfer to a 6-qt. slow cooker. Add apple and onion. In a small bowl, mix brown sugar, salt, paprika and pepper; rub over meat and place in slow cooker.

2. Whisk remaining ingredients; pour around the pork roast. Cook, covered, on low until a thermometer reads 145° and the meat is tender, 3½-4½ hours.

3. Remove the roast from slow cooker; tent with foil. Let stand 15 minutes before slicing. Strain cooking juices; serve pork slices and vegetables with juices.

4 OZ. COOKED PORK WITH ¾ CUP VEGETABLE MIXTURE: 313 cal., 7g fat (2g sat. fat), 68mg chol., 799mg sod., 34g carb. (17g sugars, 4g fiber), 29g pro. **DIABETIC EXCHANGES:** 4 lean meat, 2 starch.

KOREAN PULLED PORK TACOS

3. Remove the roast; skim fat from cooking juices. Shred pork with 2 forks; return to slow cooker and heat through. Serve in tortillas with slaw. If desired, serve with green onions and additional chili sauce.

FREEZE OPTION: Freeze the cooled pork mixture in freezer containers. To use, partially thaw in refrigerator overnight. Heat through in a saucepan, stirring occasionally and adding a little water or broth if necessary.

2 TACOS: 603 cal., 29g fat (10g sat. fat), 108mg chol., 1177mg sod., 46g carb. (11g sugars, 4g fiber), 37g pro.

SLOW-COOKER CHIPOTLE PORK CHOPS

I love the tender texture of pork chops from the slow cooker! The flavor of this sauce is similar to barbecue, but with a little extra kick. The crispy onions on top add a delectable crunch.
—*Elisabeth Larsen, Pleasant Grove, UT*

- -

PREP: 15 min. • **COOK:** 4 hours
MAKES: 8 servings

  8 bone-in pork loin chops (7 oz. each)
  1 small onion, finely chopped
  ⅓ cup chopped chipotle peppers in adobo sauce
  ¼ cup packed brown sugar
  2 Tbsp. red wine vinegar
  2 garlic cloves, minced
  ½ tsp. salt
  ¼ tsp. pepper
  1 can (15 oz.) tomato sauce
  1 can (14½ oz.) fire-roasted diced tomatoes, undrained
TOPPINGS
  1 can (6 oz.) french-fried onions
  ¼ cup minced fresh cilantro

Place all ingredients except toppings in a 5-qt. slow cooker. Cook, covered, on low until a thermometer inserted in pork reads at least 145°, 4-5 hours. Top with french-fried onions and cilantro just before serving.

1 PORK CHOP: 408 cal., 20g fat (6g sat. fat), 86mg chol., 844mg sod., 24g carb. (10g sugars, 2g fiber), 32g pro.

KOREAN PULLED PORK TACOS

I created this unique pulled pork recipe to replicate our favorite food truck tacos at home. They're a little sweet, a little spicy and totally tasty any time of year.
—*Julie Orr, Fullerton, CA*

- -

PREP: 25 min. • **COOK:** 8 hours
MAKES: 10 servings

  ½ cup reduced-sodium soy sauce
  ½ cup water
  3 Tbsp. brown sugar
  2 Tbsp. sesame oil
  1 Tbsp. baking cocoa
  3 tsp. chili powder
  1 garlic clove, minced
  ¼ tsp. ground ginger
  1 boneless pork shoulder butt roast (4-5 lbs.)

SLAW
  3 Tbsp. sugar
  2 Tbsp. reduced-sodium soy sauce
  1 Tbsp. Sriracha chili sauce
  2 tsp. sesame oil
  1 tsp. rice vinegar
  1 pkg. (14 oz.) coleslaw mix
  1 Tbsp. toasted sesame seeds, optional
ASSEMBLY
 20 flour tortillas (6 in.), warmed
     Optional toppings: Thinly sliced green onions and additional Sriracha chili sauce

1. Whisk together first 8 ingredients. Place roast in a 6-qt. slow cooker. Pour soy sauce mixture over top. Cook, covered, on low until pork is tender, 8-10 hours.
2. About 1 hour before serving, mix first 5 slaw ingredients until blended. Place coleslaw mix in a large bowl; toss with dressing and, if desired, sesame seeds. Refrigerate, covered, until serving.

SLOW-COOKER
CHIPOTLE
PORK CHOPS

SPICED APPLE OATMEAL

These easy, apple-y oats give your family a warm and cozy breakfast no matter how busy you are.

—*Teri Rasey, Cadillac, MI*

PREP: 15 min. • **COOK:** 4½ hours.
MAKES: 10 servings

- ½ cup packed brown sugar
- 2 Tbsp. lemon juice
- 2 Tbsp. molasses
- 3 tsp. ground cinnamon
- 1 tsp. ground nutmeg
- ½ tsp. ground ginger
- ½ tsp. ground allspice
- ¼ tsp. salt
- 4 medium apples, peeled and cut into 1-in. slices
- 2 cups steel-cut oats
- 2 large eggs
- 2½ cups water
- 2 cups 2% milk
- 1 cup refrigerated vanilla dairy creamer
  Chopped pecans and additional milk, optional

1. Mix first 8 ingredients. Place apples in a greased 4-qt. slow cooker. Top with brown sugar mixture, then with oats.
2. Whisk together eggs, water, milk and creamer; pour over oats. Cook, covered, on low until oats are tender, 4½-5 hours. If desired, serve oatmeal with pecans and additional milk.
NOTE: This recipe was tested with Coffee-mate Natural Bliss vanilla coffee creamer.
1 CUP: 290 cal., 7g fat (3g sat. fat), 49mg chol., 109mg sod., 53g carb. (30g sugars, 5g fiber), 7g pro.

BBQ PORK & PEPPERS

This was the first recipe I ever made in a slow cooker, and it was the first recipe my husband taught me! I usually pair this with white rice and a salad.

—*Rachael Hughes, Southampton, PA*

PREP: 10 min. • **COOK:** 8 hours
MAKES: 4 servings

- 4 bone-in pork loin chops (7 oz. each)
- 1 large onion, chopped
- 1 large sweet red pepper, chopped
- 1 large green pepper, chopped
- 1 cup barbecue sauce
  Chopped fresh parsley, optional

Place chops in a 4-qt. slow cooker coated with cooking spray. Top with onion, peppers and barbecue sauce. Cover and cook on low 8-10 hours or until pork is tender. If desired, top with chopped fresh parsley.
1 CHOP WITH ¾ CUP SAUCE: 291 cal., 10g fat (3g sat. fat), 86mg chol., 638mg sod., 17g carb. (12g sugars, 3g fiber), 33g pro.
DIABETIC EXCHANGES: 4 lean meat, 1 vegetable, ½ starch.

DID YOU KNOW?

Green peppers are unripened versions of red, yellow or orange peppers. They are less expensive because they're quicker to get to market. Colored peppers have more natural sweetness.

SPICED APPLE OATMEAL

**SLOW-COOKER CHORIZO
BREAKFAST CASSEROLE**

SLOW-COOKED CHERRY PORK CHOPS

I mixed and matched several recipes to come up with this one. I'm always happy to adapt recipes for my slow cooker. It's so easy to prepare a meal that way.
—*Mildred Sherrer, Fort Worth, TX*

- -

PREP: 10 min. • **COOK:** 3 hours
MAKES: 6 servings

6	bone-in pork loin chops (8 oz. each)
⅛	tsp. salt
	Dash pepper
1	cup canned cherry pie filling
2	tsp. lemon juice
½	tsp. chicken bouillon granules
⅛	tsp. ground mace
	Additional cherry pie filling, warmed, optional

1. In a large skillet coated with cooking spray, brown the pork chops over medium heat on both sides. Season with salt and pepper.
2. In a 3-qt. slow cooker, combine the pie filling, lemon juice, bouillon and mace. Add the pork chops. Cover and cook on low until meat is no longer pink, 3-4 hours. Serve with additional pie filling if desired.
1 SERVING: 366 cal., 18g fat (7g sat. fat), 111mg chol., 204mg sod., 11g carb. (9g sugars, 1g fiber), 36g pro.

SLOW-COOKER CHORIZO BREAKFAST CASSEROLE

My kids ask for this slow-cooked casserole for breakfast and dinner. I've served it with white country gravy or salsa for meals that are delightful either way.
—*Cindy Pruitt, Grove, OK*

- -

PREP: 25 min. • **COOK:** 4 hours + standing
MAKES: 8 servings

1	lb. fresh chorizo or bulk spicy pork sausage
1	medium onion, chopped
1	medium sweet red pepper, chopped
2	jalapeno peppers, seeded and chopped
1	pkg. (30 oz.) frozen shredded hash brown potatoes, thawed
1½	cups shredded Mexican cheese blend
12	large eggs
1	cup 2% milk
½	tsp. pepper

1. In a large skillet, cook chorizo, onion, red pepper and jalapenos over medium heat until cooked through and vegetables are tender, 7-8 minutes, breaking chorizo into crumbles; drain. Cool slightly.
2. In a greased 5-qt. slow cooker, layer a third of the potatoes, chorizo mixture and cheese. Repeat layers twice. In a large bowl, whisk eggs, milk and pepper until blended; pour over top.
3. Cook, covered, on low 4-4½ hours or until eggs are set and a thermometer reads 160°. Uncover and let stand for 10 minutes before serving.
NOTE: Wear disposable gloves when cutting hot peppers; the oils can burn skin. Avoid touching your face.
1½ CUPS: 512 cal., 32g fat (12g sat. fat), 350mg chol., 964mg sod., 25g carb. (4g sugars, 2g fiber), 30g pro.

**GREEK-STYLE
STUFFED PEPPERS**

GREEK-STYLE STUFFED PEPPERS

The bounty of peppers found at your local farmers market in the early fall, combined with some standard Greek ingredients, creates a dish that bursts with color and fresh flavor.
—*Renee Murby, Johnston, RI*

PREP: 30 min. • **COOK:** 4½ hours
MAKES: 8 servings

- 2 Tbsp. olive oil
- 1 small fennel bulb, chopped
- 1 small red onion, chopped
- 1 pkg. (10 oz.) frozen chopped spinach, thawed and squeezed dry
- 3 garlic cloves, minced
- 2 each medium sweet yellow, orange, red and green peppers
- 1 can (28 oz.) crushed tomatoes, divided
- 1 lb. ground lamb
- 1 cup cooked barley
- 1 cup crumbled feta cheese, plus more for serving
- ½ cup Greek olives, chopped
- 1½ tsp. dried oregano
- ½ tsp. salt
- ½ tsp. crushed red pepper flakes
- ½ tsp. pepper
  Chopped fresh parsley, optional

1. In a large skillet, heat oil over medium-high heat. Add fennel and onion; cook and stir until tender, 6-8 minutes. Add spinach and garlic; cook 1 minute longer. Cool slightly.
2. Cut and reserve tops from peppers; remove seeds. Pour 1 cup crushed tomatoes into bottom of a 6- or 7-qt. slow cooker. In large bowl, combine remaining ingredients; add fennel mixture. Spoon mixture into peppers; place in slow cooker. Pour the remaining crushed tomatoes over peppers; replace pepper tops. Cook, covered, on low until peppers are tender, 4½-5½ hours. If desired, serve with additional feta and chopped parsley.
1 STUFFED PEPPER: 313 cal., 16g fat (6g sat. fat), 45mg chol., 684mg sod., 26g carb. (11g sugars, 8g fiber), 17g pro. **DIABETIC EXCHANGES:** 2 starch, 2 medium-fat meat, 1 fat.

APPLE BUTTER PORK
WITH WHITE BEANS

APPLE BUTTER PORK WITH WHITE BEANS

This enticing dish is an entire dinner with meat, vegetables and beans, wonderful to come home after I've run the kids around to activities all afternoon. The apple butter with the pork is yummy and perfect for fall!
—*Elisabeth Larsen, Pleasant Grove, UT*

PREP: 20 min. • **COOK:** 4 hours
MAKES: 10 servings

- 12 oz. fresh baby carrots, roughly chopped
- 1 small onion, chopped
- 1 Tbsp. olive oil
- 1 boneless pork loin roast (3 lbs.)
- 1½ tsp. salt, divided
- ½ tsp. pepper, divided
- 1 cup apple butter
- 2 Tbsp. apple cider vinegar
- 1 Tbsp. Dijon mustard
- 3 garlic cloves, minced
- 2 cans (15 oz. each) great northern beans, rinsed and drained

1. Place carrots and onion in a 6-qt. slow cooker. Sprinkle roast with 1 tsp. salt and ¼ tsp. pepper. In a large skillet, heat oil over medium-high heat; brown roast on all sides. Transfer to slow cooker.
2. In a small bowl, combine apple butter, vinegar, mustard, garlic, remaining salt and pepper; pour over the pork and vegetables. Cook, covered, on low until vegetables are tender and a thermometer inserted into pork reads 145°, 3½-4½ hours.
3. Remove roast from slow cooker; tent with foil. Add beans to slow cooker; cook, covered, on high until heated through, about 30 minutes. Serve sliced pork with bean mixture.
4 OZ. COOKED PORK WITH ½ CUP BEAN MIXTURE: 314 cal., 8g fat (3g sat. fat), 68mg chol., 579mg sod., 28g carb. (12g sugars, 5g fiber), 31g pro.

Soups, Sides & Sandwiches

CHORIZO
CHILI

CHORIZO CHILI

I modified a bean soup recipe and came up with this wonderful chili. I make it mild, as that's how my family likes it, then I just add Tabasco sauce to spice up my bowl. Feel free to make it vegetarian by using soy chorizo and vegetable broth.
—*Jenne Delkus, Des Peres, MO*

- -

PREP: 20 min. • **COOK:** 5 hours
MAKES: 2 qt.

  2 cans (15 oz. each) black beans, rinsed and drained
  1 can (16 oz.) kidney beans, rinsed and drained
  1 jar (16 oz.) chunky salsa
  1 can (15 oz.) whole kernel corn, drained
  1 pkg. (12 oz.) fully cooked Spanish chorizo links, chopped
  1 can (10 oz.) diced tomatoes and green chiles, undrained
  1 cup reduced-sodium chicken broth
  2 Tbsp. ground cumin
  1 to 2 tsp. hot pepper sauce
  1 medium ripe avocado, peeled and cubed
  6 Tbsp. sour cream
  ¼ cup fresh cilantro leaves

Combine the first 9 ingredients in a 4- or 5-qt. slow cooker. Cook, covered, on low for 5-6 hours or until flavors are blended. Serve with avocado, sour cream and cilantro.
1 CUP: 366 cal., 17g fat (6g sat. fat), 30mg chol., 1262mg sod., 37g carb. (8g sugars, 10g fiber), 18g pro.

DID YOU KNOW?
Spanish chorizo links are fully cooked and made with smoked pork. Mexican chorizo sausage is made from fresh (uncooked) meat.

FREEZE OPTION: Place the shredded pork and vegetables in freezer containers; top with cooking juices. Cool and freeze. To use, partially thaw in refrigerator overnight. Heat through in a covered saucepan, stirring gently. Add a little broth if necessary.

1 SANDWICH: 484 cal., 29g fat (7g sat. fat), 71mg chol., 400mg sod., 36g carb. (15g sugars, 3g fiber), 18g pro.

CHUCK WAGON BEANS WITH SAUSAGE

I followed the lead of cooks of Old West cattle ranges to come up with these savory beans. Sweet and smoky, they're made extra hearty by the addition of some sausage.
—*Nancy Moore, Bucklin, KS*

- -

PREP: 15 min. • **COOK:** 8 hours
MAKES: 24 servings (⅔ cup each)

- 2 cans (28 oz. each) baked beans
- 3 cans (16 oz. each) kidney beans, rinsed and drained
- 2 cans (15 oz. each) pinto beans, rinsed and drained
- 1 lb. smoked kielbasa or Polish sausage, sliced
- 1 jar (12 oz.) pickled jalapeno slices, drained
- 1 medium onion, chopped
- 1 cup barbecue sauce
- ½ cup spicy brown mustard
- ¼ cup steak seasoning

In a greased 6-qt. slow cooker, combine all ingredients. Cover and cook on low for 8-10 hours or until heated through.

⅔ CUP: 229 cal., 7g fat (2g sat. fat), 17mg chol., 1299mg sod., 32g carb. (3g sugars, 8g fiber), 11g pro.

MIDNIGHT CARIBBEAN PORK SANDWICHES

These sandwiches are so tasty! They've got depth of flavor — savory, sweet, piquant, subtle and sublime. They're super easy to make and worth the (slow-cooker) wait.
—*Elizabeth Bennett, Mill Creek, WA*

- -

PREP: 25 min. • **COOK:** 6 hours
MAKES: 12 servings

- 1 Tbsp. canola oil
- 3 medium onions, cut into ½-in. slices
- 1 bottle (12 oz.) amber beer or 1½ cups chicken broth
- ¼ cup packed brown sugar
- 10 garlic cloves, minced and divided
- 2 Tbsp. ground cumin
- 7 tsp. minced chipotle peppers in adobo sauce, divided
- ½ tsp. salt
- ½ tsp. pepper
- 1 boneless pork shoulder butt roast (2 to 3 lbs.)
- 1 cup mayonnaise
- ½ cup minced fresh cilantro
- 12 Hawaiian sweet hamburger buns
- 2 medium ripe avocados, peeled and sliced

1. In a large skillet, heat oil over medium-high heat. Add onions; cook and stir until tender, 6-8 minutes. Add beer, brown sugar, 8 garlic cloves, cumin, 5 tsp. chipotle peppers, salt and pepper; cook and stir until combined.
2. Place the pork roast in a 5- or 6-qt. slow cooker. Pour the onion mixture over meat. Cook, covered, on low until pork is tender, 6-8 hours.
3. Meanwhile, combine mayonnaise, cilantro, remaining 2 garlic cloves and chipotle peppers. Cover and refrigerate until serving.
4. Remove roast; shred with 2 forks. Strain cooking juices. Reserve vegetables and 1 cup juices; discard remaining juices. Skim fat from reserved juices. Return pork and reserved vegetables and cooking juices to slow cooker; heat through. Serve on buns with avocado and mayonnaise mixture.

SLOW-COOKER CHICKEN ENCHILADA MELTS

SLOW-COOKER CHICKEN ENCHILADA MELTS

After tasting a similar recipe at a sandwich shop, I knew I had to try my own version at home. Personally, I like mine even more! I like to mix equal parts salsa and ranch dressing to make a tasty sauce for these sandwiches.
—*Blair Lonergan, Rochelle, VA*

- -

PREP: 25 min. • **COOK:** 4 hours
MAKES: 6 servings

1½ lbs. boneless skinless chicken breasts
1 jar (16 oz.) salsa
1 envelope reduced-sodium taco seasoning
4 medium tomatoes, seeded and chopped
½ cup minced fresh cilantro
12 diagonally sliced French bread slices (1 in. thick)
1 cup shredded cheddar cheese
Sliced ripe olives and additional chopped tomatoes, optional

1. In a greased 3-qt. slow cooker, combine chicken, salsa and taco seasoning. Cook, covered, on low until chicken is tender, 4-5 hours.
2. To serve, preheat broiler. Shred chicken with 2 forks; stir in tomatoes and cilantro.
3. Place bread on ungreased baking sheets; broil 2-3 in. from heat until tops are lightly browned. Using tongs, place rounded ⅓ cup chicken mixture on each toast. Sprinkle with cheese. Broil until the cheese is melted, 2-3 minutes. If desired, top with olives and additional tomatoes.
FREEZE OPTION: Cool chicken mixture without tomatoes and cilantro; freeze in freezer containers. To use, partially thaw in refrigerator overnight. Heat through in a saucepan, stirring occasionally; stir in tomatoes and cilantro and serve as directed.
2 OPEN-FACED SANDWICHES: 377 cal., 10g fat (5g sat. fat), 81mg chol., 1082mg sod., 36g carb. (7g sugars, 2g fiber), 32g pro.

SPICY PERUVIAN POTATO SOUP

SPICY PERUVIAN POTATO SOUP

This robust Peruvian soup (Locro de Papas) has the comfort of potatoes and warming spiciness of chiles. Light enough for a simple lunch, it's also satisfying enough to serve as a soup-for-dinner meal.
—*Taste of Home Test Kitchen*

- -

PREP: 35 min. • **COOK:** 4 hours
MAKES: 2 qt.

1 Tbsp. olive oil
1 medium onion, chopped
1 medium sweet red pepper, cut into 1-in. pieces
3 garlic cloves, minced
1 carton (32 oz.) chicken stock
2 large Yukon Gold potatoes, peeled and cut into 1-in. cubes
1 can (4 oz.) chopped green chiles
½ cup minced fresh cilantro, divided
½ to 1 serrano pepper, seeded and finely chopped
2 tsp. ground cumin
1 tsp. dried oregano
¼ tsp. salt
¼ tsp. pepper
1 fully cooked Spanish chorizo link (3 oz.), chopped
Optional toppings: Sour cream and cubed avocado

1. In a large skillet, heat oil over medium-high heat. Add onion and sweet pepper; cook and stir until crisp-tender, 6-8 minutes. Add garlic; cook 1 minute longer. Transfer to a 4- or 5-qt. slow cooker. Add the chicken stock, potatoes, chiles, ¼ cup cilantro, serrano pepper and seasonings. Cook, covered, on low until the potatoes are tender, 4-6 hours.
2. Remove soup from heat; cool slightly. Process in batches in a blender until smooth. Return to slow cooker. Stir in chorizo and remaining ¼ cup cilantro; heat through. If desired, serve with sour cream and avocado.
1 CUP: 153 cal., 5g fat (1g sat. fat), 7mg chol., 472mg sod., 23g carb. (3g sugars, 2g fiber), 6g pro. **DIABETIC EXCHANGES:** 1½ starch, 1 fat.

SLOW-COOKED SAGE DRESSING

When oven space is at a premium, a batch of slow-cooker dressing can come to the rescue. This recipe is rich with butter and sage, and because it doesn't need the oven, very cook-friendly.

—*Ellen Benninger, Greenville, PA*

PREP: 15 min. • **COOK:** 4 hours
MAKES: 12 servings (about ¾ cup each)

1¼ cups butter, cubed
1½ tsp. rubbed sage
  1 tsp. salt
  ½ tsp. pepper
 14 to 15 cups day-old cubed bread
  3 cups chopped celery
1½ cups chopped onion

1. In a microwave, melt butter with sage, salt and pepper. Place bread, celery and onion in a large bowl; toss with butter mixture. Transfer to a 5-qt. slow cooker.
2. Cook, covered, on low until heated through, 4-5 hours, stirring once.
¾ CUP: 291 cal., 21g fat (12g sat. fat), 51mg chol., 570mg sod., 23g carb. (4g sugars, 2g fiber), 4g pro.

EASY PORTUGUESE-STYLE BEAN SOUP

One day I was looking at Portuguese recipes and decided to put together a bean soup that embraced the bright and spicy flavors of that country. My family liked it so much, it became a classic in our household. To save time and work, the sausage, vegetables and herbs can all be handled in minutes with a food processor.

—*Steven Vance, Woodland, WA*

PREP: 30 min. • **COOK:** 7 hours
MAKES: 4¼ qt.

  4 cans (15½ oz. each) navy beans, rinsed and drained
  5 cups chicken stock
  1 lb. linguica sausage or smoked sausage, thinly sliced
  2 cans (14½ oz. each) petite diced tomatoes, undrained
  1 large onion, halved and thinly sliced
  1 large sweet red pepper, thinly sliced
  2 celery ribs, thinly sliced
  2 medium carrots, thinly sliced

EASY PORTUGUESE-STYLE
BEAN SOUP

  1 cup dry white wine or additional chicken stock
  4 garlic cloves, minced
  2 bay leaves
  1 orange zest strip (3 in.)
  1 lemon zest strip (3 in.)
  1 Tbsp. sweet paprika
  1 Tbsp. hot pepper sauce
  1 tsp. dried savory
  1 tsp. dried thyme
  ½ tsp. ground cumin
  ½ tsp. salt
  ¼ tsp. pepper
  ½ cup chopped green onions
  ½ cup minced fresh cilantro
  ½ cup minced fresh parsley

1. Place the first 20 ingredients in a 7-qt. slow cooker. Cook, covered, on low until vegetables are tender, 7-9 hours. Remove bay leaves, orange and lemon zest strips.
2. Transfer 4 cups soup to a blender; cool slightly. Cover; process until smooth. Return to slow cooker; add green onions, cilantro and parsley. Heat through.
FREEZE OPTION: Freeze cooled soup in freezer containers. To use, partially thaw in refrigerator overnight. Heat through in a saucepan, stirring occasionally and adding a little broth if necessary.
NOTE: Linguica is available in many grocery stores, but any smoked sausage will do.
1 CUP: 235 cal., 8g fat (3g sat. fat), 18mg chol., 893mg sod., 28g carb. (4g sugars, 7g fiber), 14g pro.

BUFFALO CHICKEN SLIDERS

My family loves spicy foods, and this is a great combination of sweet and spicy. You won't be able to eat just one!
—*Christina Addison, Blanchester, OH*

PREP: 20 min. • **COOK:** 3 hours
MAKES: 6 servings

- 1 lb. boneless skinless chicken breasts
- 2 Tbsp. plus ⅓ cup Louisiana-style hot sauce, divided
- ¼ tsp. pepper
- ¼ cup butter, cubed
- ¼ cup honey
- 12 Hawaiian sweet rolls, warmed
  Optional ingredients: Lettuce leaves, sliced tomato, thinly sliced red onion and crumbled blue cheese

1. Place chicken in a 3-qt. slow cooker. Toss with 2 Tbsp. hot sauce and pepper; cook, covered, on low until tender, 3-4 hours.

2. Remove chicken; discard cooking juices. In a small saucepan, combine butter, honey and remaining hot sauce; cook and stir over medium heat until blended. Shred chicken with 2 forks; stir into sauce and heat through. Serve on rolls with optional ingredients as desired.

FREEZE OPTION: Freeze cooled chicken mixture in freezer containers. To use, partially thaw in refrigerator overnight. Microwave, covered, on high in a microwave-safe dish until heated through, stirring occasionally and adding a little water or broth if necessary.

2 SLIDERS: 396 cal., 15g fat (8g sat. fat), 92mg chol., 873mg sod., 44g carb. (24g sugars, 2g fiber), 24g pro.

SLOW-COOKED CORN ON THE COB

I like to eat corn all year long, so I came up with this recipe. It's my favorite side to serve when I make sloppy joes. You can use a butter substitute for a skinny version of this corn.
—*Teresa Flowers, Sacramento, CA*

PREP: 10 min. • **COOK:** 2 hours
MAKES: 4 servings

- 4 medium ears sweet corn, cut into 2-in. pieces
- 1 can (15 oz.) coconut milk
- 1 medium onion, chopped
- ¼ cup butter, cubed
- 6 fresh thyme sprigs
- 2 garlic cloves, minced
- 1 bay leaf
- ¾ tsp. salt
- ¼ tsp. pepper
- ¼ cup fresh cilantro leaves, chopped
- 2 green onions, sliced

In a 5- or 6-qt. slow cooker, combine the first 9 ingredients. Cook, covered, on high 2-3 hours or until tender. Serve with cilantro and green onions.

4 PIECES: 161 cal., 9g fat (6g sat. fat), 8mg chol., 118mg sod., 21g carb. (7g sugars, 2g fiber), 4g pro.

BUFFALO CHICKEN SLIDERS

BEEFY MINESTRONE

LUAU PORK LETTUCE WRAPS

I first made this recipe when our family took a trip to a beach house in Florida. On my night to cook, I did a luau theme and used this recipe as the appetizer. These are still a favorite today!
—*Joyce Conway, Westerville, OH*

- -

PREP: 30 min. • **COOK:** 6 hours
MAKES: 2 dozen

3	tsp. sea salt
1	tsp. pepper
1	boneless pork shoulder butt roast (3 to 4 lbs.)
½	cup ketchup
½	cup hoisin sauce
⅓	cup chili garlic sauce
1	lb. baby portobello mushrooms, chopped
1	large onion, chopped
1	can (20 oz.) unsweetened crushed pineapple
2	cans (8 oz. each) sliced water chestnuts, drained and chopped
	Bibb lettuce leaves
	Chopped green onions, optional

1. Rub salt and pepper over roast; transfer to a 5- or 6-qt. slow cooker. Combine the ketchup, hoisin and chili sauce; pour over roast. Top with mushrooms, onion and pineapple. Cook, covered, on low until pork is tender, 6-8 hours.
2. Remove roast; cool slightly. Strain cooking juices. Reserve vegetables and ½-1½ cups juices; discard remaining juices. Skim fat from reserved juices. Shred the pork with 2 forks. Return pork and reserved vegetables to slow cooker; pour desired amount of reserved cooking juices over pork mixture and stir to combine. Stir in the water chestnuts; heat through. Serve in lettuce leaves; top with green onions, if desired.
FREEZE OPTION: Freeze cooled meat mixture in freezer containers. To use, partially thaw in refrigerator overnight. Microwave, covered, on high in a microwave-safe dish until heated through, gently stirring and adding a little broth if necessary. Serve with lettuce.
2 FILLED LETTUCE WRAPS: 242 cal., 6g fat (2g sat. fat), 57mg chol., 1017mg sod., 23g carb. (16g sugars, 2g fiber), 24g pro.

BEEFY MINESTRONE

I know lots of minestrone recipes don't contain meat, but my husband thinks a meal is only a meal if it contains some sort of meat. Consequently, this is the perfect meal. It strikes that balance of flavorful, healthful and soul-satisfying.
—*Juli Snaer, Enid, OK*

- -

PREP: 20 min. • **COOK:** 6½ hours
MAKES: 8 servings (3 qt.)

6	cups chicken broth
1	can (16 oz.) kidney beans, rinsed and drained
1	can (15 oz.) crushed tomatoes
1	can (14½ oz.) diced tomatoes with basil, oregano and garlic, undrained
1	lb. beef top round steak, cut onto ½-in. cubes
15	fresh baby carrots, halved
2	celery ribs, chopped
1	small onion, chopped
½	cup dry red wine
4	garlic cloves, minced
1	tsp. dried oregano
1	tsp. dried basil
¼	tsp. pepper
1	cup uncooked ditalini or other small pasta
	Fresh oregano, shredded Parmesan cheese, optional

1. Combine the first 13 ingredients in a 5- or 6-qt. slow cooker. Cover and cook on low for 6-7 hours or until meat is tender.
2. Stir in pasta. Cover and cook on high for 30 minutes or until pasta is tender. Top with fresh oregano and shredded Parmesan cheese, if desired
1½ CUPS: 255 cal., 3g fat (1g sat. fat), 35mg chol., 1124mg sod., 33g carb. (7g sugars, 6g fiber), 21g pro

LUAU PORK LETTUCE WRAPS

POTATO & LEEK SOUP

POTATO & LEEK SOUP

Chock-full of veggies and bacon with just a little tanginess from sour cream, bowls of this comforting soup taste just as terrific with a sandwich as they do with crackers.
—*Melanie Wooden, Reno, NV*

PREP: 20 min. • **COOK:** 8 hours
MAKES: 8 servings (2 qt.)

- 4 cups chicken broth
- 3 medium potatoes, peeled and cubed
- 1½ cups chopped cabbage
- 2 medium carrots, chopped
- 1 medium leek (white portion only), chopped
- 1 medium onion, chopped
- ¼ cup minced fresh parsley
- ½ tsp. salt
- ½ tsp. caraway seeds
- ½ tsp. pepper
- 1 bay leaf
- ½ cup sour cream
- 1 lb. bacon strips, cooked and crumbled

1. Combine the first 11 ingredients in a 4- or 5-qt. slow cooker. Cover and cook on low for 8-10 hours or until vegetables are tender.

2. Before serving, combine sour cream with 1 cup soup; return all to the slow cooker. Stir in bacon and discard bay leaf.

1 CUP: 209 cal., 11g fat (4g sat. fat), 27mg chol., 1023mg sod., 18g carb. (4g sugars, 2g fiber), 10g pro.

FALL VEGETABLE SLOPPY JOES

FALL VEGETABLE SLOPPY JOES

I make this dish in the fall and sneak grated vegetables into the sloppy joe mixture. It's especially good when children don't like to eat their vegetables! Just walk away until the end of the day and let the slow cooker do all the work. Also delicious: Top the filling with a little shredded cheese before serving.
—*Nancy Heishman, Las Vegas, NV*

PREP: 30 min. • **COOK:** 4 hours
MAKES: 18 servings

- 8 bacon strips, cut into 1-in. pieces
- 2 lbs. lean ground beef (90% lean)
- 1 medium onion, chopped
- 2 garlic cloves, minced
- 2 cups shredded peeled butternut squash
- 2 medium parsnips, peeled and shredded
- 2 medium carrots, peeled and shredded
- 1 can (12 oz.) cola
- 1 can (8 oz.) tomato paste
- 1 cup water
- ⅓ cup honey mustard
- 1½ tsp. ground cumin
- 1¼ tsp. salt
- 1 tsp. ground allspice
- ½ tsp. pepper
- 18 hamburger buns, split

1. In a large skillet, cook bacon over medium heat until crisp, stirring occasionally. Remove with a slotted spoon; drain on paper towels. Discard drippings. In the same skillet, cook ground beef, onion and garlic over medium heat until beef is no longer pink and onion is tender, 10-12 minutes, breaking up beef into crumbles; drain.

2. Transfer to a 5- or 6-qt. slow cooker. Stir in the squash, parsnips, carrots, cola, tomato paste, water, mustard and seasonings. Cook, covered, on low until vegetables are tender, 4-5 hours. Stir in bacon. Serve on buns.

FREEZE OPTION: Freeze the cooled meat mixture in freezer containers. To use, partially thaw in refrigerator overnight. Heat through in a saucepan, stirring occasionally and adding a little water if necessary.

1 SANDWICH: 275 cal., 8g fat (3g sat. fat), 35mg chol., 526mg sod., 35g carb. (9g sugars, 3g fiber), 17g pro. **DIABETIC EXCHANGES:** 2 starch, 2 lean meat.

MEXICAN CHICKEN SOUP

This zesty soup is loaded with chicken, corn and black beans in a mildly spicy red broth. As a busy mom of three young children, I'm always looking for dinner recipes that can be prepared in the morning. The kids love the taco taste of this easy soup.

—Marlene Kane, Lainesburg, MI

- -

PREP: 10 min. • **COOK:** 3 hours
MAKES: 6 servings

- 1½ lbs. boneless skinless chicken breasts, cubed
- 2 tsp. canola oil
- ½ cup water
- 1 envelope reduced-sodium taco seasoning
- 1 can (32 oz.) V8 juice
- 1 jar (16 oz.) salsa
- 1 can (15 oz.) black beans, rinsed and drained
- 1 pkg. (10 oz.) frozen corn, thawed
- 6 Tbsp. reduced-fat cheddar cheese
- 6 Tbsp. reduced-fat sour cream
- 2 Tbsp. minced fresh cilantro

1. In a large nonstick skillet, saute chicken in oil until no longer pink. Add water and taco seasoning; simmer, uncovered, until chicken is well coated.

2. Transfer to a 5-qt. slow cooker. Stir in the V8 juice, salsa, beans and corn. Cover and cook on low for 3-4 hours or until heated through. Serve with cheese, sour cream and minced cilantro.

1½ CUPS: 345 cal., 7g fat (3g sat. fat), 72mg chol., 1315mg sod., 34g carb. (12g sugars, 7g fiber), 31g pro.

"Very easy to make and flavorful. I used Perdue Short Cuts Southwestern seasoned chicken. I buy them when they are on sale and I have coupons, so I'm usually stocked up in the freezer. Definitely a keeper. Next time, I will make it in a soup pot instead of the slow cooker and maybe add a little chopped green chiles."

—SKIPPY3716, TASTEOFHOME.COM

CUBAN-STYLE PORK SANDWICHES

CUBAN-STYLE PORK SANDWICHES

Loaded with tangy flavor, this is a lighter version of a favorite restaurant-style sandwich. If you don't have a panini maker, tuck the sandwiches under the broiler until the bread is browned and the cheese melted.

—Robin Haas, Cranston, RI

- -

PREP: 20 min. • **COOK:** 6 hours + standing
MAKES: 10 servings

- 1 large onion, cut into wedges
- ¾ cup reduced-sodium chicken broth
- 1 cup minced fresh parsley
- 7 garlic cloves, minced and divided
- 2 Tbsp. cider vinegar
- 1 Tbsp. plus 1½ tsp. lemon juice, divided
- 2 tsp. ground cumin
- 1 tsp. ground mustard
- 1 tsp. dried oregano
- ½ tsp. salt
- ½ tsp. pepper
- 1 boneless pork shoulder butt roast (3 to 4 lbs.)
- 1¼ cups fat-free mayonnaise
- 2 Tbsp. Dijon mustard
- 10 whole wheat hamburger buns, split
- 1¼ cups shredded reduced-fat Swiss cheese
- 1 medium onion, thinly sliced and separated into rings
- 2 whole dill pickles, sliced

1. Place onion wedges and broth in a 5-qt. slow cooker. In a small bowl, combine the parsley, 5 garlic cloves, vinegar, 1 Tbsp. lemon juice, cumin, mustard, oregano, salt and pepper; rub over pork roast. Add to slow cooker. Cover and cook on low until meat is tender, 6-8 hours.

2. Remove meat; let stand for 10 minutes before slicing. In another small bowl, combine mayonnaise, mustard and remaining garlic and lemon juice; spread over buns. Layer bun bottoms with pork, cheese, sliced onion and pickles; replace tops.

3. Cook on a panini maker or indoor grill until buns are browned and cheese is melted, 2-3 minutes.

1 SANDWICH: 415 cal., 18g fat (6g sat. fat), 90mg chol., 943mg sod., 32g carb. (8g sugars, 5g fiber), 33g pro.

SLOW-COOKED RATATOUILLE

I get my son to eat eggplant when I prepare this classic French veggie dish in the slow cooker. Garlic cheese bread on the side makes it irresistible.

—Diane Goedde, Red Lodge, MT

- -

PREP: 25 min. + standing • **COOK:** 5 hours
MAKES: 10 servings

- 1 medium eggplant, peeled and cut into 1-in. cubes
- 1 Tbsp. plus 1 tsp. salt, divided
- 2 medium onions, halved and thinly sliced
- 4 medium tomatoes, chopped
- 3 medium zucchini, cut into ¾-in. slices
- 2 celery ribs, chopped
- 3 Tbsp. olive oil
- 2 tsp. dried basil or 2 Tbsp. minced fresh basil
- 4 garlic cloves, minced
- ½ tsp. pepper
- 1 can (6 oz.) tomato paste
- 1 can (2¼ oz.) sliced ripe olives, drained
- ⅓ cup coarsely chopped fresh basil

1. Place eggplant in a colander over a plate; sprinkle with 1 Tbsp. salt and toss. Let stand 45 minutes. Rinse and drain well; blot dry with paper towels.

2. Place eggplant and remaining vegetables in a 5- or 6-qt. slow cooker. Add oil, dried basil, garlic, pepper and remaining salt; toss to combine.

3. Cook, covered, on low 5-6 hours or until onions are tender. Stir in tomato paste, olives and fresh basil; heat through.

FREEZE OPTION: Freeze cooled ratatouille in freezer containers. To use, partially thaw in refrigerator overnight. Microwave, covered, on high in a microwave-safe dish until heated through, stirring gently.

¾ CUP: 102 cal., 5g fat (1g sat. fat), 0 chol., 380mg sod., 13g carb. (7g sugars, 4g fiber), 3g pro. **DIABETIC EXCHANGES:** 2 vegetable, 1 fat.

SHREDDED STEAK SANDWICHES

I received this recipe when I was a newlywed, and it's been a favorite ever since. The saucy steak barbecue makes an easy, satisfying meal served on buns or over rice, potatoes or buttered noodles.

—Lee Steinmetz, Lansing, MI

- -

PREP: 15 min. • **COOK:** 6 hours
MAKES: 14 servings

- 3 lbs. beef top round steak, cut into large pieces
- 2 large onions, chopped
- ¾ cup thinly sliced celery
- 1½ cups ketchup
- ½ to ¾ cup water
- ⅓ cup lemon juice
- ⅓ cup Worcestershire sauce
- 3 Tbsp. brown sugar
- 3 Tbsp. cider vinegar
- 2 to 3 tsp. salt
- 2 tsp. prepared mustard
- 1½ tsp. paprika
- 1 tsp. chili powder
- ½ tsp. pepper
- ⅛ to ¼ tsp. hot pepper sauce
- 14 sandwich rolls, split

1. Place meat in a 5-qt. slow cooker. Add onions and celery. In a bowl, combine the ketchup, water, lemon juice, Worcestershire sauce, brown sugar, vinegar, salt, mustard, paprika, chili powder, pepper and hot pepper sauce. Pour over meat.

2. Cover and cook on high for 6-8 hours. Remove meat; cool slightly. Shred meat with 2 forks. Return to the slow cooker and heat through. Serve ½ cup on each roll.

1 SANDWICH: 347 cal., 7g fat (2g sat. fat), 39mg chol., 1100mg sod., 44g carb. (13g sugars, 2g fiber), 27g pro.

SLOW-COOKED RATATOUILLE

SLOW-COOKER BBQ HAM SANDWICHES

BEEF TACO CHILI

This one of my husband's absolute favorite dishes. It was also voted Best Chili in our county's autumn Harvest Festival. If you like less broth, use just 1¾ cups water and 1½ tsp. bouillon.
—*Dana Beery, Ione, WA*

- -

PREP: 25 min. • **COOK:** 7 hours
MAKES: 6 servings (2¼ qt.)

- 1   lb. ground beef
- 1   medium onion, chopped
- 2½ cups water
- 2   cans (15 oz. each) pinto beans, rinsed and drained
- 1   can (14½ oz.) diced tomatoes, undrained
- 2   cans (8 oz. each) tomato sauce
- 2½ tsp. beef bouillon granules
- 2   garlic cloves, minced
- 1   envelope taco seasoning
- 2   Tbsp. chili powder
- 2   tsp. dried oregano
- 2   tsp. baking cocoa
- 1½ tsp. ground cumin
- 1   tsp. Louisiana-style hot sauce
- ½   tsp. pepper
     Optional toppings: Sour cream, tortilla strips and sliced jalapenos

1. Cook beef and onion in a large skillet over medium heat until meat is no longer pink; drain. Transfer to a 4-qt. slow cooker. Stir in the remaining ingredients.
2. Cover and cook on low for 7-9 hours or until heated through. Serve with toppings if desired.
1½ CUPS: 337 cal., 11g fat (3g sat. fat), 47mg chol., 1657mg sod., 39g carb. (7g sugars, 10g fiber), 23g pro.

DID YOU KNOW?

Oregano comes in two types. The sweet Mediterranean one is often simply labeled oregano. It belongs to the mint family. Mexican oregano, a member of the verbena family, has a more intense flavor and citrusy notes.

SLOW-COOKER BBQ HAM SANDWICHES

Friends love these barbecue sandwiches and often ask me to make them. Since I know they are crowd-pleasers, I double the recipe and serve them at potlucks.
—*Dana Knox, Butler, PA*

- -

PREP: 20 min. • **COOK:** 2 hours
MAKES: 16 servings

- 3   cups ketchup
- ¾   cup chopped onion
- ¾   cup chopped green pepper
- ¾   cup packed brown sugar
- ½   cup lemon juice
- ⅓   cup Worcestershire sauce
- 1   Tbsp. prepared mustard
- 1¼   tsp. ground allspice
- 1½   tsp. liquid smoke, optional
- 3   lbs. thinly sliced deli ham
- 16   kaiser or ciabatta rolls, split
      Sliced pepperoncini, optional

1. In a large saucepan, combine the first 8 ingredients; if desired, stir in liquid smoke. Bring to a boil over medium-high heat. Reduce heat; simmer mixture for 5 minutes, stirring occasionally.
2. Place ham in a 5- or 6-qt. slow cooker. Add sauce; stir gently to combine. Cook, covered, on low 2-3 hours or until heated through. Serve on rolls. Top with sliced pepperoncini if desired.
1 SANDWICH: 348 cal., 4g fat (0 sat. fat), 38mg chol., 1744mg sod., 57g carb. (26g sugars, 2g fiber), 21g pro.

BEEF TACO CHILI

CRANBERRY BBQ
PULLED PORK

CRANBERRY BBQ
PULLED PORK

Cranberry sauce adds a yummy twist to pulled pork that my family can't get enough of! The pork cooks to tender perfection in the slow cooker, which also makes this dish conveniently portable.
—Carrie Wiegand, Mount Pleasant, IA

- -

PREP: 20 min.
COOK: 9 hours
MAKES: 14 servings

- 1 boneless pork shoulder roast (4 to 6 lbs.)
- ⅓ cup cranberry juice
- 1 tsp. salt
SAUCE
- 1 can (14 oz.) whole-berry cranberry sauce
- 1 cup ketchup
- ⅓ cup cranberry juice
- 3 Tbsp. brown sugar
- 4½ tsp. chili powder
- 2 tsp. garlic powder
- 1 tsp. onion powder
- ½ tsp. salt
- ¼ tsp. ground chipotle pepper
- ½ tsp. liquid smoke, optional
- 14 hamburger buns, split

1. Cut roast in half. Place in a 4-qt. slow cooker. Add cranberry juice and salt. Cover and cook on low until the meat is tender, 8-10 hours.

2. Remove roast halves and set aside. In a small saucepan, combine the cranberry sauce, ketchup, cranberry juice, brown sugar, seasonings and liquid smoke if desired. Cook and stir over medium heat until mixture is slightly thickened, about 5 minutes.

3. Skim fat from cooking juices; set aside ½ cup juices. Discard remaining juices. When cool enough to handle, shred the pork with 2 forks and return to slow cooker.

4. Stir in sauce mixture and reserved cooking juices. Cover and cook on low until heated through, about 1 hour. Serve on buns.

FREEZE OPTION: Freeze the cooled meat mixture in freezer containers. To use, partially thaw in refrigerator overnight. Heat through in a saucepan, stirring occasionally and adding a little water if necessary.

1 SANDWICH: 409 cal., 15g fat (5g sat. fat), 77mg chol., 772mg sod., 42g carb. (19g sugars, 2g fiber), 26g pro.

SIMPLE VEGETARIAN SLOW-COOKED BEANS

When I have a hungry family to feed, these tasty beans with spinach, tomatoes and carrots are a go-to dish. This veggie delight is frequently on the menu.
—*Jennifer Reid, Farmington, ME*

- -

PREP: 15 min. • **COOK:** 4 hours
MAKES: 8 servings

- 4 cans (15½ oz. each) great northern beans, rinsed and drained
- 4 medium carrots, finely chopped (about 2 cups)
- 1 cup vegetable stock
- 6 garlic cloves, minced
- 2 tsp. ground cumin
- ¾ tsp. salt
- ⅛ tsp. chili powder
- 4 cups fresh baby spinach, coarsely chopped
- 1 cup oil-packed sun-dried tomatoes, patted dry and chopped
- ⅓ cup minced fresh cilantro
- ⅓ cup minced fresh parsley

In a 3-qt. slow cooker, combine the first 7 ingredients. Cook, covered, on low until carrots are tender, 4-5 hours, adding spinach and tomatoes during the last 10 minutes of cooking. Stir in cilantro and parsley.
¾ CUP: 229 cal., 3g fat (0 sat. fat), 0 chol., 672mg sod., 40g carb. (2g sugars, 13g fiber), 12g pro.

QUICK-PREP BBQ BEEF SANDWICHES

Serve these mouthwatering sandwiches with coleslaw on the side or right on the sandwich. You can freeze any leftover meat for an easy meal later on.
—*Bunny Palmertree, Carrollton, MS*

- -

PREP: 10 min. • **COOK:** 10 hours
MAKES: 16 servings

- 1 can (10½ oz.) condensed beef broth, undiluted
- 1 cup ketchup
- ½ cup packed brown sugar
- ½ cup lemon juice
- 3 Tbsp. steak sauce
- 2 garlic cloves, minced
- 1 tsp. pepper
- 1 tsp. Worcestershire sauce
- 1 beef eye round roast (3½ lbs.), cut in half
- 1 tsp. salt
- 16 sandwich buns, split
     Dill pickle slices, optional

1. In a small bowl, whisk first 8 ingredients. Pour half of mixture into a 5-qt. slow cooker. Sprinkle beef with salt; add to slow cooker and top with the remaining broth mixture.
2. Cover and cook on low for 10-12 hours or until meat is tender. Shred meat with 2 forks and return to slow cooker. Using a slotted spoon, place ½ cup beef mixture on each bun. Top with pickles if desired.
1 SANDWICH: 370 cal., 8g fat (2g sat. fat), 46mg chol., 963mg sod., 47g carb. (16g sugars, 1g fiber), 28g pro.

"The addition of dill pickles is what sets this one apart from many very good shredded beef sandwich recipes I have. This one will be added to the collection!"
—LYNNETTE68, TASTEOFHOME.COM

SIMPLE VEGETARIAN SLOW-COOKED BEANS

BEER BRAT CHILI

MUSHROOM & RICE PILAF

This easy rice pilaf is a lifesaver when you are hosting Thanksgiving. Just place the ingredients in the slow cooker and forget about it until it's time to serve!
—*Kathleen Hedger, Godfrey, IL*

- -

PREP: 15 min. • **COOK:** 3 hours
MAKES: 10 servings

½   cup butter, cubed
2   cups uncooked long grain rice
½   lb. sliced fresh mushrooms
8   green onions, chopped
2   tsp. dried oregano
2   cans (10½ oz. each) condensed beef broth, undiluted
1½   cups water

In a large saucepan, heat butter over medium heat. Add rice; cook and stir until lightly browned, 5-6 minutes. Transfer to a 3-qt. slow cooker. Add mushrooms, green onions and oregano. Stir in broth and water. Cook, covered, on low until rice is tender and liquid is absorbed, 3-4 hours.
¾ CUP: 246 cal., 10g fat (6g sat. fat), 24mg chol., 490mg sod., 34g carb. (1g sugars, 1g fiber), 6g pro.

DID YOU KNOW?

Traditional pilaf recipes always begin with browning the rice (or bulgur, used in some Middle Eastern versions) in butter or oil. Besides giving the dish a toasty flavor, this helps to separate the grains, which creates a light and fluffy finished texture.

BEER BRAT CHILI

My husband and I love this chili because it smells so good as it simmers in the slow cooker all day. I can't think of a better way to use up leftover brats. He can't think of a better way to eat them!
—*Katrina Krumm, Apple Valley, MN*

- -

PREP: 10 min. • **COOK:** 5 hours
MAKES: 8 servings (2 ½ qt.)

1   can (15 oz.) cannellini beans, rinsed and drained
1   can (15 oz.) pinto beans, rinsed and drained
1   can (15 oz.) southwestern black beans, undrained
1   can (14½ oz.) Italian diced tomatoes, undrained
1   can (10 oz.) diced tomatoes and green chiles, undrained
1   pkg. (14 oz.) fully cooked beer bratwurst links, sliced
1½   cups frozen corn
1   medium sweet red pepper, chopped
1   medium onion, finely chopped
¼   cup chili seasoning mix
1   garlic clove, minced

In a 5-qt. slow cooker, combine all chili ingredients. Cook, covered, on low 5-6 hours.
1¼ CUPS: 383 cal., 16g fat (5g sat. fat), 34mg chol., 1256mg sod., 42g carb. (7g sugars, 10g fiber), 17g pro.

MUSHROOM
& RICE PILAF

CREAMY HASH BROWNS

My mother often took this comforting side dish to social dinners because it was such a hit. Now I get the same compliments when I make it. Bacon and onion jazz it up. The creamy mixture is quick to make, thanks to frozen hash browns and canned soups.
—*Donna Downes, Las Vegas, NV*

- -

PREP: 15 min. • **COOK:** 4 hours
MAKES: 14 servings

- 1 pkg. (2 lbs.) frozen cubed hash brown potatoes
- 2 cups (8 oz.) cubed process cheese (Velveeta)
- 2 cups sour cream
- 1 can (10½ oz.) condensed cream of celery soup, undiluted
- 1 can (10½ oz.) condensed cream of chicken soup, undiluted
- 1 lb. sliced bacon, cooked and crumbled
- 1 large onion, chopped
- ¼ cup butter, melted
- ¼ tsp. pepper

Place potatoes in an ungreased 5-qt. slow cooker. In a large bowl, combine remaining ingredients. Pour over potatoes and mix well. Cover and cook on low for 4-5 hours or until potatoes are tender and heated through.
1 SERVING: 303 cal., 20g fat (11g sat. fat), 54mg chol., 745mg sod., 18g carb. (4g sugars, 1g fiber), 10g pro.

GREEN CHILE POSOLE

This recipe combines parts of my nanny's and my mother's recipes that were taught to me when I was young. An optional sprinkling of queso fresco on top is delightful.
—*Jaime Love, Las Vegas, NV*

- -

PREP: 10 min. • **COOK:** 4 hours
MAKES: 6 servings

- 1 pork tenderloin (1 lb.), cut into 1-in. pieces
- 2 cans (15 oz. each) hominy, rinsed and drained
- 1 can (4 oz.) chopped green chiles
- ¼ tsp. salt
- ¼ tsp. pepper
- 4 cups chicken broth, divided
- 3 tomatillos, husks removed and chopped
  Optional: Sliced avocado, lime wedge, sliced jalapenos, sliced radishes, chopped cilantro and sour cream

1. Place first 5 ingredients and 3¾ cups broth in a 3- or 4-qt. slow cooker. Puree tomatillos with remaining broth in a blender; stir into pork mixture.
2. Cook, covered, on low until pork is tender, 4-5 hours. If desired, serve with avocado and other toppings.
1⅓ CUPS: 173 cal., 3g fat (1g sat. fat), 46mg chol., 1457mg sod., 17g carb. (1g sugars, 4g fiber), 17g pro.

GREEN CHILI POSOLE

SWEET & SPICY PINEAPPLE CHICKEN SANDWICHES

HEARTY BEAN SOUP

This soup is convenient to simmer all day in a slow cooker. Your family will love it.
—*Alice Schnoor, Arion, IA*

- -

PREP: 10 min. • **COOK:** 6 hours 10 min.
MAKES: 10 servings (2½ qt.)

3	cups chopped parsnips
2	cups chopped carrots
1	cup chopped onion
1½	cups dried great northern beans
5	cups water
1½	lbs. smoked ham hocks
2	garlic cloves, minced
2	tsp. salt
½	tsp. pepper
⅛	to ¼ tsp. hot pepper sauce

1. In a 5-qt. slow cooker, place parsnips, carrots and onion. Top with beans. Add water, ham, garlic, salt, pepper and hot pepper sauce. Cover and cook on high for 6-7 hours or until beans are tender.
2. Remove meat and bones from slow cooker. When cool enough to handle, cut meat into bite-sized pieces and return to slow cooker; heat through.

1 CUP: 161 cal., 2g fat (0 sat. fat), 8mg chol., 686mg sod., 29g carb. (4g sugars, 9g fiber), 10g pro. **DIABETIC EXCHANGES:** 2 starch, 1 lean meat.

SWEET & SPICY PINEAPPLE CHICKEN SANDWICHES

My kids ask for chicken sloppy joes, and this version has a bonus of sweet pineapple. The recipe is great to double for a potluck. Yummy topped with smoked Gouda cheese.
—*Nancy Heishman, Las Vegas, NV*

- -

PREP: 15 min. • **COOK:** 2¾ hours
MAKES: 8 servings

2½	lbs. boneless skinless chicken breasts
1	bottle (18 oz.) sweet and spicy barbecue sauce, divided
2	Tbsp. honey mustard
1	can (8 oz.) unsweetened crushed pineapple, undrained
8	hamburger buns, split and toasted Optional: Bibb lettuce leaves and thinly sliced red onionl

1. Place chicken breasts in a 4-qt. slow cooker. Combine ¼ cup barbecue sauce and mustard; pour over chicken. Cover and cook on low until chicken is tender, 2½-3 hours.

2. Remove chicken; discard liquid. Shred chicken with 2 forks and add back to slow cooker. Add the crushed pineapple and remaining barbecue sauce; cover and cook on high for 15 minutes.
3. Serve on toasted buns with toppings as desired.

FREEZE OPTION: Place shredded chicken in freezer containers. Cool and freeze. To use, partially thaw in refrigerator overnight. Heat through in a covered saucepan, stirring gently. Add a little broth if necessary.

1 SANDWICH: 415 cal., 6g fat (1g sat. fat), 78mg chol., 973mg sod., 56g carb. (30g sugars, 2g fiber), 34g pro.

> **TEST KITCHEN TIP**
> The chicken mixture is more sweet than spicy. If your family likes a little more heat, add a jalapeno pepper.

BBQ BACON PULLED CHICKEN SANDWICHES

This simple recipe tastes amazing. We prefer putting mayo on the bun and adding cheddar or Muenster cheese, lettuce, tomato and onion. Several of us put ranch dressing on our sandwiches, too.
—*Jennifer Darling, Ventura, CA*

- -

PREP: 20 min. • **COOK:** 3 hours
MAKES: 12 servings

- 1   bottle (18 oz.) barbecue sauce
- ½   cup amber beer or root beer
- ¼   cup cider vinegar
- 2   green onions, chopped
- 2   Tbsp. dried minced onion
- 2   Tbsp. Dijon mustard
- 2   Tbsp. Worcestershire sauce
- 4   garlic cloves, minced
- 1   Tbsp. dried parsley flakes
- 2   lbs. boneless skinless chicken breasts
- 12   hamburger buns, split and toasted
- 24   cooked bacon strips
- 12   lettuce leaves

1. In a large bowl, combine first 9 ingredients. Place chicken in a greased 4- or 5-qt. slow cooker; pour sauce over top. Cook, covered, on low until tender, 3-4 hours.
2. Remove the chicken; shred with 2 forks. Return chicken to slow cooker; heat through. Serve on buns with bacon and lettuce.
FREEZE OPTION: Freeze cooled, cooked chicken mixture in freezer containers. To use, partially thaw in refrigerator overnight. Heat through in a saucepan, stirring occasionally and adding a little water if necessary.
1 SANDWICH: 401 cal., 12g fat (4g sat. fat), 65mg chol., 1175mg sod., 43g carb. (19g sugars, 2g fiber), 28g pro.

**SLOW-COOKER
GARLIC-ROSEMARY
CAULIFLOWER PUREE**

SLOW-COOKER GARLIC-ROSEMARY CAULIFLOWER PUREE

I love this delicious fake take on mashed potatoes and it doesn't heat up my kitchen! Treat leftovers as you would leftover mashed potatoes for mock potato pancakes.
—*Sharon Gibson, Hendersonville, NC*

- -

PREP: 15 min. • **COOK:** 3 hours
MAKES: 6 servings

- 2   Tbsp. butter, melted
- 1   medium onion, chopped
- 1   large head cauliflower, cut into florets
- 1   pkg. (6½ oz.) spreadable garlic and herb cheese
- ½   cup grated Parmesan cheese
- ½   tsp. Montreal steak seasoning
- ¼   tsp. pepper
- 1   tsp. minced fresh rosemary or ½ tsp. dried rosemary, crushed
- ¼   cup heavy cream, warmed
  Optional: Additional minced fresh rosemary and pepper

1. Place melted butter and onion in a 4- or 5-qt. slow cooker. Add cauliflower; cook, covered, on high until cauliflower is tender, 3-4 hours.
2. Process in batches in a food processor to desired consistency. Add remaining ingredients and process until blended. If desired, serve with additional rosemary and pepper.
⅔ CUP: 245 cal., 20g fat (12g sat. fat), 54mg chol., 386mg sod., 11g carb. (5g sugars, 3g fiber), 6g pro.

TEST KITCHEN TIP
At only 11 grams carbohydrates per serving, this dish is a flavorful and lower-in-carbs alternative to mashed potatoes.

BBQ BACON PULLED CHICKEN SANDWICHES

LOADED BROCCOLI-CHEESE POTATO CHOWDER

LOADED BROCCOLI-CHEESE POTATO CHOWDER

For anyone who loves baked potato or broccoli-cheese soup, this is the best of both worlds. If you have bacon lovers, offer crumbled cooked bacon for topping. Then everyone is happy, carnivore or not!
—*Vivi Taylor, Middleburg, FL*

PREP: 15 min. • **COOK:** 6 hours 10 min.
MAKES: 8 servings (about 2 qt.)

- 1 pkg. (20 oz.) refrigerated O'Brien hash brown potatoes
- 1 garlic clove, minced
- 2 cups reduced-fat sour cream
- ¼ cup all-purpose flour
- ½ tsp. pepper
- ⅛ tsp. ground nutmeg
- 3 cups vegetable stock
- 1 pkg. (12 oz.) frozen broccoli florets, thawed
- 4 cups shredded cheddar cheese, divided
- ½ cup finely chopped green onions

1. Combine the hash browns and garlic in a 5- or 6-qt. slow cooker. In a large bowl, whisk the sour cream, flour, pepper and nutmeg until smooth; stir in stock. Pour into slow cooker; stir to combine. Cook, covered, on low until hash browns are tender, 6-8 hours.
2. Add the broccoli and 3 cups cheese; cover and cook until cheddar cheese is melted, about 10 minutes longer. Serve with green onions and remaining cheese.
1 CUP: 386 cal., 23g fat (13g sat. fat), 62mg chol., 921mg sod., 26g carb. (6g sugars, 2g fiber), 20g pro.

TEST KITCHEN TIP
Nutmeg is the secret spice in many savory recipes, often used in white sauces, pastas and potato dishes. Be careful not to overdo it. A small amount of the spice goes a long way.

SPAGHETTI SQUASH WITH TOMATOES & OLIVES

SPAGHETTI SQUASH WITH TOMATOES & OLIVES

This squash is a welcome side dish, but you can also top it with canned tuna to serve as a main course. I use my own canned tomatoes for the best flavor. It's easy and so tasty!
—*Carol Chase, Sioux City, IA*

PREP: 15 min. • **COOK:** 5¼ hours
MAKES: 10 servings

- 1 medium spaghetti squash, halved, seeds removed
- 1 can (14 oz.) diced tomatoes
- ¼ cup sliced green olives with pimientos, drained
- 1 tsp. dried oregano
- ½ tsp. salt
- ½ tsp. pepper
- ½ cup shredded cheddar cheese
- ¼ cup chopped fresh basil

1. Place squash in 6- or 7-qt. slow cooker, overlapping as needed to fit. Cook, covered, on low until tender, 5-7 hours.
2. Remove squash from slow cooker; drain any cooking liquid from slow cooker. Using a fork, separate squash into strands resembling spaghetti, discarding the skin. Return squash to slow cooker. Stir in tomatoes, olives, oregano, salt and pepper; cook on low until heated through, about 15 minutes. Top with cheese and basil to serve.
¾ CUP: 92 cal., 3g fat (1g sat. fat), 6mg chol., 296mg sod., 15g carb. (1g sugars, 4g fiber), 3g pro. **DIABETIC EXCHANGES:** 1 starch, ½ fat.

Snacks & Sweets

**SLOW-COOKER
CHERRY PEAR BUCKLE**

SLOW-COOKER CHERRY PEAR BUCKLE

I added pears to my cherry cobbler recipe to create this delightful slow-cooked buckle. You could also add fresh summer plums and berries to your cherries. You'll love this old-fashioned and pretty dessert.
—Mary Anne Thygesen, Portland, OR

PREP: 20 min. • **COOK:** 4½ hours
MAKES: 8 servings

- 6   medium pears, peeled and sliced
- 4   cups fresh or frozen pitted dark sweet cherries, thawed
- 1   cup sugar
- ¼   cup tapioca flour
- 1¾ cups all-purpose flour
- ¼   cup old-fashioned oats
- 3   tsp. baking powder
- ½   tsp. salt
- ¼   cup cold butter
- ¾   cup 2% milk
- 2   tsp. cinnamon sugar
     Sweetened whipped cream

1. Line inside of a 5-qt. slow cooker with a double thickness of heavy-duty foil; spray foil with cooking spray. In a large bowl, combine pears, cherries, sugar and tapioca flour; spoon into slow cooker. Cook, covered, on high until bubbly, 4-5 hours.
2. Meanwhile, combine flour, oats, baking powder and salt. Cut in butter until crumbly. Stir in milk. Drop by tablespoonfuls over pear mixture; sprinkle with cinnamon sugar. Cover and cook until a toothpick inserted in center of topping comes out clean, 30-45 minutes longer. Serve with whipped cream.
1 SERVING: 411 cal., 7g fat (4g sat. fat), 17mg chol., 386mg sod., 86g carb. (48g sugars, 6g fiber), 5g pro.

TEST KITCHEN TIP
Cutting butter into dry ingredients results in tiny bits of flour-coated butter throughout the dough, creating a biscuit topping that is both tender and crumbly at the same time. If you don't have a pastry blender, use two knives to cut in the cold butter.

NUTTY SLOW-COOKER SNACK MIX

CHOCOLATE-COVERED CHERRY PUDDING CAKE

I remember how much my grandfather cherished the chocolate-covered cherries we brought him for Christmas. After he passed away, I came up with this rich recipe in his honor. It's perfection served with a spoonful of whipped topping.
—*Meredith Coe, Charlottesville, VA*

PREP: 20 min. • **COOK:** 2 hours + standing
MAKES: 8 servings

- ½ cup reduced-fat sour cream
- 2 Tbsp. canola oil
- 1 Tbsp. butter, melted
- 2 tsp. vanilla extract
- 1 cup all-purpose flour
- ¼ cup sugar
- ¼ cup packed brown sugar
- 3 Tbsp. baking cocoa
- 2 tsp. baking powder
- ½ tsp. ground cinnamon
- ⅛ tsp. salt
- 1 cup fresh or frozen pitted dark sweet cherries, thawed
- 1 cup fresh or frozen pitted tart cherries, thawed
- ⅓ cup 60% cacao bittersweet chocolate baking chips

PUDDING
- ½ cup packed brown sugar
- 2 Tbsp. baking cocoa
- 1¼ cups hot water

1. In a large bowl, beat the sour cream, oil, butter and vanilla until blended. Combine the flour, sugars, cocoa, baking powder, cinnamon and salt. Add to sour cream mixture just until combined. Stir in cherries and chips. Pour into a 3-qt. slow cooker coated with cooking spray.
2. In a small bowl, combine brown sugar and cocoa. Stir in hot water until blended. Pour over the batter (do not stir). Cover and cook on high for 2-2½ hours or until set. Let stand for 15 minutes. Serve warm.
1 SERVING: 291 cal., 9g fat (3g sat. fat), 9mg chol., 167mg sod., 51g carb. (35g sugars, 2g fiber), 4g pro.

NUTTY SLOW-COOKER SNACK MIX

My three teenage boys inhale snacks! This easy recipe makes a big batch that keeps them snacking happily for the day—and I appreciate that the nutrient-dense nuts add a little protein.
—*Jennifer Fisher, Austin, TX*

PREP: 10 min. • **COOK:** 1½ hours
MAKES: 7 cups

- 3 cups Cheerios
- 3 cups mixed nuts
- 2 cups miniature cheddar cheese fish-shaped crackers
- ½ cup butter, melted
- 1 Tbsp. Worcestershire sauce
- 1 tsp. Greek seasoning

1. Combine Cheerios, nuts and crackers in a 4- or 5-qt. slow cooker. Whisk together butter, Worcestershire sauce and Greek seasoning. Pour over the cereal mixture; toss to coat.
2. Cook, covered, on high 1 hour, stirring frequently. Reduce heat to low; cook mix until crisp, 30-45 minutes longer, stirring frequently. Spread onto a baking sheet to cool. Store in an airtight container.
½ CUP: 337 cal., 25g fat (7g sat. fat), 19mg chol., 399mg sod., 22g carb. (2g sugars, 4g fiber), 7g pro.

SWEET POTATO & PESTO SLOW-COOKER BREAD

2. Turn onto a lightly floured surface; knead until smooth and elastic, 6-8 minutes. Place in a greased bowl, turning once to grease the top. Cover and let rise in a warm place until doubled, about 1 hour.

3. Punch down dough. Turn onto a lightly floured surface; roll into a 18x9-in. rectangle. Spread pesto to within 1 in. of edges; sprinkle with ½ cup Parmesan. Roll up jelly-roll style, starting with a long side; pinch seam and ends to seal.

4. Using a sharp knife, cut roll lengthwise in half; carefully turn each half cut side up. Loosely twist strips around each other, keeping cut surfaces facing up. Shape into a coil; place on parchment. Transfer to a 6-qt. slow cooker; sprinkle with remaining 2 Tbsp. Parmesan. Let rise until doubled, about 1 hour.

5. Cook, covered, on low until bread is lightly browned, 3-3½. Remove from slow cooker and cool slightly before slicing.

1 SLICE: 271 cal., 10g fat (3g sat. fat), 26mg chol., 464mg sod., 36g carb. (3g sugars, 2g fiber), 8g pro.

ITALIAN MEATBALLS & SAUSAGES

Here's a wonderful appetizer for the big game or any family function. Very easy to prepare and also very tasty. I've doubled and even tripled the recipe for large to huge groups. No matter how much I make, I always come home with an empty slow cooker.
—*Jan Kasinger, Graham, WA*

- -

PREP: 10 min. • **COOK:** 4 hours
MAKES: 8 cups

2 lbs. frozen fully cooked Italian meatballs, thawed
1 bottle (16 oz.) zesty Italian salad dressing
1 pkg. (14 oz.) miniature smoked sausages
2 cups medium fresh mushrooms, stems removed
1 can (2¼ oz.) sliced ripe olives, drained

Combine all ingredients in a 4- or 5-qt. slow cooker. Cook, covered, on low until heated through, 4-6 hours, stirring every hour.
⅓ CUP: 200 cal., 16g fat (6g sat. fat), 29mg chol., 663mg sod., 4g carb. (1g sugars, 1g fiber), 9g pro.

SWEET POTATO & PESTO SLOW-COOKER BREAD

I like to bake fresh bread, both as a way to offer my family a delicious accompaniment to dinner and just because I enjoy the process. Baking bread in the slow cooker allows you to achieve a tender, perfectly baked loaf without turning on the oven, especially helpful in the summer.
—*Shauna Havey, Roy, UT*

- -

PREP: 45 min. + rising
COOK: 3 hours + cooling
MAKES: 1 loaf (12 slices)

1 pkg. (¼ oz.) active dry yeast
⅔ cup warm half-and-half cream (110° to 115°)
1 large egg, room temperature
1 cup canned sweet potato puree or canned pumpkin
1 tsp. sugar
1 tsp. kosher salt
¼ tsp. ground nutmeg
3½ to 4 cups bread flour
1 container (7 oz.) refrigerated prepared pesto
½ cup plus 2 Tbsp. grated Parmesan cheese, divided

1. Dissolve yeast in warm cream. In a large bowl, combine egg, sweet potato puree, sugar, salt, nutmeg, yeast mixture and 2 cups flour; beat on medium speed until smooth. Stir in enough remaining flour to form a soft dough (dough will be sticky).

**ITALIAN MEATBALLS
& SAUSAGES**

SLOW-COOKER CHRISTMAS PUNCH

Indulge in this warm pineapple punch made in the slow cooker. We use cinnamon and Red Hots to give it that cozy spiced flavor and welcome-home aroma.
—*Angie Goins, Tazewell, TN*

PREP: 5 min. • **COOK:** 3 hours
MAKES: 10 servings

- 4 cups unsweetened pineapple juice
- 4 cups cranberry juice
- ⅓ cup Red Hots
- 2 cinnamon sticks (3 in.)
  Fresh cranberries and additional cinnamon sticks

In a 3- or 4-qt. slow cooker, combine first 4 ingredients. Cook, covered, on low until heated through and candies are melted, 3-4 hours. Garnish with cranberries and additional cinnamon sticks.

¾ CUP: 129 cal., 0 fat (0 sat. fat), 0 chol., 4mg sod., 33g carb. (28g sugars, 0 fiber), 1g pro.

HAMBURGER DIP

HAMBURGER DIP

This is hands-down the easiest dip to make, and I never have leftovers. We have used venison in place of hamburger, as well as half hamburger and half spicy sausage. Everyone seems to enjoy this wonderful dip!
—*Mary Kidder, Nappanee, IN*

PREP: 20 min. • **COOK:** 1½ hours
MAKES: 5 cups

- 1 lb. lean ground beef (90% lean)
- 12 oz. process cheese (Velveeta), cubed
- 1 can (10¾ oz.) condensed tomato soup, undiluted
- 1 can (10½ oz.) condensed cream of mushroom soup, undiluted
- 2 tsp. chili powder
- 1 tsp. ground cumin
  Tortilla chips

In a large skillet, cook beef over medium heat until no longer pink, 8-10 minutes, breaking into crumbles; drain. Transfer to a greased 3- or 4-qt. slow cooker. Stir in the Velveeta, soups and seasonings. Cook, covered, on low until heated through, 1½-2 hours, stirring halfway through cooking. Serve warm with tortilla chips.

¼ CUP: 97 cal., 6g fat (3g sat. fat), 26mg chol., 330mg sod., 5g carb. (2g sugars, 1g fiber), 7g pro.

SLOW-COOKER TROPICAL ORANGE CAKE

Inspired by the fruity tropical flavors of my all-time favorite yogurt, this makes for a fresh, fun and comforting treat. Try it for a beautiful dessert that is ridiculously easy to prepare!
—*Lisa Renshaw, Kansas City, MO*

PREP: 15 min. • **COOK:** 4 hours + standing
MAKES: 8 servings

- 3   cups cold 2% milk
- 1   pkg. (3.4 oz.) instant coconut cream pudding mix
- 1   pkg. orange cake mix (regular size)
- ¾ cup unsweetened pineapple tidbits
- 2   cups toasted coconut marshmallows, quartered

1. In a large bowl, whisk milk and pudding mix 2 minutes. Transfer to a greased 5-qt. slow cooker. Prepare cake mix batter according to package directions, folding pineapple into batter. Pour into slow cooker.
2. Cook, covered, on low until edges of cake are golden brown, about 4 hours.
3. Remove slow-cooker insert; sprinkle cake with marshmallows. Let stand, uncovered, 10 minutes before serving.
1 SERVING: 518 cal., 20g fat (6g sat. fat), 77mg chol., 596mg sod., 73g carb. (50g sugars, 1g fiber), 9g pro.

GREEK SHRIMP CANAPES

I grew up by the ocean and then moved to a land-locked state. I wanted to show people in my area how to easily cook seafood, and this is the recipe I came up with. It's become a neighborhood favorite.
—*Amy Harris, Springville, UT*

PREP: 15 min. • **COOK:** 65 min.
MAKES: about 2½ dozen

- 1½ cups olive oil
- ¾   cup lemon juice
- ⅔   cup dry white wine
- ¼   cup Greek seasoning
- 4   garlic cloves, minced
- 1   lb. uncooked shrimp (31-40 per lb.), peeled and deveined
- 2   large cucumbers
- 1   pkg. (8 oz.) cream cheese, softened
       Minced fresh parsley

1. In a large bowl, whisk first 5 ingredients until blended. Pour 1½ cups marinade into a large bowl. Add shrimp and stir to coat. Cover and refrigerate 45 minutes.
2. Meanwhile, pour remaining marinade into a 4- or 5-qt. slow cooker. Cook, covered, on high, 45 minutes. Drain shrimp, discarding marinade in bowl. Add shrimp to slow cooker. Cook, covered, on high until shrimp turn pink, about 20 minutes, stirring once. Drain.
3. Cut each cucumber into ¼-in.-thick slices. Scoop out centers, leaving bottoms intact. Pipe cream cheese onto each cucumber slice; top with shrimp and parsley.
1 CANAPE: 68 cal., 6g fat (2g sat. fat), 26mg chol., 139mg sod., 1g carb. (1g sugars, 0 fiber), 3g pro.

SLOW-COOKER TROPICAL ORANGE CAKE

SPICY HONEY
SRIRACHA
GAME DAY DIP

SPICY HONEY SRIRACHA GAME DAY DIP

You can easily whip up this creamy, spicy and salty dip. I love dips for parties in the slow cooker—just turn the slow cooker to low once it is cooked and let your guests help themselves. No need to worry about the dip getting cold and having to reheat it.
—*Julie Peterson, Crofton, MD*

- -

PREP: 20 min. • **COOK:** 3 hours
MAKES: 3 cups

- 1 lb. ground chicken
- 1 pkg. (8 oz.) cream cheese, cubed
- 1 cup shredded white cheddar cheese
- ¼ cup chicken broth
- 2 to 4 Tbsp. Sriracha chili sauce
- 2 Tbsp. honey
  Tortilla chips
  Chopped green onions, optional

1. In a large skillet, cook ground chicken over medium heat until no longer pink, 6-8 minutes, breaking into crumbles; drain. Transfer to a greased 3-qt. slow cooker. Stir in cream cheese, cheddar cheese, broth, chili sauce and honey.
2. Cook, covered, on low until cheese is melted, 3-4 hours, stirring every 30 minutes. Serve with tortilla chips. If desired, sprinkle with green onions.
¼ CUP: 168 cal., 13g fat (6g sat. fat), 54mg chol., 243mg sod., 5g carb. (4g sugars, 0 fiber), 9g pro.

TEST KITCHEN TIP
If you don't have Sriracha, improvise with a moderately spicy hot sauce. Add some pepper flakes, lime juice or extra honey to suit your taste.

CINNAMON ROLL CASSEROLE

CINNAMON ROLL CASSEROLE
Because we love cinnamon rolls, I created a slow-cooker recipe to make for a weekend breakfast or brunch. This is a delectable, no-fuss recipe and perfect for company and family.
—*Joan Hallford, North Richland Hills, TX*

- -

PREP: 20 min. • **COOK:** 2½ hours
MAKES: 10 servings

- 2 tubes (12.4 oz. each) refrigerated cinnamon rolls with icing, cut into quarters
- ½ cup chopped toasted pecans, divided
- ½ cup miniature semisweet chocolate chips, divided
- ½ cup evaporated milk
- 3 Tbsp. maple syrup
- 2 tsp. vanilla extract
- 1 tsp. ground cinnamon
- ½ cup all-purpose flour
- ½ cup packed brown sugar
- ¼ tsp. pumpkin pie spice
- ½ cup cold butter, cubed

1. Place half of the cinnamon roll pieces in a greased 4- or 5-qt. slow cooker. Sprinkle with ¼ cup pecans and ¼ cup chocolate chips. In a small bowl, whisk the milk, syrup, vanilla and cinnamon until blended; pour over rolls. Top with the remaining cinnamon roll pieces and remaining miniature chocolate chips. Top with 1 packet icing.
2. For topping, mix flour, brown sugar and pie spice; cut in butter until crumbly. Stir in remaining pecans. Sprinkle over icing. Cook, covered, on low 2½-3 hours or until rolls are set. Remove crock insert to a cooling rack and top with remaining icing. Serve warm.
1 SERVING: 492 cal., 25g fat (11g sat. fat), 28mg chol., 638mg sod., 65g carb. (36g sugars, 2g fiber), 5g pro.

BUFFALO CHICKEN EGG ROLLS

One of my favorite slow-cooker recipes starts with just four ingredients. Then it's time to wrap Buffalo chicken and cheeses in egg roll wraps before baking. For a bite-sized version, use smaller wonton wraps.
—*Tara Odegaard, Omaha, NE*

PREP: 35 min. • **COOK:** 3 hours
MAKES: 16 servings

- 1½ lbs. boneless skinless chicken breasts
- 2 Tbsp. ranch salad dressing mix
- ½ cup Buffalo wing sauce
- 2 Tbsp. butter
- 16 egg roll wrappers
- ⅓ cup crumbled feta cheese
- ⅓ cup shredded part-skim mozzarella cheese
  Ranch salad dressing, optional

1. In a 3-qt. slow cooker, combine chicken, dressing mix and wing sauce. Cook, covered, on low until chicken is tender, 3-4 hours.
2. Preheat oven to 425°. Shred chicken with 2 forks; stir in butter.
3. With a corner of an egg roll wrapper facing you, place 3 Tbsp. chicken mixture just below center of wrapper; top with 1 tsp. each feta and mozzarella cheeses. (Cover remaining wrappers with a damp paper towel until ready to use.) Fold bottom corner over filling; moisten remaining wrapper edges with water. Fold side corners toward center over filling; roll up tightly, pressing at the tip to seal. Place on parchment-lined baking sheets, seam side down. Repeat.
4. Bake until golden brown, 15-20 minutes. Let stand 5 minutes before serving.
1 EGG ROLL: 174 cal., 4g fat (2g sat. fat), 33mg chol., 716mg sod., 21g carb. (0 sugars, 1g fiber), 13g pro.

TEST KITCHEN TIP
We tried brushing some of the egg rolls with oil before baking and they turned out about the same as the plain version. The egg rolls get lightly browned and crisp. They aren't quite as crunchy as deep-fried egg rolls, but close!

THAI CHICKEN LETTUCE CUPS

Lettuce wraps make light, lively appetizers. These are easy to make because the slow cooker does most of the work. Just load it up and let things get cooking. When the chicken is cooked, simply shred and serve.
—*Robin Haas, West Roxbury, MA*

PREP: 10 min. • **COOK:** 2½ hours
MAKES: 12 servings

- 1 lb. boneless skinless chicken breasts
- ½ cup reduced-sodium chicken broth
- 4 garlic cloves, minced
- 1 Tbsp. sugar
- 1 Tbsp. reduced-sodium soy sauce
- 2 tsp. oyster sauce
- ½ tsp. crushed red pepper flakes
- 2 cups torn basil leaves, divided
- 2 Tbsp. hoisin sauce
- 12 Bibb or Boston lettuce leaves
- 2 cups cooked long grain rice
- 4 green onions, chopped
  Shredded carrots and thinly sliced radishes

1. In a 1½-qt. slow cooker, combine the first 7 ingredients. Cook, covered, on low until a thermometer inserted in chicken reads 165°, about 2½ hours. Remove chicken; shred with 2 forks. Return meat to slow cooker. Stir in 1½ cups basil and hoisin sauce; heat through.
2. Serve in lettuce leaves with rice, green onions, carrots, radishes and remaining basil.
FREEZE OPTION: Freeze cooled chicken mixture and juices in freezer containers. To use, partially thaw in refrigerator overnight. Heat through in a saucepan, stirring occasionally and adding a little broth if necessary.
1 LETTUCE CUP: 93 cal., 1g fat (0 sat. fat), 21mg chol., 162mg sod., 11g carb. (2g sugars, 1g fiber), 9g pro.

**THAI CHICKEN
LETTUCE CUPS**

RANCH CHICKEN SLIDERS

PULLED PORK NACHOS

While home from college, my daughter made these tempting pork nachos, her first recipe ever. My son and I couldn't get enough.
—*Carol Kurpjuweit, Humansville, MO*

- -

PREP: 30 min. • **COOK:** 8 hours
MAKES: 16 servings

- 1 tsp. garlic powder
- 1 tsp. mesquite seasoning
- ¼ tsp. pepper
- ⅛ tsp. celery salt
- 3 lbs. boneless pork shoulder butt roast
- 1 medium green pepper, chopped
- 1 medium sweet red pepper, chopped
- 1 medium onion, chopped
- 1 can (16 oz.) baked beans
- 1 cup barbecue sauce
- 1 cup shredded cheddar cheese
   Corn or tortilla chips
   Optional toppings: Chopped tomatoes, shredded lettuce and chopped green onions

1. In a small bowl, mix seasoning ingredients. Place roast in a 5- or 6-qt. slow cooker; rub with seasonings. Add peppers and onion. Cook, covered, on low 8-10 hours.
2. Remove roast; cool slightly. Strain cooking juices, reserving vegetables and ½ cup juices; discard remaining juices. Skim fat from reserved juices. Shred pork with 2 forks.
3. Return pork, reserved juices and vegetables to slow cooker. Stir in beans, barbecue sauce and cheese; heat through. Serve over chips with toppings as desired.
FREEZE OPTION: Freeze cooled pork mixture in freezer containers. To use, partially thaw in refrigerator overnight. Heat through in a saucepan, stirring occasionally and adding a little broth or water if necessary.
½ CUP PORK MIXTURE: 233 cal., 11g fat (5g sat. fat), 60mg chol., 416mg sod., 14g carb. (6g sugars, 2g fiber), 18g pro.

RANCH CHICKEN SLIDERS

My 13-year-old grandson loves crack chicken. We always joked how nothing could make it taste better, until one day Avery's eyes lit up and he said, "Let's fry it!" Then our fried crack chicken burger was born. You won't believe how good these little sliders are.
—*Tamara Hire, Decatur, IL*

- -

PREP: 2¾ hours + chilling
COOK: 10 min./batch • **MAKES:** 6 servings

- 1 lb. boneless skinless chicken breast halves
- 1 envelope ranch salad dressing mix
- 1 pkg. (8 oz.) cream cheese, cubed
- 2 cups crushed pretzels
- 2 cups crushed potato chips or crushed barbecue potato chips
- ¼ cup grated Parmesan cheese
- 2 large eggs
- 1 Tbsp. 2% milk
- 1 cup all-purpose flour
- 1 tsp. garlic salt
- ½ tsp. pepper
- ¼ tsp. paprika
   Oil for frying
- 12 mini buns
   Optional toppings: Lettuce, tomato, bacon, cheddar cheese

1. Place chicken in a 3- or 4-qt. slow cooker. Sprinkle with dressing mix; top with cubed cream cheese. Cook, covered, on low until a thermometer reads 165°, 2½-3½ hours (mixture may appear curdled). Meanwhile, place pretzels, chips and Parmesan in a food processor; pulse until combined. Reserve 1 cup for sliders. Transfer remaining to a shallow bowl.
2. Remove chicken from slow cooker; shred with 2 forks. Return chicken to slow cooker; stir to combine. Add reserved 1 cup pretzel mixture; cool completely. Refrigerate at least 30 minutes.
3. In a shallow bowl, whisk eggs and milk. Combine flour, garlic salt, pepper and paprika in another shallow bowl.
4. Divide and shape chicken mixture into twelve ½-in.-thick patties. Dip patties in flour mixture to coat both sides; shake off excess. Dip in egg mixture, then in remaining pretzel mixture, patting to help coating adhere.
5. In an cast-iron or other heavy skillet, heat ¼ in. oil to 375°. Fry sliders, a few at a time, until golden brown, 3-4 minutes on each side. Drain on paper towels. Serve in buns with toppings as desired.
2 SLIDERS: 705 cal., 40g fat (12g sat. fat), 138mg chol., 1299mg sod., 59g carb. (5g sugars, 2g fiber), 29g pro.

SLOW-COOKER SAUSAGE & APPLES

OLE BEAN DIP

This rich, cheesy bean dip is a crowd-pleaser and so easy to prepare. Two kinds of cheese and sour cream balance the spicy flavor of chiles and taco sauce. Leftovers are great served cold in lunches.
—*Lorraine Wilson, Moses Lake, WA*

PREP: 20 min. • **COOK:** 4 hours
MAKES: 12 cups

    4 cups shredded Monterey Jack cheese
    4 cups shredded cheddar cheese
    1 can (16 oz.) refried beans
    1 bottle (16 oz.) taco sauce
    2 cups sour cream
    2 medium tomatoes, chopped
    1 medium onion, chopped
    1 can (6 oz.) pitted ripe olives,
       drained and chopped
    1 can (4 oz.) chopped green chiles
    1 Tbsp. lemon juice
       Tortilla chip scoops and thinly sliced
       green onions

Combine the first 10 ingredients in a greased 5- or 6-qt. slow cooker. Cook, covered, on low until cheese is melted, 4-5 hours, stirring every hour. Serve with tortilla chips and green onions.
¼ CUP: 114 cal., 9g fat (5g sat. fat), 20mg chol., 235mg sod., 3g carb. (1g sugars, 1g fiber), 5g pro.

TEST KITCHEN TIP

For a truly smooth dip, it's best to shred your own cheese. Preshredded cheese tends not to melt as smoothly, leaving bits of cheese in your dip.

SLOW-COOKER SAUSAGE & APPLES

This recipe belongs to my friend Patty, who made me a wonderful cookbook of her dishes. This is one of her most popular. I often double it for parties.
—*Tammy Zywicki, Elmira, NY*

PREP: 10 min. • **COOK:** 3 hours
MAKES: 24 servings

    2 lbs. smoked kielbasa or
       Polish sausage, sliced
    1 jar (24 oz.) chunky applesauce
    ½ cup packed brown sugar
    ½ cup chopped onion

Combine all ingredients in a 4- or 5-qt. slow cooker. Cook, covered on low, until heated through, 3-4 hours.
¼ CUP: 155 cal., 10g fat (4g sat. fat), 25mg chol., 254mg sod., 11g carb. (9g sugars, 0 fiber), 5g pro.

OLE BEAN DIP

SHREDDED
LAMB SLIDERS

SLOW-COOKER STRAWBERRY SODA CAKE

When you want a sweet cake without the heat of the oven, this slow-cooked spin on cola cake comes in handy. The topping smells divinely like chocolate-covered strawberries. (Remember this one for Valentine's Day!) Delicious served with whipped cream or powdered sugar.
—*Laura Herbage, Covington, LA*

- -

PREP: 30 min. • **COOK:** 2 hours
MAKES: 8 servings

- 1 cup 1% chocolate milk
- ½ cup butter, melted and slightly cooled
- 2 tsp. vanilla extract
- 2 cups all-purpose flour
- ½ cup sugar
- 2½ tsp. baking powder
- ½ tsp. salt
- ¼ cup semisweet chocolate chips

TOPPING
- 1 cup strawberry soda
- ¾ cup packed brown sugar
- ¼ cup sugar
- ¼ cup dark chocolate chips
- ¼ cup seedless strawberry jam
- ¼ cup molasses
  Whipped cream and sliced fresh strawberries

1. In a large bowl, mix the chocolate milk, melted butter and vanilla until well blended. In another bowl, whisk flour, sugar, baking powder and salt; gradually mix into chocolate milk mixture. Stir in chocolate chips. Spread into a greased 3- or 4-qt. slow cooker.
2. For topping, in a small saucepan, combine soda and sugars. Cook and stir over medium heat until sugar is dissolved; remove from heat. Stir in dark chocolate chips, jam and molasses; pour over batter.
3. Cook, covered, on high until a toothpick inserted in the center comes out clean, 2-2½ hours. Serve with whipped cream and strawberries.
1 SERVING: 504 cal., 16g fat (10g sat. fat), 32mg chol., 423mg sod., 88g carb. (63g sugars, 2g fiber), 5g pro.

SHREDDED LAMB SLIDERS

These savory sliders feature lamb, a wonderful special-occasion meat. Once at the Great American Beer Fest, I made about 1,500 sliders in two days, and they went fast—I used every little bit I had to serve the very last customer.
—*Craig Kuczek, Aurora, CO*

- -

PREP: 45 min. • **COOK:** 6 hours
MAKES: 2 dozen

- 1 boneless lamb shoulder roast (3½ to 4¼ lbs.)
- 1½ tsp. salt
- ½ tsp. pepper
- 1 Tbsp. olive oil
- 2 medium carrots, chopped
- 4 shallots, chopped
- 6 garlic cloves
- 2 cups beef stock

PESTO
- ¾ cup fresh mint leaves
- ¾ cup loosely packed basil leaves
- ⅓ cup pine nuts
- ¼ tsp. salt
- ¾ cup olive oil
- ¾ cup shredded Parmesan cheese
- ⅓ cup shredded Asiago cheese
- 24 slider buns
- 1 pkg. (4 oz.) crumbled feta cheese

1. Sprinkle roast with salt and pepper. In a large skillet, heat oil over medium-high heat; brown meat. Transfer meat to a 6- or 7-qt. slow cooker. In the same skillet, cook and stir carrots, shallots and garlic until crisp-tender, about 4 minutes. Add stock, stirring to loosen browned bits from pan. Pour over lamb. Cook, covered, on low until lamb is tender, 6-8 hours.
2. Meanwhile for pesto, place mint, basil, pine nuts and salt in a food processor; pulse until chopped. Continue processing while gradually adding oil in a steady stream. Add cheeses; pulse just until blended.
3. When cool enough to handle, remove meat from bones; discard bones. Shred meat with 2 forks. Strain cooking juices, adding vegetables to shredded meat; skim fat. Return cooking juices and meat to slow cooker. Heat through. Serve on buns with pesto and feta.
1 SLIDER: 339 cal., 22g fat (7g sat. fat), 56mg chol., 459mg sod., 16g carb. (2g sugars, 1g fiber), 18g pro.

**SLOW-COOKER
STRAWBERRY SODA CAKE**

FARMERS MARKET PASTA
PAGE 139

133

147

94

115

Stovetop Suppers

Quick, everyday, delicious...those are the recipes we reach for time and again. When you want a simple dinner that comes together fast and fabulous, turn here. You will find 90-plus express-lane dinners, dishes that highlight the season's best, and even ways to take advantage of sale ingredients. Smart cooking starts with these timesaving suppers!

Beef & Ground Beef

BRIEF BURRITOS

With three children in school, evenings are often hectic and short on time. I can put this dish together after school and still have time to run back to town for evening activities. Best of all, the kids love it.
—*Ginger Burow, Fredericksburg, TX*

TAKES: 20 min. • **MAKES:** 8 servings

- 1 lb. ground beef
- 1 can (16 oz.) refried beans
- 1 can (10 oz.) diced tomatoes and green chiles, drained
- ½ cup chili sauce
- 8 flour tortillas (10 in.), warmed
- ½ cup shredded cheddar cheese
- ½ cup sour cream

1. In a large skillet, cook beef over medium heat 6-8 minutes or until no longer pink, breaking into crumbles; drain. Stir in beans, tomatoes and chili sauce; heat through.
2. Place about ½ cup meat mixture near the center on each tortilla; top with cheese and sour cream. Fold bottom and sides of tortilla over filling and roll up. Serve immediately.

1 BURRITO: 430 cal., 14g fat (7g sat. fat), 50mg chol., 1022mg sod., 46g carb. (5g sugars, 9g fiber), 21g pro.

BLACK BEAN BURRITOS: Substitute black beans for the refried beans and 1 cup salsa for the canned tomatoes and chili sauce. Double the cheese.

BLT BURRITOS: Combine 6 cups shredded lettuce, 3 cups diced tomatoes, 1½ cups crumbled cooked bacon, ½ cup mayonnaise and ¼ tsp. pepper; spoon onto tortillas and roll up.

CHEESY CRAB BURRITOS: Combine 8 oz. each softened cream cheese, shredded cheddar cheese and flaked imitation crabmeat; spoon onto tortillas and roll up. Bake on an ungreased baking sheet at 350° until heated through, about 20 minutes. Serve with salsa.

BRIEF BURRITOS

**ONE-POT BACON
CHEESEBURGER
PASTA**

a boil. Reduce heat; simmer, covered, until pasta is al dente, stirring occasionally, about 10 minutes.

3. Stir in 1 cup cheese, pickle and bacon; cook and stir until cheese is melted. Serve with remaining cheese and, if desired, tomatoes, lettuce, pickles and red onions.

1⅓ CUPS: 390 cal., 18g fat (8g sat. fat), 73mg chol., 1023mg sod., 31g carb. (7g sugars, 3g fiber), 25g pro.

SKILLET BEEF STEW

Think you can't prepare a hot and hearty stew in under 40 minutes? Think again! This super stew recipe uses frozen vegetables and prepared gravy, so you can serve up steaming bowlfuls in no time.
—Taste of Home *Test Kitchen*

- -

PREP: 10 min. • **COOK:** 25 min.
MAKES: 4 servings

1	lb. beef top sirloin steak
2	Tbsp. canola oil
1	pkg. (16 oz.) frozen vegetables for stew
1	jar (12 oz.) beef gravy
2	Tbsp. Worcestershire sauce
½	tsp. dried thyme
¼	tsp. pepper
¼	tsp. garlic powder

Cut steak into 2x¼-in. strips. In a large skillet, cook beef over medium heat until no longer pink. Drain if necessary. Stir in remaining the ingredients; bring to a boil. Reduce heat; cover and simmer for 15 minutes or until heated through.

1 CUP: 314 cal., 12g fat (3g sat. fat), 53mg chol., 642mg sod., 21g carb. (2g sugars, 1g fiber), 27g pro. **DIABETIC EXCHANGES:** 3 lean meat, 1½ starch, 1½ fat.

ONE-POT BACON CHEESEBURGER PASTA

When the weather's too chilly to grill burgers, I whip up a big pot of this cheesy pasta. Believe it or not, it tastes just like a bacon cheeseburger, and it's much easier for my young children to enjoy.
—Carly Terrell, Granbury, TX

- -

PREP: 15 min. • **COOK:** 35 min.
MAKES: 12 servings

8	bacon strips, chopped
2	lbs. ground beef
½	large red onion, chopped
12	oz. uncooked spiral pasta
4	cups chicken broth
2	cans (15 oz. each) crushed tomatoes
1	can (8 oz.) tomato sauce
1	cup water
¼	cup ketchup
3	Tbsp. prepared mustard
2	Tbsp. Worcestershire sauce
¼	tsp. salt
¼	tsp. pepper
2	cups shredded cheddar cheese, divided
⅓	cup chopped dill pickle Chopped tomatoes, shredded lettuce, sliced pickles and sliced red onion, optional

1. In a 6-qt. stockpot, cook bacon over medium heat, stirring occasionally, until crisp, 6-8 minutes. Remove with a slotted spoon; drain on paper towels. Discard drippings.
2. In the same pot, cook the beef and onion over medium heat until meat is no longer pink, breaking into crumbles, 6-8 minutes; drain. Add the next 10 ingredients; bring to

CORNED BEEF STIR-FRY

MOM'S ROAST BEEF

This well-seasoned roast is Mom's specialty. Everyone loves slices of the fork-tender roast beef and its savory gravy, and people always ask what her secret ingredients are. Now you have the delicious recipe for our favorite dish!
—*Linda Gaido, New Brighton, PA*

PREP: 20 min.
COOK: 2½ hours + standing
MAKES: 8 servings

- 1 Tbsp. canola oil
- 1 beef eye round roast (about 2½ lbs.)
- 1 garlic clove, minced
- 2 tsp. dried basil
- 1 tsp. salt
- 1 tsp. dried rosemary, crushed
- ½ tsp. pepper
- 1 medium onion, chopped
- 1 tsp. beef bouillon granules
- 1 cup brewed coffee
- ¾ cup water

GRAVY

- ¼ cup all-purpose flour
- ¼ cup cold water

1. In a Dutch oven, heat oil over medium heat; brown the roast on all sides. Remove from pan. Mix garlic and seasonings; sprinkle over roast.

2. Add chopped onion to same pan; cook and stir over medium heat until tender; stir in bouillon, coffee and ¾ cup water. Add roast; bring to a boil. Reduce heat; simmer, covered, until meat is tender, about 2½ hours.

3. Remove roast from pan, reserving cooking juices. Tent with foil; let stand 10 minutes before slicing.

4. Mix flour and cold water until smooth; stir into cooking juices. Bring to a boil, stirring constantly. Cook and stir until thickened, 1-2 minutes. Serve with roast.

1 SERVING: 198 cal., 6g fat (2g sat. fat), 65mg chol., 453mg sod., 5g carb. (1g sugars, 1g fiber), 28g pro.

CORNED BEEF STIR-FRY

The celery seed really comes through in this colorful combination of carrots, cabbage and corned beef. A woman at church shared the recipe with me. My husband and son love its subtle sweetness.
—*Alesah Padgett, Franklin, GA*

TAKES: 30 min. • **MAKES:** 6 servings

- 7 Tbsp. canola oil, divided
- 3 Tbsp. white vinegar
- 2 Tbsp. sugar
- 1 tsp. celery seed
- ¼ tsp. salt
- 6 cups coarsely chopped cabbage
- 1 cup shredded carrots
- ¼ cup chopped green onions
- ½ lb. thinly sliced deli corned beef
   Hot cooked rice, optional

1. In a small bowl, whisk 4 Tbsp. oil, vinegar, sugar, celery seed and salt until the sugar is dissolved; set aside.

2. In a large skillet, saute the cabbage, carrots and onions in remaining oil for 15-16 minutes or until crisp-tender. Stir in the vinegar-oil mixture and corned beef. Cover and simmer for 10 minutes or until heated through. Serve with rice if desired.

1 SERVING: 243 cal., 19g fat (3g sat. fat), 25mg chol., 629mg sod., 12g carb. (8g sugars, 3g fiber), 9g pro.

MOM'S ROAST BEEF

VEGGIE STEAK SOFT TACOS

Since I used to live in Mexico, I love re-creating the flavors I enjoyed there. This is one of my favorite quick meals!
—*Becky Toney, Tarpon Springs, FL*

- -

TAKES: 25 min. • **MAKES:** 4 servings

- 1 lb. beef top sirloin steak, thinly sliced
- 2 tsp. ground cumin
- ⅛ tsp. salt
- 3 tsp. canola oil, divided
- 1 large onion, sliced
- 1 small sweet red pepper, julienned
- 1 small green pepper, julienned
- 2 Tbsp. minced fresh cilantro
- 4 whole wheat tortillas (8 in.), warmed
  Optional ingredients: Shredded lettuce, chopped tomato and reduced-fat sour cream

1. Sprinkle beef with cumin and salt. In a large skillet, saute beef in 2 tsp. oil until no longer pink. Remove and set aside.

2. In same skillet, saute onion and peppers in remaining oil until tender. Stir in cilantro. Return beef to the pan; heat through.

3. Spoon onto tortillas. Serve with lettuce, tomato and sour cream if desired.

1 TACO: 344 cal., 11g fat (2g sat. fat), 46mg chol., 299mg sod., 28g carb. (4g sugars, 4g fiber), 29g pro. **DIABETIC EXCHANGES:** 3 lean meat, 1½ starch, 1 vegetable, 1 fat.

TEST KITCHEN TIP

To chop cilantro or parsley without dirtying a cutting board, place sprigs in a small glass container and snip with kitchen shears until chopped to desired fineness.

BEEF PAPRIKASH WITH FIRE-ROASTED TOMATOES

BEEF PAPRIKASH WITH FIRE-ROASTED TOMATOES

Beef cooked Hungarian-style with paprika, peppers and tomatoes makes a marvelous Sunday dinner. We prefer it with kluski egg noodles, or try mashed potatoes.
—*Gloria Bradley, Naperville, IL*

- -

PREP: 15 min. • **COOK:** 1¾ hours
MAKES: 8 servings

- ⅓ cup all-purpose flour
- 2 Tbsp. sweet Hungarian or regular paprika, divided
- 1¼ tsp. salt, divided
- 2 lbs. boneless beef chuck roast, cut into 1-in. pieces
- 2 Tbsp. canola oil, divided
- 1 large onion, chopped
- 1 small sweet red pepper, finely chopped
- 2 cans (8 oz. each) tomato sauce
- 1 can (14½ oz.) fire-roasted diced tomatoes, undrained
- 1 can (14½ oz.) beef broth
- 1 pkg. (16 oz.) kluski or other egg noodles
- 3 Tbsp. butter
  Minced fresh parsley, optional

1. In a small bowl, mix flour, 1 Tbsp. paprika and ½ tsp. salt. Sprinkle over beef and toss to coat; shake off excess.

2. In a Dutch oven, heat 1 Tbsp. oil over medium heat. Brown beef pieces in batches, adding remaining oil as needed. Remove from pan with a slotted spoon, reserving drippings in the pan.

3. Add onion and pepper to drippings; cook and stir 4-5 minutes or until tender. Stir in the tomato sauce, tomatoes, broth and remaining 1 Tbsp. paprika and ¾ tsp. salt; bring to a boil. Reduce heat; simmer, covered, 1½-2 hours or until beef is tender.

4. Cook the noodles according to package directions. Drain; return to pot. Add butter and toss to coat. Serve with stew. If desired, sprinkle with parsley.

1 CUP STEW WITH ¾ CUP COOKED NOODLES: 534 cal., 21g fat (8g sat. fat), 133mg chol., 953mg sod., 51g carb. (5g sugars, 4g fiber), 33g pro.

WALKING TACOS

Take these tacos for a walk any time you need an on-the-go dinner, campfire meal or easy game-night supper. The ingredients go right into the chip bags!
—*Beverly Matthews, Richland, WA*

- -

PREP: 10 min. • **COOK:** 30 min.
MAKES: 5 servings

- 1 lb. ground beef
- 1 envelope reduced-sodium chili seasoning mix
- ¼ tsp. pepper
- 1 can (10 oz.) diced tomatoes and green chiles
- 1 can (15 oz.) Ranch Style beans (pinto beans in seasoned tomato sauce)
- 5 pkg. (1 oz. each) corn chips
  Toppings: Shredded cheddar cheese, sour cream and sliced green onions

1. In a large skillet, cook beef over medium heat until no longer pink, breaking into crumbles, 6-8 minutes; drain. Stir in chili seasoning mix, pepper, tomatoes and beans; bring to a boil. Reduce heat; simmer, uncovered, until thickened, 20-25 minutes, stirring occasionally.
2. Just before serving, cut open corn chip bags. Add beef mixture and toppings.
1 SERVING: 530 cal., 28g fat (6g sat. fat), 56mg chol., 1017mg sod., 44g carb. (5g sugars, 6g fiber), 24g pro.

LIVER SKILLET SUPPER

Whenever I serve this to people for the first time, someone exclaims, "I can't believe it's liver!" Around here, that's what we call this recipe. As longtime custom harvesters, we've provided meals for many hungry farmhands. This lets me pursue my dual passions for creating new recipes and quantity cooking.
—*Karen Ann Bland, Gove City, KS*

- -

TAKES: 30 min. • **MAKES:** 6 servings

- ½ lb. sliced bacon
- ¾ cup all-purpose flour
- 1 tsp. garlic salt, divided
- 1 tsp. onion salt, divided
- 1 tsp. pepper, divided
- 1 lb. beef liver
- 6 large potatoes, peeled and thinly sliced
- 1 large onions, thinly sliced
  Green pepper rings, optional

In a large skillet, cook bacon until crisp. Remove to a paper towel to drain; reserve drippings in skillet. Combine flour and half of the garlic salt, onion salt and pepper. Cut liver into 2x½-in. strips; dredge in the flour mixture, coating well. Lightly brown liver in drippings. Add potatoes and onion. Sprinkle with remaining seasonings; cook until the potatoes are browned and tender, stirring occasionally. Crumble bacon over top. Garnish with green pepper rings if desired.
1 CUP: 540 cal., 10g fat (3g sat. fat), 278mg chol., 882mg sod., 85g carb. (7g sugars, 7g fiber), 29g pro.

WALKING TACOS

ASPARAGUS
BEEF LO MEIN

ASPARAGUS BEEF LO MEIN

This springtime beef stir-fry is as easy as it gets. Ramen noodles make it extra fun.
—*Dottie Wanat, Modesto, CA*

- -

TAKES: 20 min. • **MAKES:** 4 servings

- 1   beef top sirloin steak (1 lb.), cut into thin strips
- 2   pkg. (3 oz. each) beef ramen noodles
- ⅔   cup hoisin sauce
- 2¼ cups water, divided
- 2   Tbsp. olive oil, divided
- 1   lb. fresh asparagus, trimmed and cut into 2½-in. pieces
- 1   small garlic clove, minced

1. Toss beef with ½ tsp. seasoning from a ramen seasoning packet (discard remaining opened packet). In a small bowl, mix hoisin sauce and ¼ cup water.
2. In a saucepan, bring remaining water to a boil. Add noodles and contents of the unopened seasoning packet; cook, uncovered, 3 minutes. Remove from heat; let stand, covered, until noodles are tender.
3. Meanwhile, in a large skillet, heat 1 Tbsp. oil over medium-high heat; stir-fry beef until browned, 3-4 minutes. Remove from pan.
4. In same pan, heat remaining oil over medium-high heat; stir-fry asparagus with garlic until crisp-tender, 1-3 minutes. Stir in hoisin sauce mixture; bring to a boil. Cook until slightly thickened. Stir in beef; heat through. Serve over noodles.
1 SERVING: 511 cal., 21g fat (7g sat. fat), 47mg chol., 1367mg sod., 48g carb. (13g sugars, 3g fiber), 31g pro.

"My husband really likes this dish. I make it with broccoli and it turns out really delicious."
—SUGARRADISH, TASTEOFHOME.COM

RHODE ISLAND HOT WIENERS

RHODE ISLAND HOT WIENERS

Many Rhode Islanders spell wiener with an "ei" and serve theirs "all the way" with meat sauce, mustard, onion and a sprinkle of celery salt. Give it a try.
—*Karen Barros, Bristol, RI*

- -

PREP: 15 min. • **COOK:** 50 min.
MAKES: 8 servings

- ¼   cup butter, cubed
- 1   medium onion, finely chopped
- 2   Tbsp. Worcestershire sauce
- 2   Tbsp. paprika
- 2   Tbsp. chili powder
- 3   tsp. ground cumin
- 1   tsp. ground mustard
- ¾   tsp. ground cinnamon
- ½   tsp. ground allspice
- 1   lb. ground beef
- ¼   cup water
- 8   hot dogs
- 8   hot dog buns, split and warmed
  Toppings: Yellow mustard, finely chopped onion and celery salt

1. In a large skillet, heat butter over medium heat. Add onion; cook and stir 3-4 minutes or until tender. Stir in Worcestershire sauce and seasonings. Add beef; cook 6-8 minutes or until no longer pink, breaking into crumbles. Stir in water; bring to a boil. Reduce heat; simmer, uncovered, 30 minutes.
2. In a large skillet, cook hot dogs over medium heat 8-10 minutes or until lightly browned, turning occasionally. Serve in buns with meat sauce and toppings as desired.
1 HOT DOG: 447 cal., 29g fat (12g sat. fat), 75mg chol., 803mg sod., 28g carb. (5g sugars, 3g fiber), 20g pro.

MOROCCAN BEEF & APPLE STEW

I like to cook various dishes from around the world, so when I found a recipe for Moroccan tagine, I adapted it to our family's tastes. It starts off a bit sweet and ends with a spicy bite.
—*Dawn Elliott, Greenville, MI*

PREP: 25 min. + chilling • **COOK:** 2½ hours
MAKES: 8 servings

- 1¾ lbs. beef stew meat
- 5 Tbsp. Mrs. Dash Caribbean Citrus seasoning blend, divided
- ½ cup butter, cubed, divided
- 4 medium onions, coarsely chopped
- 2 celery ribs, cut into ⅛-in. slices
- 4 garlic cloves, minced
- 2 cups beef broth
- 3 medium sweet potatoes, peeled and cubed (about 5 cups)
- 4 medium Granny Smith apples, peeled and cut into 1½-in. pieces
- 4 medium carrots, cut into ½-in. slices
- 1 cup apple butter
- ¼ cup minced fresh cilantro
  Hot cooked couscous

1. In a large bowl, toss beef with 4 Tbsp. seasoning blend. Refrigerate, covered, 30 minutes.

2. In a Dutch oven, heat ¼ cup butter over medium heat. Brown beef in batches. Remove with a slotted spoon.

3. In same pan, melt remaining butter. Add the onions, celery and remaining seasoning blend; cook and stir until the vegetables are tender, 6-8 minutes Add garlic; cook 1 minute longer. Stir in broth. Return beef to pan; bring to a boil. Reduce heat; simmer, covered, 1½ hours.

4. Stir in sweet potatoes, apples, carrots and apple butter. Cook, covered, 30-40 minutes longer or until the meat and vegetables are tender. Sprinkle with minced cilantro. Serve with hot couscous.

1⅓ CUPS: 449 cal., 19g fat (10g sat. fat), 92mg chol., 398mg sod., 48g carb. (30g sugars, 6g fiber), 22g pro.

SOUTHWESTERN BEEF & RICE SKILLET

I like to serve this spiced-up skillet dish with warm flour tortillas and a side of guacamole. If you like things a little spicier, add more jalapenos and enjoy the heat!
—*Pat Hockett, Ocala, FL*

TAKES: 30 min. • **MAKES:** 4 servings

- 1 lb. lean ground beef (90% lean)
- 1 medium onion, chopped
- 1 medium green pepper, chopped
- 1 jalapeno pepper, seeded and finely chopped
- 1½ cups uncooked instant rice
- 1 can (14½ oz.) diced tomatoes with mild green chiles
- 1½ cups beef broth
- 1 tsp. ground cumin
- ¼ tsp. salt
- ¼ tsp. pepper
- 1 cup shredded Mexican cheese blend

1. In a large skillet, cook beef, onion, green pepper and jalapeno over medium heat until meat is no longer pink and vegetables are tender, breaking up beef into crumbles, 8-10 minutes; drain.

2. Add rice, tomatoes, broth and seasonings. Bring to a boil, then reduce heat. Simmer, covered, until the liquid is absorbed, about 5 minutes. Fluff with a fork. Remove from heat; sprinkle with cheese. Let stand, covered, until cheese is melted.

1½ CUPS: 482 cal., 19g fat (8g sat. fat), 96mg chol., 962mg sod., 41g carb. (5g sugars, 4g fiber), 33g pro.

SOUTHWESTERN BEEF & RICE SKILLET

**BEEF BARLEY
SKILLET**

MINUTE STEAKS PARMESAN

We often use cubed steaks to make steak sandwiches. In this recipe, I dress them up with a cheesy Parmesan coating and zesty pizza sauce.
—*Carol Dalke, Elk Creek, MT*

- -

TAKES: 25 min. • **MAKES:** 4 servings

- 1 large egg white, lightly beaten
- 2 tsp. water
    Dash pepper
- ½ cup finely crushed saltine crackers
- ½ cup grated Parmesan cheese
- 4 beef cubed steaks (4 oz. each)
- 2 Tbsp. butter
- 1 can (8 oz.) pizza sauce

1. In a shallow bowl, combine the egg white, water and pepper. Set aside. On a plate, combine cracker crumbs and cheese. Dip each cube steak into the egg mixture, then coat with cracker-cheese mixture.
2. In a large skillet, melt butter; brown steaks on both sides. Add pizza sauce and simmer for 3-5 minutes. Garnish with remaining crumb mixture. Serve immediately.
1 SERVING: 185 cal., 10g fat (6g sat. fat), 39mg chol., 521mg sod., 10g carb. (3g sugars, 1g fiber), 13g pro.

"It was nice to find something different...this one is a keeper. Only change I would make is next time, I will add some cheese at the last minute. But very good."
—SHARONRABURN, TASTEOFHOME.COM

BEEF BARLEY SKILLET

This versatile dish goes together fast since it's made with quick-cooking barley. You can make it with ground turkey or chicken, and any color bell pepper that you have on hand.
—*Irene Tetreault, South Hadley, MA*

- -

TAKES: 30 min. • **MAKES:** 4 servings

- 1 lb. lean ground beef (90% lean)
- 1 small onion, chopped
- ¼ cup chopped celery
- ¼ cup chopped green pepper
- 1 can (14½ oz.) diced tomatoes, undrained
- 1½ cups water
- ¾ cup quick-cooking barley
- ½ cup chili sauce
- 1 tsp. Worcestershire sauce
- ½ tsp. dried marjoram
- ⅛ tsp. pepper
    Chopped parsley, optional

In a large skillet, cook beef, onion, celery and green pepper over medium-high heat until beef is no longer pink and vegetables are tender, breaking up meat into crumbles; drain. Stir in remaining ingredients. Bring to a boil. Reduce heat; simmer, uncovered, until barley is tender, 5-10 minutes. If desired, top with chopped parsley.
1½ CUPS: 362 cal., 10g fat (4g sat. fat), 71mg chol., 707mg sod., 41g carb. (11g sugars, 8g fiber), 27g pro. **DIABETIC EXCHANGES:** 3 lean meat, 2 starch, 1 vegetable.

QUICK
PEPPER
STEAK

CURRIED BEEF PITA POCKETS

If there are people in your family who think they won't like the taste of curry, serve this. They'll be curry lovers forever!

—*Mary Ann Kosmas, Minneapolis, MN*

PREP: 5 min. • **COOK:** 30 min.
MAKES: 4 servings

- 1 lb. ground beef
- 1 medium onion, chopped
- 1 garlic clove, halved
- 1 Tbsp. curry powder
- ½ cup water
- ½ tsp. salt
- ½ tsp. sugar
- ¼ tsp. pepper
- 1 medium tomato, seeded and diced
- 1 medium zucchini, diced
- 8 pita pocket halves
  Refrigerated tzatziki sauce, optional

1. In a large skillet, brown ground beef with the onion, garlic and curry; drain and discard garlic. Stir in water, salt, sugar and pepper. Cover and simmer 15 minutes.
2. Add tomato and zucchini; cook just until heated through. Spoon the meat mixture into pita breads. Serve with tzatziki sauce, if desired.
2 FILLED PITA HALVES: 393 cal., 14g fat (5g sat. fat), 70mg chol., 665mg sod., 38g carb. (4g sugars, 3g fiber), 27g pro.

QUICK PEPPER STEAK

When I need a speedy skillet supper, this pepper steak comes to my rescue. The tender meat is slightly sweet, with a hint of brown sugar and molasses.

—*Monica Williams, Burleson, TX*

TAKES: 25 min. • **MAKES:** 6 servings

- 2 Tbsp. cornstarch
- 2 Tbsp. brown sugar
- 2 Tbsp. minced fresh gingerroot
- ¾ tsp. garlic powder
- 1 can (14½ oz.) beef broth
- 3 Tbsp. reduced-sodium soy sauce
- 1 Tbsp. molasses
- 1½ lbs. beef top sirloin steak, cut into ¼-in. strips
- 1 Tbsp. canola oil
- 2 large green peppers, cut into ½-in. strips
- 1½ cups sliced celery
- 3 green onions, chopped
- 4 tsp. lemon juice
  Hot cooked noodles, optional

1. In a bowl, combine the cornstarch, brown sugar, ginger and garlic powder. Stir in broth until smooth. Add soy sauce and molasses; set aside.
2. In a nonstick skillet or wok, stir-fry steak in oil for 4-5 minutes; remove and keep warm. Stir-fry peppers, celery and onions until crisp-tender, about 5 minutes. Stir broth mixture and add to the vegetables. Return meat to the pan. Bring to a boil; cook and stir until thickened, about 2 minutes. Stir in lemon juice. Serve over noodles if desired.
¾ CUP: 233 cal., 7g fat (2g sat. fat), 46mg chol., 672mg sod., 14g carb. (9g sugars, 2g fiber), 26g pro. **DIABETIC EXCHANGES:** 3 lean meat, 1 vegetable, ½ starch, ½ fat.

TEST KITCHEN TIP

Greek in origin, tzatziki sauce is a blend of yogurt, cucumber, garlic, and often lemon and dill. You can make your own version with plain yogurt or sour cream, plus whichever of these flavor components you like.

**CURRIED BEEF
PITA POCKETS**

COUNTRY-FRIED STEAK

This down-home main course is simple
to make and so delicious!
—*Betty Claycomb, Alverton, PA*

TAKES: 20 min. • **MAKES:** 4 servings

- ½ cup all-purpose flour
- ½ tsp. salt
- ½ tsp. pepper
- ¾ cup buttermilk
- 1 cup crushed saltines
- 4 beef cubed steaks (1 lb.)
- 3 Tbsp. canola oil
- 1 can (10¾ oz.) condensed cream
   of mushrooms soup, undiluted
- 1 cup whole milk

1. In a shallow bowl, combine flour, salt and
pepper. Place buttermilk in a shallow bowl.
Place saltine crumbs in a third bowl. Coat
steaks with flour mixture, then dip into
buttermilk and coat with crumbs.
2. In a large skillet over medium-high heat,
cook steaks in oil for 2-3 minutes on each side
or until golden and no longer pink. Remove
and keep warm. Add soup and milk to skillet;
bring to a boil, stirring to loosen browned bits
from pan. Serve gravy with steaks.
1 SERVING: 469 cal., 22g fat (6g sat. fat),
77mg chol., 1134mg sod., 34g carb. (6g
sugars, 2g fiber), 34g pro.

CURLY NOODLE DINNER

The calendar on my kitchen wall is often
filled with church work, 4-H leader
meetings and school activities for our
three daughters. Recipes like this one
are perfect for our busy family.
—*Gwen Clemon, Soldier, IA*

TAKES: 25 min. • **MAKES:** 4 servings

- 1 lb. ground beef
- 1 pkg. (3 oz.) beef ramen noodles
- 1 can (14½ oz.) stewed tomatoes
- 1 can (8½ oz.) whole kernel
   corn, drained

In a skillet, brown beef; drain. Stir in noodles
with contents of accompanying seasoning
packet, tomatoes and corn; mix well. Bring
to a boil. Reduce heat; cover and simmer for
10 minutes or until the noodles are tender.
1 SERVING: 359 cal., 18g fat (7g sat. fat),
70mg chol., 794mg sod., 26g carb. (9g sugars,
3g fiber), 24g pro.

**BEEF TENDERLOIN
STROGANOFF**

BEEF TENDERLOIN
STROGANOFF

Here's a delightful main course that's meant
for weeknight celebrations. The creamy sauce
drenches the beef tenderloin and noodles.
While it comes together quickly, your family
will think you toiled for hours!
—*Elizabeth Deguit, Richmond Hill, GA*

TAKES: 30 min. • **MAKES:** 6 servings

- 2 Tbsp. all-purpose flour
- 1½ lbs. beef tenderloin, cut
   into thin strips
- 2 Tbsp. olive oil
- 2 Tbsp. butter
- 1½ cups beef broth
- ¼ cup sour cream
- 2 Tbsp. tomato paste
- ½ tsp. paprika
   Salt to taste
   Hot cooked noodles

1. Place flour in a large bowl or dish; add beef,
a few pieces at a time, and toss to coat. In a
large skillet, brown beef in oil and butter over
medium heat.
2. Gradually stir in broth; bring to a boil.
Reduce heat to low. In a small bowl, combine
sour cream, tomato paste, paprika and salt;
slowly stir in sour cream mixture (do not
boil). Cook, uncovered, over low heat for
15-20 minutes, stirring frequently. Serve
with hot noodles.
1 SERVING: 275 cal., 17g fat (7g sat. fat),
62mg chol., 260mg sod., 3g carb. (1g sugars,
0 fiber), 26g pro.

BEEF STEW WITH CHEDDAR DUMPLINGS

My family asks for this rich stew just about every week. Perfect for company, it's surprisingly easy to make. Everyone comments on the flavorful cheddar cheese in the dumplings.
—Jackie Riley, Garrettsville, OH

- -

PREP: 25 min. • **COOK:** 1½ hours
MAKES: 8 servings

- ½ cup all-purpose flour
- ½ tsp. salt
- ½ tsp. pepper
- 2 to 3 lbs. beef stew meat, cut into 1-in. pieces
- 2 Tbsp. canola oil
- 5 cups water
- 5 tsp. beef bouillon granules
- 1 Tbsp. browning sauce, optional
- ½ tsp. onion salt
- ½ tsp. garlic salt
- 4 medium carrots, sliced
- 1 medium onion, cut into wedges
- 1 can (14½ oz.) cut green beans, drained

DUMPLINGS

- 2 cups biscuit/baking mix
- 1 cup shredded cheddar cheese
- ⅔ cup whole milk

1. In a large bowl or dish, combine the flour, salt and pepper. Add beef, a few pieces at a time, and toss to coat. In a Dutch oven, brown beef in oil in batches.
2. Stir in the water, bouillon, browning sauce if desired, onion salt and garlic salt. Bring to a boil. Reduce heat; cover and simmer for 1 hour.
3. Add carrots and onion. Cover and simmer 10-15 minutes longer or until vegetables are tender. Stir in green beans.
4. For dumplings, combine biscuit mix and cheese. Stir in enough milk to form a soft dough. Drop dough by tablespoonfuls onto simmering stew. Cover and simmer for 10-12 minutes (do not lift cover) or until a toothpick inserted in a dumpling comes out clean. Serve immediately.
1 SERVING: 441 cal., 21g fat (8g sat. fat), 88mg chol., 1627mg sod., 33g carb. (6g sugars, 3g fiber), 30g pro.

PEANUT BEEF STIR-FRY

Peanut butter lends a subtle flavor to this no-fuss beef dish. For a change of pace, try ground beef. It's always tasty over noodles.
—Rita Reifenstein, Evans City, PA

- -

TAKES: 20 min. • **MAKES:** 4 servings

- 5 tsp. cornstarch
- 1 can (14½ oz.) beef broth
- 2 Tbsp. soy sauce
- 2 Tbsp. creamy peanut butter
- ½ tsp. sugar
  Dash pepper
- 1 lb. beef top sirloin steak, thinly sliced
- 1 cup sliced onion
- 1 cup sliced celery
- 2 Tbsp. canola oil
- 1 tsp. minced garlic

1. In a large bowl, combine the cornstarch, broth, soy sauce, peanut butter, sugar and pepper until smooth; set aside. In a large skillet or wok, stir-fry the beef, onion and celery in oil for 5-8 minutes or until meat is no longer pink. Add garlic; cook 1 minute longer.
2. Stir cornstarch mixture and add to the pan. Bring to a boil; cook and stir for 1-2 minutes or until thickened.
1 CUP: 305 cal., 17g fat (5g sat. fat), 76mg chol., 609mg sod., 11g carb. (4g sugars, 2g fiber), 26g pro.

"This was really good. I served it over rice with egg rolls on the side."
—KATLAYDEE3, TASTEOFHOME.COM

BEEF STEW WITH CHEDDAR DUMPLINGS

EASY ASIAN BEEF & NOODLES

EASY ASIAN BEEF & NOODLES

I created this dish on a whim to feed my hungry teenagers. It's since become a dinnertime staple—and now two of my grandchildren make it in their own kitchens.
—Judy Batson, Tampa, FL

TAKES: 25 min. • **MAKES:** 4 servings

- 1 beef top sirloin steak (1 lb.), cut into ¼-in.-thick strips
- 6 Tbsp. reduced-sodium teriyaki sauce, divided
- 8 oz. uncooked whole grain thin spaghetti
- 2 Tbsp. canola oil, divided
- 3 cups broccoli coleslaw mix
- 1 medium onion, halved and thinly sliced
   Chopped fresh cilantro, optional

1. Toss beef with 2 Tbsp. teriyaki sauce. Cook spaghetti according to package directions; drain.
2. In a large skillet, heat 1 Tbsp. oil over medium-high heat; stir-fry beef pieces until browned, 1-3 minutes. Remove from pan.
3. In same skillet, heat remaining oil over medium-high heat; stir-fry coleslaw mix and onion until crisp-tender, 3-5 minutes. Add spaghetti and remaining teriyaki sauce; toss and heat through. Stir in beef. If desired, sprinkle with cilantro.
2 CUPS: 462 cal., 13g fat (2g sat. fat), 46mg chol., 546mg sod., 52g carb. (9g sugars, 8g fiber), 35g pro.

SWEET BBQ MEATBALLS

❄ SWEET BBQ MEATBALLS

These sauced-up meatballs have big Asian flair. If your family likes sweet-and-sour chicken, this beefy version hits the spot.
—Taste of Home *Test Kitchen*

TAKES: 25 min. • **MAKES:** 6 servings

- 2 tsp. olive oil
- ½ lb. sliced fresh mushrooms
- 1 medium green pepper, cut into 1-in. pieces
- 1 medium onion, cut into 1-in. pieces
- 1 pkg. (12 oz.) frozen fully cooked Italian meatballs, thawed
- 1 bottle (18 oz.) barbecue sauce
- 1 jar (10 oz.) apricot preserves
- 1 cup unsweetened pineapple chunks
- ½ cup water
- ¾ tsp. ground mustard
- ⅛ tsp. ground allspice
   Hot cooked rice

1. In a Dutch oven, heat oil over medium-high heat. Add mushrooms, pepper and onion; cook and stir 7-9 minutes or until tender.
2. Stir in meatballs, barbecue sauce, preserves, pineapple, water, mustard and allspice. Reduce heat to medium; cook and stir 6-8 minutes or until meatballs are heated through. Serve with rice.
FREEZE OPTION: Freeze cooled meatball mixture in freezer containers. To use, partially thaw in refrigerator overnight. Heat through in a covered saucepan, stirring and adding a little water if necessary. Serve as directed.
1 CUP: 512 cal., 16g fat (6g sat. fat), 27mg chol., 1507mg sod., 85g carb. (61g sugars, 3g fiber), 13g pro.

Poultry

**SHREDDED BARBECUE
CHICKEN OVER GRITS**

SHREDDED BARBECUE CHICKEN OVER GRITS

There's nothing like juicy, saucy chicken sitting atop a pile of steaming grits. And the pumpkin in these grits gives them a kiss of fall flavor. Your family will come running to the table for this dish.

—*Erin Mylroie, Santa Clara, UT*

PREP: 20 min. • **COOK:** 25 min.
MAKES: 6 servings

- 1 lb. boneless skinless chicken breasts
- ¼ tsp. pepper
- 1 can (14½ oz.) reduced-sodium chicken broth, divided
- 1 cup hickory smoke-flavored barbecue sauce
- ¼ cup molasses
- 1 Tbsp. ground ancho chili pepper
- ½ tsp. ground cinnamon
- 2¼ cups water
- 1 cup quick-cooking grits
- 1 cup canned pumpkin
- ¾ cup shredded pepper jack cheese
- 1 medium tomato, seeded and chopped
- 6 Tbsp. reduced-fat sour cream
- 2 green onions, chopped
- 2 Tbsp. minced fresh cilantro

1. Sprinkle chicken with pepper; place in a large skillet coated with cooking spray.
2. Combine 1 cup broth, barbecue sauce, molasses, chili pepper and cinnamon; pour over chicken. Bring to a boil. Reduce heat; cover and simmer for 20-25 minutes or until a thermometer reads 165°. Shred meat with 2 forks and return to the skillet.
3. Meanwhile, in a large saucepan, bring water and remaining broth to a boil. Slowly stir in grits and pumpkin. Reduce heat; cook and stir for 5-7 minutes or until thickened. Stir in cheese until melted.
4. Divide grits among 6 bowls; top each with ½ cup chicken mixture. Serve with tomato, sour cream, green onions and cilantro.
1 SERVING: 345 cal., 9g fat (4g sat. fat), 62mg chol., 718mg sod., 42g carb. (17g sugars, 4g fiber), 25g pro. **DIABETIC EXCHANGES:** 3 lean meat, 2½ starch, 1 fat.

CRANBERRY MAPLE CHICKEN

CHICKEN IN BASIL CREAM

When I first read this recipe, I thought it looked difficult. But because I had all the ingredients readily at hand, I gave it a try. Am I glad I did! Not only was it simple to prepare, it tastes amazing.
—*Judy Baker, Craig, CO*

- -

TAKES: 25 min. • **MAKES:** 4 servings

- ¼ cup whole milk
- ¼ cup dry bread crumbs
- 4 boneless skinless chicken breast halves (4 oz. each)
- 3 Tbsp. butter
- ½ cup chicken broth
- 1 cup heavy whipping cream
- 1 jar (4 oz.) sliced pimientos, drained
- ½ cup grated Parmesan cheese
- ¼ cup minced fresh basil
- ⅛ tsp. pepper

1. Place milk and bread crumbs in separate shallow bowls. Dip chicken in milk, then coat with crumbs.
2. In a large skillet over medium-high heat, cook chicken in butter 5 minutes on each side or until a thermometer inserted in chicken reads 165°. Remove and keep warm.
3. Add broth to the skillet. Bring to a boil over medium heat; stir to loosen browned bits. Stir in the cream and pimientos; boil and stir for 1 minute. Reduce heat. Add the cheese, basil and pepper; cook and stir until heated through. Serve with chicken.
1 SERVING: 493 cal., 37g fat (22g sat. fat), 177mg chol., 536mg sod., 9g carb. (3g sugars, 1g fiber), 30g pro.

CRANBERRY MAPLE CHICKEN

Cranberries and a hint of maple syrup make a sweet sauce for these easy chicken breast halves. They're a quick but lovely main course for weeknights and other occasions.
—*Kim Pettipas, Oromocto, NB*

- -

TAKES: 30 min. • **MAKES:** 6 servings

- 2 cups fresh or frozen cranberries
- ¾ cup water
- ⅓ cup sugar
- 6 boneless skinless chicken breast halves (4 oz. each)
- ½ tsp. salt
- ¼ tsp. pepper
- 1 Tbsp. canola oil
- ¼ cup maple syrup

1. In a small saucepan, combine the cranberries, water and sugar. Cook over medium heat until the berries pop, about 15 minutes.
2. Meanwhile, sprinkle chicken with salt and pepper. In a large nonstick skillet, cook chicken in oil over medium heat until juices run clear, 4-5 minutes on each side. Stir syrup into cranberry mixture; serve with chicken.
1 CHICKEN BREAST HALF WITH 3 TBSP. SAUCE: 236 cal., 5g fat (1g sat. fat), 63mg chol., 253mg sod., 24g carb. (22g sugars, 1g fiber), 23g pro.

"Delicious! One of my favorite recipes. I never remember to buy pimientos, so I always use chopped roasted red peppers and it's great. I double the sauce (or just use 2 chicken breasts and make the sauce as is) since it goes great over the chicken and pasta, too. Love!"
—KGHMAMA, TASTEOFHOME.COM

FIG-GLAZED CHICKEN WITH WHITE BEANS

TERIYAKI-GLAZED CHICKEN

I love to experiment with food. We're able to buy sweet onions grown on Maui, so I stir-fry them with chicken and carrots for a tasty teriyaki meal.
—*Kel Brenneman, Riverdale, CA*

- -

TAKES: 30 min. • **MAKES:** 4 servings

- 4   boneless skinless chicken breast halves, cut into strips
- 3   Tbsp. canola oil, divided
- 4   medium carrots, julienned
- 1   medium sweet onion, julienned
- ½   cup soy sauce
- ¼   cup packed brown sugar
      Hot cooked rice
      Optional: Sesame seeds, toasted, and sliced green onions

1. In a large skillet or wok, stir-fry chicken in 2 Tbsp. oil until no longer pink, 6-8 minutes. Remove chicken and set aside. In the same skillet, stir-fry carrots in remaining oil for 2 minutes. Add onion; stir-fry until the vegetables are tender, 2-4 minutes longer.
2. Combine soy sauce and brown sugar; add to skillet. Bring to a boil. Return chicken to pan. Boil until sauce is slightly thickened, about 5 minutes. Serve with rice. Sprinkle with toasted sesame seeds and green onions if desired.
1 SERVING: 324 cal., 13g fat (2g sat. fat), 63mg chol., 1922mg sod., 23g carb. (20g sugars, 3g fiber), 28g pro.

TEST KITCHEN TIP
A simple swap to reduced-sodium soy sauce will decrease sodium to about 1,200 milligrams per serving, but that's still high. To cut it further, replace some of the soy sauce with reduced-sodium broth or water.

FIG-GLAZED CHICKEN WITH WHITE BEANS

Sauteed shallots, fig jam, rosemary, lemon and sherry vinegar make a delightful sauce for both the chicken and the beans. My husband couldn't believe how well the white beans absorbed the flavor, making this a grand slam. Matchstick carrots can be added to the bean mixture for extra color, flavor and crunch.
—*Arlene Erlbach, Morton Grove, IL*

- -

PREP: 15 min. • **COOK:** 30 min.
MAKES: 6 servings

- ¾   cup fig preserves
- ⅓   cup water
- 2   Tbsp. lemon juice
- 2   Tbsp. sherry vinegar
- 4   tsp. minced fresh rosemary or 1 tsp. dried rosemary, crushed
- 1   Tbsp. Worcestershire sauce
- ¼   tsp. salt
- ¼   tsp. pepper
- 6   bone-in chicken thighs (about 2¼ lbs.)
- 4   shallots, coarsely chopped
- 1   can (15 oz.) cannellini beans, rinsed and drained

1. Mix first 8 ingredients. In a large skillet over medium-high heat, brown chicken in batches, starting skin side down. Remove from pan, reserving drippings.
2. In drippings, saute the shallots until golden brown, 2-3 minutes. Stir in preserves mixture; bring to a boil, stirring to loosen browned bits from pan. Add chicken. Reduce heat; simmer, covered, 5 minutes.
3. Add the beans; return to a boil. Cook, uncovered, until a thermometer inserted in chicken reads 170°-175°, 12-15 minutes.
1 SERVING: 405 cal., 15g fat (4g sat. fat), 81mg chol., 287mg sod., 42g carb. (25g sugars, 3g fiber), 26g pro.

**TERIYAKI
GLAZED CHICKEN**

**APPLE-GLAZED
CHICKEN THIGHS**

APPLE-GLAZED
CHICKEN THIGHS

My "pickatarian" child is choosy but willing to
eat this chicken glazed with apple juice and
thyme. I dish it up with mashed potatoes
and green beans.
—*Kerry Picard, Spokane, WA*

TAKES: 25 min. • **MAKES:** 6 servings

- 6 **boneless skinless chicken**
  thighs (1½ lbs.)
- ¾ **tsp. seasoned salt**
- ¼ **tsp. pepper**
- 1 **Tbsp. canola oil**
- 1 **cup unsweetened apple juice**
- 1 **tsp. minced fresh thyme**
  or ¼ tsp. dried thyme

1. Sprinkle chicken with seasoned salt and
pepper. In a large skillet, heat the oil over
medium-high heat. Brown chicken on both
sides. Remove from pan.

2. Add juice and thyme to skillet. Bring to a
boil, stirring to loosen browned bits from
pan; cook until liquid is reduced by half.
Return chicken to pan; cook, covered, over
medium heat 3-4 minutes longer or until a
thermometer inserted in chicken reads 170°.
**1 CHICKEN THIGH WITH ABOUT 1 TBSP.
GLAZE:** 204 cal., 11g fat (2g sat. fat), 76mg
chol., 255mg sod., 5g carb. (4g sugars,
0 fiber), 21g pro. **DIABETIC EXCHANGES:**
3 lean meat, ½ fat.

CAJUN COUNTRY
FRIED CHICKEN

I like to make my own Cajun seasoning using a
blend of herbs and spices, but in this recipe a
store-bought blend works just as well.
—*Dave Fisher, Ten Mile, TN*

PREP: 15 min. + marinating
COOK: 10 min. /batch • **MAKES:** 12 servings

- 2 **cups whole milk**
- 2 **Tbsp. Cajun seasoning, divided**

- 8 **boneless skinless chicken**
  breast halves (4 oz. each)
- 4 **boneless skinless chicken**
  thighs (about 1 lb.), halved
- 1¼ **cups all-purpose flour**
- ½ **tsp. lemon-pepper seasoning**
- ½ **tsp. garlic salt**
  Oil for frying

1. In a large bowl, combine milk and 1 Tbsp.
Cajun seasoning; add chicken. Cover and
refrigerate for at least 2 hours.
2. In a large shallow dish, combine the flour,
lemon pepper, garlic salt and remaining Cajun
seasoning. Drain chicken and discard milk
mixture. Place chicken in flour mixture and
turn to coat.
3. In a skillet, heat ¼ in. of oil; fry chicken in
batches until golden brown and juices run
clear, 7-8 minutes.
1 SERVING: 289 cal., 16g fat (2g sat. fat),
68mg chol., 291mg sod., 11g carb. (1g sugars,
0 fiber), 24g pro.

KUNG PAO WINGS

Served as an entree over hot cooked rice, these delicious wings have plenty of personality—with sweet red pepper for color, red pepper flakes for zip and peanuts for crunch. They're quick and easy to fix, too.
—*Kathy Evans, Lacey, WA*

- -

TAKES: 30 min. • **MAKES:** 4 servings

- 8 whole chicken wings (about 1½ lbs.)
- 2 Tbsp. sugar
- 2 tsp. cornstarch
- ¼ cup water
- ¼ cup soy sauce
- 2 Tbsp. lemon juice
- ¼ tsp. crushed red pepper flakes
- 1 Tbsp. canola oil
- 1 small sweet red pepper, diced
- ½ cup diced onion
- 1 to 2 garlic cloves, minced
- ⅓ cup peanuts
   Hot cooked rice
   Chopped green onions, optional

1. Cut chicken wings into 3 sections; discard wing tip section. Set the wings aside. In a small bowl, combine the sugar, cornstarch, water, soy sauce, lemon juice and pepper flakes until blended; set aside.

2. In a large skillet over medium-high heat, heat oil. Cook chicken wings, uncovered, for 10-15 minutes or until chicken juices run clear, turning occasionally.

3. Add the red pepper and onion; cook, uncovered, for 3-5 minutes or until the vegetables are crisp-tender. Add garlic; cook 1 minute longer. Stir cornstarch mixture; gradually add to skillet. Bring to a boil; cook and stir for 2 minutes or until the sauce is thickened and vegetables are tender. Sprinkle with peanuts. Serve with rice. If desired, top with green onions.

NOTE: Uncooked chicken wing sections (wingettes) may be substituted for whole chicken wings.

1 SERVING: 345 cal., 22g fat (5g sat. fat), 55mg chol., 1027mg sod., 14g carb. (8g sugars, 2g fiber), 23g pro.

SMOKY SPANISH CHICKEN

After enjoying a similar dish at a Spanish tapas restaurant, my husband and I were eager to make our own version of this saucy chicken at home. If I want to make it extra healthy, I remove the skin from the chicken after browning it.
—*Ryan Haley, San Diego, CA*

- -

TAKES: 30 min. • **MAKES:** 4 servings

- 3 tsp. smoked paprika
- ½ tsp. salt
- ¼ tsp. pepper
- 1 Tbsp. water
- 4 bone-in chicken thighs
- 1½ cups baby portobello mushrooms, quartered
- 1 cup chopped green onions, divided
- 1 can (14½ oz.) fire-roasted diced tomatoes, undrained

1. Mix first 4 ingredients; rub over chicken.

2. Place a large skillet over medium heat. Add chicken, skin side down. Cook until browned, 4-5 minutes per side; remove from the pan. Remove all but 1 Tbsp. drippings from pan.

3. In drippings, saute mushrooms and ½ cup green onions over medium heat until tender, 1-2 minutes. Stir in tomatoes. Add chicken; bring to a boil. Reduce heat; simmer, covered, until a thermometer inserted in chicken reads 170°, 10-12 minutes. Top with the remaining green onions.

1 SERVING: 272 cal., 15g fat (4g sat. fat), 81mg chol., 646mg sod., 10g carb. (4g sugars, 2g fiber), 25g pro.

KUNG PAO WINGS

CHICKEN JAMBALAYA

CHICKEN JAMBALAYA

This is a great dish to serve at parties. It's just as good as—if not tastier than—many high-fat versions. And it reheats well.
—*Lynn Desjardins, Atkinson, NH*

PREP: 20 min. • **COOK:** 1 hour
MAKES: 6 servings

- ¾ lb. boneless skinless chicken breasts, cubed
- 3 cups reduced-sodium chicken broth
- 1½ cups uncooked brown rice
- 4 oz. reduced-fat smoked turkey sausage, diced
- ½ cup thinly sliced celery with leaves
- ½ cup chopped onion
- ½ cup chopped green pepper
- 2 to 3 tsp. Cajun or Creole seasoning
- 1 to 2 garlic cloves, minced
- ⅛ tsp. hot pepper sauce
- 1 bay leaf
- 1 can (14½ oz.) no-salt-added diced tomatoes, undrained
  Chopped green onions, optional

1. In a large skillet lightly coated with cooking spray, saute chicken for 2-3 minutes or until the chicken is no longer pink. Stir in the next 10 ingredients. Bring to a boil. Reduce heat; cover and simmer for 50-60 minutes or until heated through.

2. Stir in the tomatoes; cover and simmer 10 minutes longer or until liquid is absorbed and rice is tender. Remove from the heat; let stand for 5 minutes. Discard bay leaf. Serve with green onions if desired.

NOTE: The following spices may be substituted for 1 tsp. Creole seasoning: ¼ tsp. each salt, garlic powder and paprika; and a pinch each of dried thyme, ground cumin and cayenne pepper.

1 CUP: 302 cal., 4g fat (1g sat. fat), 43mg chol., 452mg sod., 45g carb. (0 sugars, 3g fiber), 21g pro. **DIABETIC EXCHANGES:** 2½ starch, 1½ lean meat, 1 vegetable.

CASHEW CHICKEN WITH GINGER

CASHEW CHICKEN WITH GINGER

There are lots of recipes for cashew chicken, but my family thinks this one stands alone. We love the flavor from the fresh ginger and the crunch of cashews. Plus, it's easy to prepare.
—*Oma Rollison, El Cajon, CA*

TAKES: 30 min. • **MAKES:** 6 servings

- 2 Tbsp. cornstarch
- 1 Tbsp. brown sugar
- 1¼ cups chicken broth
- 2 Tbsp. soy sauce
- 3 Tbsp. canola oil, divided
- 1½ lbs. boneless skinless chicken breasts, cut into 1-in. pieces
- ½ lb. sliced fresh mushrooms
- 1 small green pepper, cut into strips
- 1 can (8 oz.) sliced water chestnuts, drained
- 1½ tsp. grated fresh gingerroot
- 4 green onions, sliced
- ¾ cup salted cashews
  Hot cooked rice

1. Mix first 4 ingredients until smooth. In a large skillet, heat 2 Tbsp. oil over medium-high heat; stir-fry chicken until no longer pink. Remove from pan.

2. In same pan, heat remaining oil over medium-high heat; stir-fry mushrooms, pepper, water chestnuts and ginger until pepper is crisp-tender, 3-5 minutes. Stir broth mixture and add to pan with green onions; bring to a boil. Cook and stir until sauce is thickened, 1-2 minutes.

3. Stir in chicken and cashews; heat through. Serve with rice.

¾ CUP CHICKEN MIXTURE: 349 cal., 19g fat (3g sat. fat), 64mg chol., 650mg sod., 18g carb. (6g sugars, 2g fiber), 28g pro. **DIABETIC EXCHANGES:** 3 lean meat, 3 fat, 1 starch.

RAVIOLI WITH APPLE CHICKEN SAUSAGE

I love butternut squash ravioli, but was never quite sure what flavors would best complement the squash. Turns out that creamy spinach, chicken sausage and a hint of sweet spice are the perfect go-alongs.
—*Mary Brodeur, Millbury, Ma*

TAKES: 30 min. • MAKES: 4 servings

1 pkg. (18 oz.) frozen butternut squash ravioli
2 pkg. (10 oz. each) frozen creamed spinach
1 Tbsp. olive oil
1 pkg. (12 oz.) fully cooked apple chicken sausage links or flavor of your choice, cut into ½-in. slices
1 tsp. maple syrup
¼ tsp. pumpkin pie spice

1. Cook ravioli according to the package directions. Prepare spinach according to package directions. Meanwhile, in a large skillet, heat oil over medium heat. Add sausage; cook and stir until browned, 2-4 minutes.
2. Drain ravioli. Add ravioli, spinach, maple syrup and pie spice to sausage; heat through.
1½ CUPS: 531 cal., 16g fat (4g sat. fat), 64mg chol., 1409mg sod., 69g carb. (19g sugars, 4g fiber), 26g pro.

BUFFALO SLOPPY JOES FOR TWO

Lean ground turkey makes this a lighter sloppy joe than the standard beef version. A hefty splash of hot sauce and optional blue cheese provide an authentic Buffalo-style flavor.
—*Maria Regakis, Saugus, MA*

TAKES: 30 min. • MAKES: 2 servings

½ lb. extra-lean ground turkey
¼ cup chopped celery
3 Tbsp. chopped onion
2 Tbsp. grated carrots
1 garlic clove, minced
3 Tbsp. tomato sauce
2 Tbsp. reduced-sodium chicken broth
1 Tbsp. Louisiana-style hot sauce
1½ tsp. brown sugar
1½ tsp. red wine vinegar
¾ tsp. Worcestershire sauce
    Dash pepper
2 hamburger buns, split
¼ cup crumbled blue cheese, optional

1. In a Dutch oven, cook first 5 ingredients over medium heat until turkey is no longer pink. Stir in the tomato sauce, chicken broth, Louisiana-style hot sauce, brown sugar, red wine vinegar, Worcestershire sauce and pepper; heat through.
2. Serve on buns; sprinkle with crumbled blue cheese if desired.
1 SANDWICH: 276 cal., 3g fat (0 sat. fat), 45mg chol., 445mg sod., 30g carb. (8g sugars, 2g fiber), 33g pro. DIABETIC EXCHANGES: 4 lean meat, 2 starch.

BUFFALO SLOPPY JOES FOR TWO

SPICY TURKEY TENDERLOIN

LEMON CHICKEN SPAGHETTI

Lemon-pepper seasoning and lemon zest give a bright flavor to this tempting chicken and veggie pasta.

—Taste of Home *Test Kitchen*

- -

TAKES: 30 min. • **MAKES:** 8 servings

- 1 lb. boneless skinless chicken breasts, cut into strips
- 2 green onions, chopped
- 2 garlic cloves, minced
- 2 Tbsp. olive oil
- 1 cup chicken broth
- ½ cup heavy whipping cream
- 8 oz. uncooked thin spaghetti or angel hair pasta
- 1 cup frozen peas
- ½ cup chopped seeded tomatoes
- ½ cup shredded Parmesan cheese
- 2 Tbsp. grated lemon zest
- ⅛ tsp. lemon-pepper seasoning

1. In a large skillet, saute the chicken, onions and garlic in oil until chicken is no longer pink. Remove chicken with a slotted spoon; keep warm. Add broth to the skillet; bring to a boil and cook until reduced by half. Reduce heat; add cream. Cook and stir for 5 minutes.
2. Cook spaghetti according to package directions. Add the peas, tomatoes, cheese and chicken to the cream mixture; heat through. Drain spaghetti; toss with the chicken mixture. Sprinkle with lemon zest and lemon pepper.
1 CUP: 289 cal., 12g fat (5g sat. fat), 55mg chol., 265mg sod., 26g carb. (3g sugars, 2g fiber), 19g pro.

SPICY TURKEY TENDERLOIN

Here's an easy turkey dish sure to really wake up your taste buds. It's the perfect choice for a weeknight dinner, or you can easily increase it for get-togethers.
—Sharon Skildum, Maple Grove, MN

- -

PREP: 20 min. • **COOK:** 25 min.
MAKES: 2 servings

- ½ tsp. chili powder
- ½ tsp. ground cumin
- ¼ to ½ tsp. salt
- ⅛ tsp. cayenne pepper
- 1 turkey breast tenderloin (½ lb.)
- 3 tsp. olive oil, divided
- ¼ cup chicken broth
- 2 Tbsp. lime juice
- 3 Tbsp. chopped onion
- 2 Tbsp. chopped jalapeno pepper
- 1 cup canned black beans, rinsed and drained
- ½ cup frozen corn, thawed
- 3 Tbsp. chopped fresh tomato
- 4 tsp. picante sauce
- 1 Tbsp. minced fresh cilantro
- 2 lime wedges

1. In a small bowl, combine the chili powder, cumin, salt and cayenne. Sprinkle half the spice mixture over turkey. In a skillet, brown turkey in 2 tsp. oil for 3-4 minutes on each side. Add the broth and lime juice to skillet. Reduce heat; cover and simmer until turkey juices run clear and thermometer reads 170°, turning once, 15-18 minutes.
2. In a small skillet, saute chopped onion and jalapeno in remaining oil until crisp-tender. Transfer to a bowl. Add the beans, corn, tomato, picante sauce, cilantro and remaining spice mixture. Serve turkey with salsa and lime wedges.
NOTE: Wear disposable gloves when cutting hot peppers; the oils can burn skin. Avoid touching your face.
1 SERVING: 342 cal., 9g fat (1g sat. fat), 56mg chol., 767mg sod., 32g carb. (4g sugars, 7g fiber), 35g pro. **DIABETIC EXCHANGES:** 3 lean meat, 2 starch, 1½ fat.

CHICKEN
BULGUR
SKILLET

CHICKEN BULGUR SKILLET

This recipe was passed on to me by a friend, and I've altered it slightly to suit our tastes. We like it with a fresh green salad.
—Leann Hillmer, Sylvan Grove, KS

PREP: 15 min. • **COOK:** 30 min.
MAKES: 4 servings

- 1 lb. boneless skinless chicken breasts, cut into 1-in. cubes
- 2 tsp. olive oil
- 2 medium carrots, chopped
- ⅔ cup chopped onion
- 3 Tbsp. chopped walnuts
- ½ tsp. caraway seeds
- ¼ tsp. ground cumin
- 1½ cups bulgur
- 2 cups reduced-sodium chicken broth
- 2 Tbsp. raisins
- ¼ tsp. salt
- ⅛ tsp. ground cinnamon

1. In a large cast-iron or other heavy skillet, cook chicken in oil over medium-high heat until meat is no longer pink. Remove and keep warm. In the same skillet, cook and stir the chopped carrots, onion, nuts, caraway seeds and cumin until the onion starts to brown, 3-4 minutes.

2. Stir in bulgur. Gradually add broth; bring to a boil over medium heat. Reduce heat; add the raisins, salt, cinnamon and chicken. Cover and simmer until bulgur is tender, 12-15 minutes.

1½ CUPS: 412 cal., 8g fat (1g sat. fat), 66mg chol., 561mg sod., 51g carb. (8g sugars, 12g fiber), 36g pro.

"Easy weeknight meal. I paired it with steamed broccoli. I doubled the cumin and cinnamon. I also used currants instead of raisins and increased the amount to about ¼ cup. I reheated leftovers for lunch, which worked well. I also think you could eat it as a cold salad. Bulgur should be with the grains in the grocery store."
— SCRAPBOOKMEISTER, TASTEOFHOME.COM

SKILLET TACOS

SKILLET TACOS

If you like Mexican food, you'll be whipping up these fast, healthy skillet tacos often.
—Maria Gobel, Greenfield, WI

TAKES: 30 min. • **MAKES:** 2 servings

- 1 Tbsp. olive oil
- ¼ lb. lean ground turkey
- 2 Tbsp. chopped onion
- 2 Tbsp. chopped green pepper
- 1 can (8 oz.) tomato sauce
- ½ cup uncooked elbow macaroni
- ½ cup water
- ¼ cup picante sauce
- 2 Tbsp. shredded reduced-fat cheddar cheese
- ¼ cup crushed baked tortilla chip scoops
- ¼ cup chopped avocado
  Optional: Iceberg lettuce wedges and sour cream

1. Heat olive oil in a large nonstick skillet over medium-high heat; add the turkey, onion and green pepper and cook until vegetables are tender and turkey is no longer pink.

2. Stir in the tomato sauce, macaroni, water and picante sauce. Bring to a boil. Reduce heat; cover and simmer until macaroni is tender, 10-15 minutes.

3. Divide between 2 plates; top with cheese, tortilla chips and avocado. Serve with lettuce and sour cream if desired.

1 CUP: 337 cal., 17g fat (4g sat. fat), 44mg chol., 861mg sod., 30g carb. (4g sugars, 5g fiber), 19g pro.

TURKEY FETTUCCINE SKILLET

I came up with this simple dish as a way to use up leftover turkey from holiday dinners. It's become a family tradition to enjoy it the day after Thanksgiving and Christmas.
—*Kari Johnston, Marwayne, AB*

PREP: 10 min. • **COOK:** 30 min.
MAKES: 6 servings

- 8 oz. uncooked fettuccine
- ½ cup chopped onion
- ½ cup chopped celery
- 4 garlic cloves, minced
- 1 tsp. canola oil
- 1 cup sliced fresh mushrooms
- 2 cups fat-free milk
- 1 tsp. salt-free seasoning blend
- ¼ tsp. salt
- 2 Tbsp. cornstarch
- ½ cup fat-free half-and-half
- ⅓ cup grated Parmesan cheese
- 3 cups cubed cooked turkey breast
- ¾ cup shredded part-skim
   mozzarella cheese

1. Cook fettuccine according to package directions. Meanwhile, in a large ovenproof skillet coated with cooking spray, saute the onion, celery and garlic in oil for 3 minutes. Add the mushrooms; cook and stir until vegetables are tender. Stir in the milk, seasoning blend and salt. Bring to a boil.
2. Combine cornstarch and half-and-half until smooth; stir into skillet. Cook and stir for 2 minutes or until thickened and bubbly. Stir in Parmesan cheese just until melted.
3. Stir in turkey. Drain fettuccine; add to turkey mixture. Heat through. Sprinkle with mozzarella cheese. Broil 4-6 in. from the heat for 2-3 minutes or until cheese is melted.
1 CUP: 361 cal., 7g fat (3g sat. fat), 76mg chol., 343mg sod., 38g carb. (8g sugars, 2g fiber), 34g pro. **DIABETIC EXCHANGES:** 4 lean meat, 2½ starch, ½ fat.

ATHENIAN CHICKEN GRILLED CHEESE SANDWICHES

ATHENIAN CHICKEN GRILLED CHEESE SANDWICHES

Mozzarella and feta cheese make one delicious duo in this upscale grilled cheese that also features tender chicken and fresh herb flavor.
—*Michael Cohen, Los Angeles, CA*

TAKES: 30 min. • **MAKES:** 4 servings

- 1 lb. boneless skinless
   chicken breasts, cubed
- ¼ tsp. kosher salt
- ¼ tsp. pepper
- 3 garlic cloves, minced
- 1 Tbsp. plus ¼ cup olive oil, divided
- 6 oz. fresh mozzarella
   cheese, shredded
- ½ cup crumbled feta cheese
- ½ cup grated Parmesan cheese
- ½ cup fresh mint leaves, chopped
- 2 Tbsp. minced fresh oregano
- 2 Tbsp. capers, drained
- 8 slices olive or Italian
   bread (½ in. thick)

1. Sprinkle chicken with salt and pepper. In a large skillet, cook chicken and garlic in 1 Tbsp. oil over medium heat until meat is no longer pink. Set aside and keep warm.
2. In a small bowl, combine the cheeses, mint, oregano and capers. Distribute half the cheese mixture evenly among 4 bread slices. Layer with chicken and remaining cheese mixture. Top with remaining bread. Brush outsides of sandwiches with remaining oil.
3. On a griddle, toast the sandwiches for 2-3 minutes on each side or until cheese is melted.
1 SANDWICH: 605 cal., 36g fat (13g sat. fat), 112mg chol., 918mg sod., 27g carb. (1g sugars, 3g fiber), 41g pro.

CHICKEN PESTO MEATBALLS

These tender pesto-stuffed meatballs get gobbled up in our house. They're short on ingredients, but packed with flavor. I always make a double batch, freezing the other half for a busy night.

—*Ally Billhorn, Wilton, IA*

TAKES: 30 min. • **MAKES:** 4 servings

    6   oz. uncooked whole grain spaghetti
    ¼   cup dry bread crumbs
    2   Tbsp. prepared pesto
    2   Tbsp. grated Parmesan cheese
    1   tsp. garlic powder
    1   lb. lean ground chicken
   1½   cups marinara sauce
    ¼   cup water
        Torn fresh basil and additional
        Parmesan cheese, optional

1. Cook spaghetti according to package directions; drain.

2. In a large bowl, combine bread crumbs, pesto, cheese and garlic powder. Add the chicken; mix lightly but thoroughly. Shape into 1-in. balls.

3. In a large skillet, brown the meatballs over medium heat, turning occasionally. Add the sauce and water; bring to a boil. Reduce heat; simmer, covered, until meatballs are cooked through, about 5 minutes. Serve with the spaghetti. If desired, top with fresh basil and additional cheese.

FREEZE OPTION: Freeze cooled meatball mixture in freezer containers. To use, partially thaw in refrigerator overnight. Heat through in a covered saucepan over low heat, stirring gently; add water if necessary.

¾ CUP MEATBALL MIXTURE WITH 1 CUP SPAGHETTI: 422 cal., 12g fat (3g sat. fat), 85mg chol., 706mg sod., 45g carb. (7g sugars, 7g fiber), 32g pro. **DIABETIC EXCHANGES:** 3 starch, 3 lean meat, 1½ fat.

CHICKEN BRUNSWICK STEW

Everyone will warm up to this hearty stew after a long day of sledding, skiing or other fun activities in the frosty outdoors. Use leftover or rotisserie chicken to keep the prep easy.

—*Patty Stremsterfer, Pleasant Plains, IL*

PREP: 25 min. • **COOK:** 1 hour
MAKES: 14 servings (about 5 qt.)

    ¼   cup butter, cubed
    2   medium onions, chopped
    6   cups chicken broth, divided
    5   cups cubed cooked chicken
    1   pkg. (16 oz.) frozen corn, thawed
    1   pkg. (16 oz.) frozen lima beans,
        thawed
    4   medium potatoes, peeled and diced
    3   cans (14½ oz. each) diced
        tomatoes, undrained
    2   celery ribs, chopped
    1   cup water
    ¼   tsp. each dried basil,
        marjoram and thyme
    ¼   tsp. hot pepper sauce
    1   Tbsp. cornstarch

1. In a stockpot, melt butter. Add onions; saute until tender. Stir in 5 cups broth, chicken, corn, beans, potatoes, tomatoes, celery, water, herbs and pepper sauce. Bring to a boil. Reduce heat; cover and simmer for 45 minutes.

2. Combine cornstarch and remaining broth until smooth; gradually stir into stew. Bring to a boil; cook and stir for 2 minutes or until slightly thickened.

1½ CUPS: 393 cal., 15g fat (5g sat. fat), 91mg chol., 1124mg sod., 29g carb. (6g sugars, 5g fiber), 35g pro.

CHICKEN PESTO MEATBALLS

GNOCCHI WITH SPINACH & CHICKEN SAUSAGE

TURKEY PICADILLO

I got this wonderful recipe from my son Greg, who is a philosophy professor and an innovative cook.
—*Anita Pinney, Santa Rosa, CA*

- -

TAKES: 30 min. • **MAKES:** 4 servings

- 5⅓ cups uncooked whole wheat egg noodles
- 1 lb. lean ground turkey
- 1 medium green pepper, chopped
- 1 small onion, chopped
- 2 garlic cloves, minced
- 2 tsp. chili powder
- ¼ tsp. pepper
- 1 can (14½ oz.) Italian diced tomatoes, undrained
- ½ cup golden raisins
  Optional: Reduced-fat sour cream and chopped green onions

1. Cook the egg noodles according to the package directions.
2. Meanwhile, in a large nonstick skillet, cook the turkey, green pepper and onion over medium heat until turkey is no longer pink; drain. Add the garlic, chili powder and pepper; cook 1 minute longer. Stir in the tomatoes and raisins; heat through. Drain noodles; serve with turkey mixture. Garnish with sour cream and green onions if desired.
1 CUP TURKEY MIXTURE WITH 1 CUP NOODLES: 463 cal., 11g fat (3g sat. fat), 90mg chol., 535mg sod., 69g carb. (19g sugars, 9g fiber), 30g pro.

DID YOU KNOW?

Picadillo has several variations in Spanish-speaking countries. Ground meat, tomatoes, onion, garlic, raisins and olives are typical ingredients. This version is slightly Americanized by omitting the olives and serving the picadillo over egg noodles instead of rice.

GNOCCHI WITH SPINACH & CHICKEN SAUSAGE

Dinner's easy when I can use ingredients typically found in my fridge and pantry.
—*Laura Miller, Lake Ann, MI*

- -

TAKES: 25 min. • **MAKES:** 4 servings

- 1 pkg. (16 oz.) potato gnocchi
- 2 Tbsp. olive oil
- 1 pkg. (12 oz.) fully cooked Italian chicken sausage links, halved and sliced
- 2 shallots, finely chopped
- 2 garlic cloves, minced
- 1 cup white wine or chicken broth
- 1 Tbsp. cornstarch
- ½ cup reduced-sodium chicken broth
- 3 cups fresh baby spinach
- ½ cup heavy whipping cream
- ¼ cup shredded Parmesan cheese

1. Cook gnocchi according to the package directions. Meanwhile, in a large skillet, heat oil over medium-high heat; cook sausage and shallots until sausage is browned and shallots are tender. Add garlic; cook 1 minute longer.
2. Stir in wine. Bring to a boil; cook until liquid is reduced by half, 3-4 minutes. In a small bowl, mix cornstarch and broth until smooth; stir into sausage mixture. Return to a boil, stirring constantly; cook and stir until thickened, 1-2 minutes. Add spinach and cream; cook and stir until spinach is wilted.
3. Drain gnocchi; add to pan and heat through. Sprinkle with cheese.
NOTE: Look for potato gnocchi in the pasta or frozen foods section.
1 CUP: 604 cal., 28g fat (12g sat. fat), 119mg chol., 1226mg sod., 58g carb. (3g sugars, 4g fiber), 27g pro.

TURKEY
PICADILLO

GOUDA-STUFFED CHICKEN

My brother gave me the recipe for this hearty dish we often serve at family gatherings. Men, especially, seem to enjoy it, and it's become one of our special favorites.

—*Mary Ann Dell, Phoenixville, PA*

PREP: 15 min. • **COOK:** 40 min.
MAKES: 4 servings

- 4 boneless skinless chicken breast halves (6 oz. each)
- 2 oz. smoked Gouda cheese, cut into thin pieces
- 2 Tbsp. all-purpose flour
- ¼ tsp. salt
- ⅛ tsp. pepper
- 2 tsp. canola oil, divided
- 1 garlic clove, minced
- 1 cup reduced-sodium chicken broth
- 1 cup apple cider or unsweetened apple juice
- 2 large tart apples, thinly sliced
- 1 Tbsp. honey

1. Cut a slit lengthwise through the thickest part of each chicken breast; fill with cheese. In a shallow bowl, combine the flour, salt and pepper. Dip chicken in flour mixture on both sides; shake off excess.

2. In a large nonstick skillet coated with cooking spray, cook chicken in 1½ tsp. oil over medium heat for 8-10 minutes on each side or until juices run clear. Remove chicken and keep warm.

3. In the same skillet, saute garlic in remaining oil for 30 seconds. Add the broth and cider, stirring to loosen browned bits. Bring to a boil. Reduce heat; simmer, uncovered, for 12-14 minutes or until mixture is reduced to about 1 cup.

4. Stir in apples and honey; return to a boil. Reduce heat; simmer, uncovered, 5-7 minutes or until the apples are crisp-tender. Serve with chicken.

1 SERVING: 350 cal., 10g fat (4g sat. fat), 110mg chol., 507mg sod., 24g carb. (18g sugars, 1g fiber), 39g pro. **DIABETIC EXCHANGES:** 5 very lean meat, 1 fruit, 1 fat, ½ starch.

ITALIAN CHICKEN TENDERLOINS

ITALIAN CHICKEN TENDERLOINS

My friend made this meal for my husband and me after our first child was born. I trimmed the dish down, and now it's low in fat and carbohydrates. When shopping for chicken tenderloins, remember that some companies label the product chicken tenders.

—*Beth Ann Stein, Richmond, IN*

TAKES: 30 min. • **MAKES:** 6 servings

- ½ cup chopped onion
- 1⅛ tsp. paprika, divided
- 3 tsp. olive oil, divided
- 1¼ cups water
- ¼ cup tomato paste
- 1 bay leaf
- ½ tsp. reduced-sodium chicken bouillon granules
- ½ tsp. Italian seasoning
- ¼ cup all-purpose flour
- 1½ tsp. grated Parmesan cheese
- ½ tsp. salt
- ¼ tsp. garlic powder
- ¼ tsp. dried oregano
- 1½ lbs. chicken tenderloins

1. In a small saucepan, saute onion and ⅛ tsp. paprika in 1 tsp. oil until tender. Stir in the water, tomato paste, bay leaf, bouillon and Italian seasoning. Bring to a boil. Reduce heat; simmer, uncovered, for 10 minutes.

2. Meanwhile, in a large shallow dish, combine the flour, cheese, salt, garlic powder, oregano and remaining paprika. Add the chicken; turn to coat.

3. In a large skillet coated with cooking spray, cook half of the chicken tenderloins in 1 tsp. oil until no longer pink, 2-3 minutes on each side. Remove and keep warm; repeat with remaining chicken and oil. Discard bay leaf. Serve sauce with chicken.

1 SERVING: 163 cal., 3g fat (0 sat. fat), 67mg chol., 287mg sod., 8g carb. (3g sugars, 1g fiber), 27g pro. **DIABETIC EXCHANGES:** 3 lean meat, ½ starch, ½ fat.

TURKEY WITH LIME BUTTER SAUCE

When I'm in Florida, I buy Key limes to make the butter sauce. But regular fresh limes work fine. If I'm using leftover turkey, I brown the meat a little so the sauce picks up the flavor.
—*Patricia Kile, Elizabethtown, PA*

TAKES: 30 min. • **MAKES:** 4 servings

- ½ cup all-purpose flour
- ⅛ tsp. salt
- ⅛ tsp. Italian seasoning
- ⅛ tsp. paprika
- ⅛ tsp. pepper
- 1 pkg. (17.6 oz.) turkey breast cutlets
- 2 Tbsp. canola oil

LIME BUTTER SAUCE
- 1 green onion, chopped
- 2 garlic cloves, minced
- ¼ cup reduced-sodium chicken broth
- ¼ cup lime juice
- ½ cup butter, cubed
- ½ tsp. minced chives
- ½ tsp. minced fresh dill
- ½ tsp. grated lime zest
  Salt and pepper to taste

1. In a large shallow dish, combine the first 5 ingredients. Add turkey, a few pieces at a time; turn to coat.

2. In a large skillet, heat oil over medium heat. Add turkey in batches and cook 1-2 minutes on each side or until no longer pink. Remove; keep warm.

3. In same skillet, cook green onion and garlic 1 minute. Add broth and lime juice, stirring to loosen browned bits from pan. Bring to a boil. Reduce heat to low; stir in remaining ingredients. Cook and stir until butter is melted. Serve turkey with butter sauce.

1 SERVING: 465 cal., 31g fat (16g sat. fat), 138mg chol., 333mg sod., 14g carb. (1g sugars, 1g fiber), 33g pro.

GREEK SAUSAGE PITAS

I nicknamed my sandwich Thor's Pita because it's robust and lightning-quick. The ingredient amounts don't really matter—use more or less, depending on what you have.
—*Teresa Aleksandrov, Ypsilanti, MI*

TAKES: 20 min. • **MAKES:** 4 servings

- 4 whole wheat pita breads (6 in.)
- 1 cup plain yogurt
- 2 green onions, chopped
- 2 Tbsp. minced fresh parsley
- 1 tsp. lemon juice
- 1 garlic clove, minced
- ¾ lb. Italian turkey sausage links or other sausage links of your choice, casings removed
- 1 medium cucumber, seeded and chopped
- 1 medium tomato, chopped
  Additional minced fresh parsley

1. Preheat oven to 325°. Wrap pita breads in foil; warm in oven while preparing toppings.

2. In a small bowl, mix yogurt, green onions, parsley, lemon juice and garlic. In a large skillet, cook the sausage over medium heat 4-6 minutes or until no longer pink, breaking into crumbles.

3. To assemble, spoon sausage over pitas. Top with cucumber, tomato and yogurt mixture; sprinkle with additional parsley.

1 OPEN-FACED SANDWICH: 309 cal., 9g fat (3g sat. fat), 39mg chol., 667mg sod., 42g carb. (5g sugars, 6g fiber), 19g pro. **DIABETIC EXCHANGES:** 3 starch, 2 lean meat.

TURKEY WITH LIME BUTTER SAUCE

Pork

SAUSAGE
RICE SKILLET

SAUSAGE RICE SKILLET

Flavorful sausage, garden zucchini and instant rice make this stovetop sensation a fresh favorite. Everyone I have shared the recipe with tells me how delicious it is.
—*Connie Putnam, Clayton, NC*

TAKES: 30 min. • **MAKES:** 4 servings

- 1 lb. bulk pork sausage
- 2 medium zucchini, halved and sliced
- 1 small onion, chopped
- ½ cup chopped green pepper
- 1 tsp. dried oregano
- ½ tsp. garlic salt or garlic powder
- 1 can (11½ oz.) V8 juice
- ⅔ cup uncooked instant rice

1. In a large skillet, cook the sausage until no longer pink; drain. Add the zucchini, onion, green pepper, oregano and garlic salt; cook and stir until onion is tender, about 5 minutes. Stir in V8 juice; bring to a boil. Reduce heat; cover and simmer for 10-14 minutes or until the vegetables are tender.

2. Return to a boil. Stir in instant rice; cover and remove from the heat. Let stand for 5-7 minutes or until rice is tender. Fluff with a fork.

1¼ CUPS: 381 cal., 25g fat (8g sat. fat), 61mg chol., 1153mg sod., 24g carb. (6g sugars, 3g fiber), 16g pro.

TEST KITCHEN TIP

Bring the sodium down to 700 milligrams per serving by using reduced-sodium V8 juice and replacing half the sausage with plain ground pork. Sprinkle in extra oregano and garlic powder to boost the flavor.

GARLIC-PORK TORTILLA ROLLS

PORK FRIED RICE FOR TWO

My husband and I often make a meal of this appealing stir-fry. It's nicely seasoned and chock-full of vegetables.
—*Laura Kittleson, Casselberry, FL*

- -

TAKES: 25 min. • **MAKES:** 2 servings

- ⅛ tsp. Chinese five-spice powder
- 6 oz. boneless pork loin, cut into ¼-in. cubes
- ½ tsp. fennel seed, crushed
- 1½ tsp. canola oil, divided
- 2 cups fresh broccoli florets
- 1 celery rib with leaves, sliced
- ½ cup shredded carrot
- ¼ cup chopped green onions
- 1½ cups cold cooked brown rice
- 1 Tbsp. reduced-sodium soy sauce
- ⅛ tsp. pepper

1. Sprinkle five-spice powder over the pork and toss to coat. In a large skillet or wok coated with cooking spray, stir-fry the pork for 3 minutes or until brown. Remove and keep warm.
2. Stir-fry crushed fennel seed in ¾ tsp. oil for 30 seconds. Add the broccoli, celery, carrot and onions; stir-fry for 3 minutes or until crisp-tender. Remove and keep warm.
3. Stir-fry rice in remaining oil for 2 minutes. Stir in soy sauce and pepper. Return the pork and vegetables to the pan; cook and stir until heated through.
1¾ CUPS: 367 cal., 10g fat (2g sat. fat), 50mg chol., 417mg sod., 44g carb. (0 sugars, 5g fiber), 26g pro. **DIABETIC EXCHANGES:** 2 starch, 2 lean meat, 2 vegetable, ½ fat.

TERIYAKI PORK TACOS

Flour tortillas take an Asian-style twist when filled with flavorful teriyaki pork strips, mandarin oranges, lettuce and crispy french-fried onions.
—*Jodi Nobile, Scotia, NY*

- -

TAKES: 25 min. • **MAKES:** 4 servings

- 1 Tbsp. canola oil
- 1 lb. thin boneless pork loin chops (½ in. thick), cut into strips
- ½ cup reduced-sodium teriyaki sauce
- 3 garlic cloves, minced
- 1 tsp. onion powder
- 4 flour tortillas (8 in.)
- 2 cups shredded romaine
- 1 can (11 oz.) mandarin oranges, drained
- ½ cup french-fried onions

1. In a large cast-iron or other heavy skillet, heat oil over medium heat. Add pork; cook and stir until no longer pink, 4-5 minutes. Add teriyaki sauce, garlic and onion powder; cook 3 minutes longer, stirring occasionally.
2. Using tongs, place about ⅔ cup pork mixture down center of each tortilla. Top with romaine, oranges and onions. Serve immediately. If desired, serve with remaining pan sauce.
1 SERVING: 472 cal., 17g fat (4g sat. fat), 55mg chol., 976mg sod., 51g carb. (18g sugars, 3g fiber), 29g pro.

**LEMON PORK
WITH MUSHROOMS**

ITALIAN SAUSAGE WITH ARTICHOKES & FETA

To impress dinner guests, I love to serve Italian sausage and artichoke hearts with pasta. This meal tastes like a gourmet masterpiece!
—*Aysha Schurman, Ammon, ID*

TAKES: 25 min. • **MAKES:** 4 servings

1 lb. bulk Italian sausage
1 small red onion, finely chopped
1 garlic clove, minced
1 jar (7½ oz.) marinated quartered artichoke hearts, drained and coarsely chopped
½ cup tomato sauce
¼ cup dry red wine or chicken broth
½ tsp. Italian seasoning
½ cup crumbled feta cheese
   Hot cooked gemelli or spiral pasta
   Minced fresh parsley, optional

1. In a large skillet, cook sausage, onion and garlic over medium heat 6-8 minutes or until sausage is no longer pink and onion is tender, breaking up sausage into crumbles; drain.
2. Stir in artichoke hearts, tomato sauce, wine and Italian seasoning; heat through. Gently stir in cheese. Serve with pasta. If desired, sprinkle with parsley.

FREEZE OPTION: Freeze cooled sausage mixture in freezer containers. To use, partially thaw in refrigerator overnight. Place sausage mixture in a saucepan; heat through, stirring occasionally and adding a little broth or water if necessary.

1 CUP SAUCE: 435 cal., 35g fat (11g sat. fat), 69mg chol., 1149mg sod., 9g carb. (5g sugars, 1g fiber), 16g pro.

LEMON PORK WITH MUSHROOMS

This is my family's favorite go-to healthy dish you wouldn't guess is good for you. A little squeeze of lemon gives these crispy, seasoned chops a bright boost.
—*Christine Datian, Las Vegas, NV*

TAKES: 30 min. • **MAKES:** 4 servings

1 large egg, lightly beaten
1 cup seasoned bread crumbs
8 thin boneless pork loin chops (2 oz. each)
¼ tsp. salt
⅛ tsp. pepper
1 Tbsp. olive oil
1 Tbsp. butter
½ lb. sliced fresh mushrooms
2 garlic cloves, minced
2 tsp. grated lemon zest
1 Tbsp. lemon juice
   Lemon wedges, optional

1. Place egg and bread crumbs in separate shallow bowls. Sprinkle pork chops with salt and pepper; dip in egg, then coat with crumbs, pressing to adhere.
2. In a large skillet, heat oil over medium heat. In batches, cook pork until golden brown, 2-3 minutes per side. Remove from pan; keep warm.
3. Wipe pan clean. In skillet, heat butter over medium heat; saute sliced mushrooms until tender, 2-3 minutes. Stir in garlic, lemon zest and lemon juice; cook and stir 1 minute. Serve over pork chops. If desired, serve with lemon wedges.

2 PORK CHOPS: 331 cal., 15g fat (5g sat. fat), 109mg chol., 601mg sod., 19g carb. (2g sugars, 1g fiber), 28g pro. **DIABETIC EXCHANGES:** 3 lean meat, 1½ fat, 1 starch.

ITALIAN SAUSAGE WITH ARTICHOKES & FETA

PARMESAN PORK
MEDALLIONS

PARMESAN PORK MEDALLIONS

I was so happy to find this recipe for tender pork. With my own special tweaks, I have served it countless times for family and friends. It takes very little prep time and adapts easily to serve any number.
—Angela Ciocca, Saltsburg, PA

- -

TAKES: 20 min. • **MAKES:** 2 servings

- ½ lb. pork tenderloin
- 2 Tbsp. seasoned bread crumbs
- 1 Tbsp. grated Parmesan cheese
- ¼ tsp. salt
  Dash pepper
- 2 tsp. canola oil
- ¼ cup sliced onion
- 1 garlic clove, minced

1. Cut pork into 4 slices; flatten to ¼-in. thickness. In a large shallow dish, combine the bread crumbs, cheese, salt and pepper. Add pork, 1 slice at a time, and turn to coat.
2. In a large skillet over medium heat, cook pork slices in oil until meat is no longer pink, 2-3 minutes on each side. Remove and keep warm.
3. Add onion to the pan; cook and stir until tender. Add garlic, cook 1 minute longer. Serve with pork.
2 SLICES: 220 cal., 9g fat (2g sat. fat), 65mg chol., 487mg sod., 8g carb. (1g sugars, 1g fiber), 25g pro. **DIABETIC EXCHANGES:** 3 lean meat, 1 fat, ½ starch.

"Super easy. I didn't have a fresh onion or garlic, so I just used onion flakes and garlic powder. It tasted great."
—EMIL LOVE, TASTEOFHOME.COM

HAM & SCALLOPED POTATOES

HAM & SCALLOPED POTATOES

I fix this saucy skillet dish often, especially when I'm running late. It's easy and takes so little time to prepare. The recipe won first prize in our local paper some years back.
—Emma Magielda, Amsterdam, NY

- -

TAKES: 30 min. • **MAKES:** 4 servings

- 4 medium potatoes, peeled and thinly sliced
- 2 Tbsp. butter
- ⅓ cup water
- ½ cup 2% milk
- 2 to 3 Tbsp. onion soup mix
- 3 Tbsp. minced fresh parsley
- 1 cup cubed process cheese (Velveeta)
- 1 cup cubed fully cooked ham

1. In a large skillet, cook potatoes in butter until potatoes are lightly browned. Add water; bring to a boil. Reduce heat; cover and simmer for 14-15 minutes or until potatoes are tender.
2. Meanwhile in a small bowl, combine the milk, soup mix and parsley; stir in cheese. Pour over potatoes. Add ham; cook and stir gently over medium heat until cheese is melted and sauce is bubbly.
1 SERVING: 353 cal., 17g fat (10g sat. fat), 56mg chol., 1170mg sod., 36g carb. (6g sugars, 2g fiber), 16g pro.

PASTA ARRABBIATA (ANGRY PASTA)

I learned how to make this while I was in Italy one summer. You can add more or less crushed red pepper...and decide how angry you would like your pasta.
—Stacie Gomm, Providence, UT

- -

PREP: 15 min. • **COOK:** 25 min.
MAKES: 6 servings

- ½ lb. bacon strips, chopped
- 2 garlic cloves, minced
- ⅓ cup olive oil
- 3 cans (15 oz. each) tomato puree
- 6 fresh basil leaves, thinly sliced
- ½ to 1 tsp. crushed red pepper flakes
- 3 cups uncooked penne pasta
   Grated Parmesan cheese

1. In a large skillet, cook bacon over medium heat until crisp. Remove to paper towels with a slotted spoon; discard drippings.

2. In the same skillet, saute garlic in olive oil for 1 minute. Add the tomato puree, basil, pepper flakes and bacon. Bring to a boil; reduce heat and simmer 15 minutes to allow flavors to blend, stirring occasionally.

3. Meanwhile, cook penne pasta according to package directions; drain. Serve with sauce; sprinkle with Parmesan cheese.

1 CUP PASTA WITH ¾ CUP SAUCE: 460 cal., 28g fat (7g sat. fat), 42mg chol., 925mg sod., 31g carb. (4g sugars, 3g fiber), 20g pro.

PORK MEDALLIONS WITH SQUASH & GREENS

The colors of the dish remind me of autumn, my favorite season. Butternut squash is nutritious as well as colorful. This is an example of cooking it in a way other than mashed and sweetened. The pork tenderloin medallions are mildly seasoned with rosemary and very tender.
—Louise Nowak, Columbia, CT

- -

PREP: 35 min. • **COOK:** 10 min.
MAKES: 8 servings

- 2 qt. water
- 4 cups chopped mustard greens
- 1 medium butternut squash, peeled and cut into ½-in. cubes
- 3 medium leeks (white portion only), halved and sliced
- 3 Tbsp. olive oil
- 2 garlic cloves, minced
- ⅛ tsp. crushed red pepper flakes
- 1½ cups reduced-sodium chicken broth
- ½ tsp. salt

PORK MEDALLIONS
- 2 pork tenderloins (¾ lb. each), cut into 8 slices
- ⅓ cup all-purpose flour
- ½ tsp. salt
- ¼ tsp. pepper
- ¼ tsp. dried rosemary, crushed
- 1 tsp. cornstarch
- ½ cup apple cider or juice
- ⅓ cup reduced-sodium chicken broth
- 1 Tbsp. olive oil
- 1 Tbsp. butter
- 1 medium tart apple, peeled and chopped

1. In a large saucepan, bring water to a boil. Add mustard greens; cook, uncovered, for 3-5 minutes or until tender.

2. Meanwhile, in a Dutch oven, saute squash and leeks in oil until tender. Add garlic and pepper flakes; saute 1 minute longer. Stir in broth and salt. Bring to a boil. Reduce heat;

simmer, uncovered, for 8 minutes or until liquid has almost evaporated. Drain greens and add to squash mixture; set aside and keep warm.

3. Flatten pork slices to ¼-in. thickness. In a large shallow dish, combine the flour, salt, pepper and rosemary. Add pork, a few pieces at a time, and toss to coat.

4. In a small bowl, whisk cornstarch, apple cider and broth until smooth; set aside.

5. In a large skillet, cook pork in oil and butter until meat juices run clear. Remove and keep warm. Add apple to the pan; cook and stir for 2-4 minutes or until crisp-tender.

6. Stir cornstarch mixture; add to the pan. Bring to a boil; cook and stir for 2 minutes or until thickened. Add pork; heat through. Top with the apple mixture; serve with squash mixture.

3 OZ. COOKED PORK WITH ¾ CUP SQUASH MIXTURE: 272 cal., 11g fat (3g sat. fat), 51mg chol., 669mg sod., 24g carb. (8g sugars, 5g fiber), 20g pro.
DIABETIC EXCHANGES: 2 lean meat, 1½ starch, 1½ fat.

PORK MEDALLIONS WITH SQUASH & GREENS

ITALIAN SUB SANDWICHES

I serve these sandwiches for a special party treat. The red and green peppers add color along with flavor.
—*Judy Long, Effingham, IL*

PREP: 15 min. • **COOK:** 40 min.
MAKES: 8 servings

- 1½ lbs. Italian sausage links, cut into ½-in. pieces
- 2 medium red onions, thinly sliced
- 2 medium sweet red peppers, thinly sliced
- 2 medium green peppers, thinly sliced
- 1 garlic clove, minced
- 3 medium tomatoes, chopped
- 1 tsp. dried oregano
  Salt and pepper to taste
- 8 submarine sandwich buns (about 10 in.), split

1. In a large skillet, cook sausage over medium heat just until no longer pink; drain. Add the onions, peppers and garlic. Cover and cook for 25 minutes or until vegetables are tender, stirring occasionally. Add the tomatoes and oregano. Cover and simmer for 5-6 minutes or until tomatoes are cooked. Season with salt and pepper.

2. Meanwhile, hollow out bottom of each roll, leaving a ½-in. shell. (Discard removed bread or save for another use.) Toast rolls. Fill with sausage mixture.

FREEZE OPTION: Freeze cooled meat mixture in freezer containers. To use, partially thaw in refrigerator overnight. Heat through in a saucepan, stirring occasionally and adding a little water if necessary.

1 SANDWICH: 442 cal., 24g fat (7g sat. fat), 46mg chol., 843mg sod., 42g carb. (7g sugars, 4g fiber), 17g pro.

SPICY CHORIZO & SHRIMP RICE

Looking for an easy one-skillet meal for dinner tonight? This satisfying dish has a fresh southwestern flavor your family will warm up to!
—*Cheryl Perry, Hertford, NC*

TAKES: 30 min. • **MAKES:** 4 servings

- ½ lb. uncooked chorizo or bulk spicy pork sausage
- 4 tomatillos, husks removed, chopped
- 1 cup uncooked long grain rice
- ¼ cup chopped onion
- ¼ cup chopped celery leaves
- ¼ cup chopped carrot
- ½ tsp. garlic powder
- ¼ tsp. pepper
- 2 cups chicken broth
- ½ lb. uncooked medium shrimp, peeled and deveined
- ¼ cup crumbled queso fresco or diced part-skim mozzarella cheese
- 2 tsp. minced fresh cilantro

1. In a large skillet, crumble chorizo; add tomatillos. Cook over medium heat for 6-8 minutes or until meat is fully cooked. Add the rice, onion, celery leaves, carrot, garlic powder and pepper; cook and stir for 2 minutes.

2. Add broth; bring to a boil. Reduce heat; cover and simmer for 10 minutes. Stir in shrimp; cover and cook 5 minutes longer or until shrimp turn pink and rice is tender. Sprinkle with cheese and cilantro.

1¼ CUPS: 478 cal., 20g fat (7g sat. fat), 126mg chol., 1282mg sod., 43g carb. (3g sugars, 2g fiber), 27g pro.

DID YOU KNOW?

Tomatillos are also known as Mexican green tomatoes. They are smaller, more tart and firm than regular tomatoes, and are covered with a papery husk that should be removed before cooking. Substitute small (golf ball-size) unripe tomatoes, if you can't find tomatillos.

ITALIAN SUB SANDWICHES

APPLE-CHERRY PORK MEDALLIONS

BREADED MUSTARD & SAGE PORK CUTLETS

I left my daughter's back-to-school night with a complimentary package of instant potatoes. To make something with them, I created these pork cutlets, and they were fantastic.
—*Carrie Farias, Oak Ridge, NJ*

- -

TAKES: 25 min. • **MAKES:** 4 servings

- 1 large egg
- 2 Tbsp. fat-free milk
- 2 Tbsp. Dijon mustard
- ¾ cup panko (Japanese) bread crumbs
- ¾ cup mashed potato flakes
- 2 tsp. ground mustard
- 2 tsp. minced fresh sage
- ⅓ cup all-purpose flour
- 8 thin boneless pork loin chops (2 oz. each)
- ½ tsp. salt
- 4 tsp. canola oil, divided

1. In a shallow bowl, whisk egg, milk and Dijon mustard. In another shallow bowl, mix bread crumbs, potato flakes, ground mustard and sage. Place flour in another shallow bowl. Sprinkle pork with salt.
2. Dip pork in flour to coat both sides; shake off the excess. Dip in egg mixture, then in bread crumb mixture, patting to help the coating adhere.
3. In a large skillet, heat 2 tsp. oil over medium heat. Add pork chops in batches; cook 2-3 minutes on each side or until a thermometer reads at least 145°, adding additional oil as needed.

2 PORK CUTLETS: 328 cal., 13g fat (3g sat. fat), 101mg chol., 567mg sod., 23g carb. (1g sugars, 1g fiber), 27g pro. **DIABETIC EXCHANGES:** 3 lean meat, 1½ starch, 1 fat.

APPLE-CHERRY PORK MEDALLIONS

If you think you're too busy to cook a first-class meal, my pork medallions with tangy apple-cherry sauce, rosemary and thyme deliver the goods in a hurry.
—*Gloria Bradley, Naperville, IL*

- -

TAKES: 30 min. • **MAKES:** 4 servings

- 1 pork tenderloin (1 lb.)
- 1 tsp. minced fresh rosemary or ¼ tsp. dried rosemary, crushed
- 1 tsp. minced fresh thyme or ¼ tsp. dried thyme
- ½ tsp. celery salt
- 1 Tbsp. olive oil
- 1 large apple, sliced
- ⅔ cup unsweetened apple juice
- 3 Tbsp. dried tart cherries
- 1 Tbsp. honey
- 1 Tbsp. cider vinegar
- 1 pkg. (8.8 oz.) ready-to-serve brown rice

1. Cut tenderloin crosswise into 12 slices; sprinkle with rosemary, thyme and celery salt. In a large nonstick skillet, heat oil over medium-high heat. Brown pork on both sides; remove from pan.
2. In same skillet, combine apple, apple juice, cherries, honey and vinegar. Bring to a boil, stirring to loosen browned bits from pan. Reduce heat; simmer, uncovered, 3-4 minutes or just until apple is tender.
3. Return pork to pan, turning to coat with sauce; cook, covered, 3-4 minutes or until pork is tender. Meanwhile, prepare rice according to package directions; serve with pork mixture.

3 OZ. COOKED PORK WITH ⅓ CUP RICE AND ¼ CUP APPLE MIXTURE: 349 cal., 9g fat (2g sat. fat), 64mg chol., 179mg sod., 37g carb. (16g sugars, 4g fiber), 25g pro.
DIABETIC EXCHANGES: 3 lean meat, 2½ starch.

BREADED MUSTARD
& SAGE PORK CUTLETS

WARM PORK & PEAR SALAD

Convenient items—like a salad mix and marinated pork loin—are the secret to this flavorful salad. It comes together in a hurry, yet it looks and tastes so special.
—*Patricia Harmon, Baden, PA*

PREP: 35 min. • **COOK:** 20 min.
MAKES: 4 servings

- 1 cup sliced sweet onion
- 1 Tbsp. plus ⅓ cup canola oil, divided
- ¼ cup cider vinegar
- 1 tsp. molasses
- 1 tsp. sugar
- ½ tsp. salt
- ⅛ tsp. pepper

SALAD

- 1 pkg. (1.7 lbs.) lemon-garlic center cut pork loin fillet
- 2 Tbsp. canola oil
- 1 pkg. (10 oz.) Italian romaine and radicchio salad mix
- 2 medium pears, sliced
- ½ cup seedless red grapes
- ½ cup coarsely chopped walnuts, toasted
- ½ cup crumbled Gorgonzola cheese

1. In a large skillet, cook onion in 1 Tbsp. oil over medium heat for 10-15 minutes or until golden brown. Cool to room temperature.
2. Place onion and vinegar in a blender; cover and process until onion is chopped. Add the molasses, sugar, salt and pepper; cover and process until blended. While processing, gradually add the remaining oil in a steady stream. Pour dressing into a microwave-safe bowl; set aside.
3. Cut pork into ¼-in. slices. In a large skillet, cook pork in oil until no longer pink. Remove and cut into strips; keep warm.
4. Microwave salad dressing on high for 30-60 seconds or until warmed; whisk until blended. Toss salad mix with ½ cup dressing; place on a serving platter. Top with pears, grapes and pork. Drizzle with remaining dressing; sprinkle with walnuts and cheese. Serve immediately.
1¾ CUPS: 680 cal., 49g fat (8g sat. fat), 83mg chol., 548mg sod., 27g carb. (16g sugars, 6g fiber), 36g pro.

HONEY LEMON SCHNITZEL

These pork cutlets are coated in a sweet sauce with honey, lemon juice and butter. They're certainly good enough for company, but perfect for a quick, weeknight meal, too.
—*Carole Fraser, North York, ON*

TAKES: 20 min. • **MAKES:** 4 servings

- 3 Tbsp. all-purpose flour
- ¾ tsp. salt
- ¾ tsp. pepper
- 4 pork sirloin cutlets (4 oz. each)
- 2 Tbsp. butter
- ¼ cup lemon juice
- ¼ cup honey

1. Mix flour, salt and pepper; sprinkle over both sides of cutlets. In a large cast-iron or other heavy skillet, heat butter over medium heat. Add pork; cook until a thermometer reads 145°, 2-3 minutes per side. Remove from pan.
2. Add lemon juice and honey to skillet; cook and stir over medium heat until thickened, about 3 minutes. Add pork; heat through.
1 SERVING: 291 cal., 10g fat (5g sat. fat), 87mg chol., 561mg sod., 23g carb. (18g sugars, 0 fiber), 26g pro.

HONEY LEMON SCHNITZEL

FARMERS MARKET PASTA

FARMERS MARKET PASTA

When we moved into our house, little did we know that we had a wild asparagus patch. For decades, that little patch has given us plenty of asparagus. This recipe can be used almost any time of year, with almost any assortment of vegetables the season has to offer. By cooking without butter or oil, you can cut fat and calories, but the flavors are still there.
—*Wendy Ball, Battle Creek, MI*

PREP: 20 min. • **COOK:** 20 min.
MAKES: 6 servings

- 9 oz. uncooked whole wheat linguine
- 1 lb. fresh asparagus, trimmed and cut into 2-in. pieces
- 2 medium carrots, thinly sliced
- 1 small red onion, chopped
- 2 medium zucchini or yellow summer squash, thinly sliced
- ½ lb. sliced fresh mushrooms
- 2 garlic cloves, minced
- 1 cup half-and-half cream
- ⅔ cup reduced-sodium chicken broth
- 1 cup frozen petite peas
- 2 cups cubed fully cooked ham
- 2 Tbsp. julienned fresh basil
- ¼ tsp. pepper
- ½ cup grated Parmesan cheese
  Optional: Additional fresh basil and Parmesan cheese

1. In a 6-qt. stockpot, cook whole wheat linguine according to package directions, adding asparagus and carrots during the last 3-5 minutes of cooking. Drain; return to pot.
2. Place a large skillet coated with cooking spray over medium heat. Add onion; cook and stir 3 minutes. Add squash, mushrooms, and garlic; cook and stir until crisp-tender, 4-5 minutes.
3. Add cream and broth; bring to a boil, stirring to loosen browned bits from pan. Reduce heat; simmer, uncovered, until sauce is thickened slightly, about 5 minutes. Stir in peas, cubed ham, 2 Tbsp. basil and pepper; heat through.
4. Add to linguine mixture; stir in ½ cup cheese. If desired, top with additional basil and cheese.
2 CUPS: 338 cal., 9g fat (4g sat. fat), 53mg chol., 817mg sod., 46g carb. (8g sugars, 8g fiber), 23g pro. **DIABETIC EXCHANGES:** 2½ starch, 2 lean meat, 1 vegetable, ½ fat.

TROPICAL PORK CHOPS

I was fortunate to visit my grandmother's birthplace in Hawaii, where I met relatives who taught me how to make this dish. It has been a family favorite since I brought the recipe home. The pineapple is a luscious sweet surprise.
—*Jeanette Babineau, Grand Junction, CO*

PREP: 20 min. • **COOK:** 30 min.
MAKES: 4 servings

- ⅓ cup ketchup
- 2 Tbsp. prepared mustard
- 2 Tbsp. brown sugar
- 1 Tbsp. cider vinegar
- 1½ tsp. soy sauce
- ⅛ tsp. garlic salt
- ⅛ tsp. onion salt
  Dash cayenne pepper
- 4 boneless pork loin chops
  Salt and pepper to taste
- ¼ cup chopped onion
- 2 garlic cloves, minced
- 1 Tbsp. canola oil
- ⅓ cup water
- ¼ cup pineapple tidbits
  Hot cooked rice

In a saucepan, combine first 8 ingredients. Cover and simmer until sugar is dissolved, about 10 minutes. Remove from the heat; set aside. Season pork chops with salt and pepper. In a skillet, cook pork, onion and garlic in oil until meat is browned. Add water and reserved sauce. Cover and cook over medium-low heat for 20-25 minutes or until the meat is no longer pink, adding more water if needed. Stir in pineapple and heat through. Serve over rice.
1 SERVING: 248 cal., 10g fat (3g sat. fat), 55mg chol., 584mg sod., 16g carb. (11g sugars, 1g fiber), 23g pro.

CREAMY PAPRIKA PORK

TENDERLOIN WITH HERB SAUCE

Tender pork is treated to a rich and creamy sauce with a slight kick, thanks to red pepper flakes. This hearty dish is very simple to prepare and always a dinnertime winner.
—*Monica Shipley, Tulare, CA*

TAKES: 25 min. • **MAKES:** 6 servings

- 2 pork tenderloins (1 lb. each)
- ½ tsp. salt
- 4 tsp. butter
- ⅔ cup half-and-half cream
- 2 Tbsp. minced fresh parsley
- 2 tsp. herbes de Provence
- 2 tsp. reduced-sodium soy sauce
- 1 tsp. beef bouillon granules
- ½ to ¾ tsp. crushed red pepper flakes

1. Cut each tenderloin into 12 slices; sprinkle with salt. In a large nonstick skillet, heat the butter over medium heat; brown pork in batches, 3-4 minutes per side. Return all pork to pan.
2. Mix remaining ingredients; pour over pork slices. Cook, uncovered, over low heat until the sauce is thickened and a thermometer inserted in pork reads 145°, 2-3 minutes, stirring occasionally. Let stand 5 minutes before serving.
NOTE: Look for herbes de Provence in the spice aisle.
4 OZ. COOKED PORK: 238 cal., 10g fat (5g sat. fat), 104mg chol., 495mg sod., 2g carb. (1g sugars, 0 fiber), 31g pro. **DIABETIC EXCHANGES:** 4 lean meat, 1 fat.

"This was INCREDIBLE! Easiest and tastiest pork loin I have ever had! I wouldn't change a single thing about it. I loved it, my kids loved it (and they don't even like pork!), and my husband liked it so much he asked if we could have it again later this week!"
—JENNB76, TASTEOFHOME.COM

CREAMY PAPRIKA PORK

When I was little, I would often ask my mom to make "favorite meat." She knew what I was really requesting was this homey pork recipe. It's been in my family for more than 30 years and is still a favorite!
—*Alexandra Barnett, Forest, VA*

TAKES: 30 min. • **MAKES:** 4 servings

- 1 pork tenderloin (1 lb.), cut into 1-in. cubes
- 1 tsp. all-purpose flour
- 4 tsp. paprika
- ¾ tsp. salt
- ¼ tsp. pepper
- 1 Tbsp. butter
- ¾ cup heavy whipping cream
  Hot cooked egg noodles or rice
  Minced fresh parsley, optional

1. Toss pork with flour and seasonings. In a large skillet, heat butter over medium heat; saute pork until lightly browned, 4-5 minutes.
2. Add the cream; bring to a boil, stirring to loosen browned bits from pan. Cook, uncovered, until cream is slightly thickened, 5-7 minutes.
3. Serve with noodles. If desired, sprinkle with parsley.
¾ CUP PORK MIXTURE: 320 cal., 23g fat (14g sat. fat), 122mg chol., 524mg sod., 3g carb. (1g sugars, 1g fiber), 24g pro.

**TENDERLOIN WITH
HERB SAUCE**

SOUTHWEST SKILLET CHOPS

SOUTHWEST SKILLET CHOPS

This is one of my go-to meals because I usually have the ingredients to make these chops in my kitchen. I can't get enough of the slightly spicy corn relish.

—Linda Cifuentes, Mahomet, IL

- -

TAKES: 25 min. • **MAKES:** 4 servings

- 4 boneless pork loin chops (6 oz. each)
- ¾ tsp. salt
- ¼ tsp. pepper
- 2 Tbsp. butter, divided
- 1 Tbsp. olive oil
- ½ small red onion, sliced
- 1 jalapeno pepper, seeded and finely chopped
- ½ cup frozen corn, thawed
- 3 Tbsp. lime juice
- ¼ cup sliced ripe olives or green olives with pimientos, optional

1. Sprinkle pork chops with salt and pepper. In a large skillet, heat 1 Tbsp. butter and oil over medium-high heat. Brown pork chops on both sides. Remove from pan.

2. In same skillet, heat the remaining butter. Add onion and jalapeno; cook and stir for 2-3 minutes or until tender. Return chops to skillet. Add corn, lime juice and, if desired, olives; cook, covered, 4-6 minutes or until a thermometer inserted in pork reads 145°. Let stand 5 minutes before serving.

NOTE: Wear disposable gloves when cutting hot peppers; the oils can burn skin. Avoid touching your face.

1 PORK CHOP WITH ¼ CUP RELISH: 330 cal., 19g fat (8g sat. fat), 97mg chol., 542mg sod., 6g carb. (1g sugars, 1g fiber), 33g pro.

PORK SCALLOPINI WITH MUSHROOMS

PORK SCALLOPINI WITH MUSHROOMS

This is a great "date night" recipe: simple to prepare, but quite impressive and delicious! I use reduced-sodium chicken broth because I add salt to season the meat and mushrooms.

—Lana Dramstad, Havre, MT

- -

TAKES: 30 min. • **MAKES:** 4 servings

- 1 pork tenderloin (1 lb.), cut into 8 slices
- 1 tsp. salt, divided
- ½ tsp. pepper, divided
- 4 Tbsp. butter, divided
- ½ lb. sliced fresh mushrooms
- 2 celery ribs, sliced
- 1 cup reduced-sodium chicken broth
- ⅓ cup heavy whipping cream
- 3 Tbsp. minced fresh parsley, divided
  Hot cooked egg noodles

1. Pound pork slices with a meat mallet to ½-in. thickness; sprinkle with ½ tsp. salt and ¼ tsp. pepper. In a large skillet, heat 1 Tbsp. butter over medium-high heat. Add pork in batches; cook 2-3 minutes on each side or until pork is golden brown, using 1 Tbsp. butter as needed. Remove; keep warm.

2. In same pan, heat remaining butter over medium heat. Add the mushrooms, celery, and remaining salt and pepper; cook and stir 6-8 minutes or until tender. Add the broth, stirring to loosen browned bits from pan. Bring to a boil; cook 5-6 minutes or until liquid is reduced to ⅔ cup.

3. Return pork to pan. Stir in cream and 2 tablespoons parsley; heat through. Serve with noodles; sprinkle with remaining parsley.

1 SERVING: 323 cal., 23g fat (13g sat. fat), 117mg chol., 895mg sod., 4g carb. (1g sugars, 1g fiber), 26g pro.

PEANUT BUTTER PORK CURRY

PORK WITH MUSTARD SAUCE

Back when I was a girl, I couldn't wait until I was grown up and could start cooking for my own family. Now that I am, I really enjoy using pork. The tender meat and the rich mustard sauce in this recipe are delectable together.
—Irma Pomeroy, Enfield, CT

TAKES: 30 min. • **MAKES:** 4 servings

- 1   lb. pork tenderloin
- 2   Tbsp. butter
- ½   cup beef broth
- ¾   tsp. dried tarragon
- ½   cup heavy whipping cream
- 1   Tbsp. Dijon mustard
     Salt and pepper to taste
     Hot cooked noodles, optional

1. Cut tenderloin into 8 pieces. Slice each piece again, but do not cut all of the way through; open and flatten each piece, pounding slightly with meat mallet to create medallions.

2. In a large skillet over medium-high heat, cook pork in butter until no longer pink, 5-6 minutes on each side. Remove to serving dish and keep warm; discard drippings.

3. In the same skillet, cook the broth and tarragon over high heat until reduced by half. Reduce heat; stir in the cream and mustard. Season with salt and pepper. Spoon over pork. Serve with noodles if desired.

2 SLICES PORK WITH 3 TBSP. SAUCE: 292 cal., 21g fat (12g sat. fat), 119mg chol., 311mg sod., 2g carb. (1g sugars, 0 fiber), 24g pro.

PEANUT BUTTER PORK CURRY

For an anniversary with my boyfriend, I cooked pork Asian-style with peanut, coconut and curry flavors. The butcher cubed the pork for me, which was a welcome timesaver.
—Angela Robinson, Findlay, OH

PREP: 15 min. • **COOK:** 20 min.
MAKES: 6 servings

- 1½ lbs. pork tenderloins, cubed
- 1   tsp. salt, divided
- ½   tsp. pepper
- 1   Tbsp. olive oil
- 1   cup sliced fresh carrots
- 1   medium onion, chopped
- 2   garlic cloves, minced
- 1   can (14½ oz.) diced tomatoes, drained
- 1   cup chicken broth
- 1   cup cream of coconut or coconut milk
- ½   cup creamy peanut butter
- 3   tsp. curry powder
- ¼   tsp. cayenne pepper
     Cooked brown rice

1. Sprinkle pork with ½ tsp. salt and pepper. In a large nonstick skillet, heat oil over medium-high heat. Add pork; cook and stir until no longer pink, 4-6 minutes. Remove.

2. In same skillet, cook carrots and onion until softened, 4-6 minutes. Add garlic; cook 2 minutes. Return pork to skillet. Add tomatoes and broth. Reduce heat; simmer, covered, 6-8 minutes.

3. Stir in cream of coconut, peanut butter, curry and cayenne and remaining salt until smooth. Simmer, uncovered, until thickened slightly, 2 minutes. Serve with brown rice.

1 CUP: 463 cal., 24g fat (9g sat. fat), 64mg chol., 837mg sod., 36g carb. (29g sugars, 4g fiber), 29g pro.

DID YOU KNOW?

Dijon, a town in eastern France's famous Burgundy wine-growing region, is the home of Dijon mustard. Mustard is commonly grown as a cover crop among grape vines. The plants attract beneficial insects and give nutrients back to the soil. They also release countless tiny mustard seeds, meaning the crop replants itself year after year. Dijon mustard completes the cycle, getting its distinctive flavor from white wine rather than vinegar (a standard ingredient in most mustards).

**PORK WITH
MUSTARD SAUCE**

Fish & Seafood

**SHRIMP
LETTUCE
WRAPS**

SHRIMP LETTUCE WRAPS

Lettuce forms a crispy shell that's full of possibilities, depending on what's in your fridge. Swap chicken, pork or tofu for the shrimp, and mix in any veggies you want. Carrots, broccoli, snow peas and chopped zucchini are all fantastic add-ins.
—Taste of Home *Test Kitchen*

- -

TAKES: 30 min. • **MAKES:** 4 servings

¼	cup reduced-sodium soy sauce
3	Tbsp. lime juice
2	Tbsp. plus 1 tsp. apricot preserves
2	Tbsp. water
2	garlic cloves, minced
¼	tsp. ground ginger
2	medium carrots
6	green onions
3	tsp. olive oil, divided
1	lb. uncooked medium shrimp, peeled and deveined
1	large sweet red pepper, chopped
2	cups hot cooked rice
8	large lettuce leaves

1. In a small bowl, mix the first 6 ingredients. Using a vegetable peeler, shave carrots lengthwise into very thin strips. Slice white parts of green onions; cut each green top in half lengthwise.
2. In a large skillet, heat 2 tsp. oil over medium-high heat. Add shrimp; stir-fry until pink. Remove from pan.
3. Stir-fry chopped red pepper and carrots in remaining oil 4 minutes. Add white parts of onions; stir-fry 1-2 minutes longer or until vegetables are crisp-tender.
4. Add ⅓ cup soy sauce mixture to pan. Bring to a boil. Add shrimp; heat through. Place ¼ cup rice on each lettuce leaf; top with ½ cup shrimp mixture. Drizzle with remaining soy sauce mixture and roll up. Tie each with a green onion strip.
2 LETTUCE WRAPS: 306 cal., 5g fat (1g sat. fat), 138mg chol., 777mg sod., 41g carb. (9g sugars, 3g fiber), 23g pro. **DIABETIC EXCHANGES:** 3 lean meat, 2 starch, 1 vegetable, ½ fat.

CRAB CAKE SANDWICHES

I originally created these golden cakes to use up some leftover crab, but you can make them anytime by using convenient canned crab. I've served them to family and friends, and they always ask for the recipe. I've also used the crab mixture to stuff mushroom caps and bake them as an appetizer.
—Yvonne Bellomo, Ebensburg, PA

TAKES: 30 min. • **MAKES:** 6 servings

- 3 cans (6 oz. each) crabmeat, drained, flaked and cartilage removed
- ½ cup crushed Ritz crackers (about 10 crackers)
- 1 medium onion, chopped
- ½ cup chopped green pepper
- ¼ cup mayonnaise
- 1 large egg, lightly beaten
- 1 tsp. salt
- 1 tsp. ground mustard
- 1 tsp. Worcestershire sauce
- ½ tsp. lemon juice
- ¼ tsp. garlic powder
- ¼ cup all-purpose flour
- ¼ cup canola oil
- 6 hard rolls, split
  Lettuce leaves, tomato and onion slices, optional

1. In a large bowl, combine the crabmeat, crushed crackers, onion and green pepper. In a small bowl, combine the mayonnaise, egg, salt, mustard, Worcestershire sauce, lemon juice and garlic powder. Stir into crab mixture until blended. Shape into six 3-in. patties; coat with flour.

2. In a large skillet, fry crab patties in oil for 5 minutes on each side or until browned. Serve on rolls with lettuce, tomato and onion if desired.

1 SANDWICH: 430 cal., 22g fat (3g sat. fat), 64mg chol., 931mg sod., 43g carb. (6g sugars, 2g fiber), 14g pro.

PARMESAN-CRUSTED TILAPIA

I usually serve this crispy fish with tartar sauce and seasoned steamed veggies. It's like a Friday night fish fry without all the calories!
—Christi McElroy, Neenah, WI

TAKES: 25 min. • **MAKES:** 4 servings

- ½ cup all-purpose flour
- 1 large egg, beaten
- ½ cup crushed Ritz crackers (about 10 crackers)
- ¼ cup grated Parmesan cheese
- ½ tsp. salt
- 4 tilapia fillets (5 oz. each)
- 2 Tbsp. olive oil
  Lemon wedges

1. Place flour and egg in separate shallow bowls. In another shallow bowl, combine the crackers, cheese and salt. Dip fillets in the flour, then egg, then cracker mixture; turn until coated.

2. In a large cast-iron or other heavy skillet, cook fillets in oil over medium heat until fish just begins to flake easily with a fork. Serve with lemon wedges.

1 FILLET: 287 cal., 13g fat (3g sat. fat), 125mg chol., 440mg sod., 12g carb. (1g sugars, 0 fiber), 31g pro.

"I used chicken instead of tilapia and my children just raved about it. They ate all of it and asked for more! It's a great coating and turns out very crispy. A real keeper!"
—SSPOONEY, TASTEOFHOME.COM

The caption in the photo reads: **PARMESAN-CRUSTED TILAPIA**

DILLED SOLE WITH ALMONDS

I make this attractive dish often because I can have it ready in less than half an hour. Served with a fresh vegetable and simple cooked potatoes, it makes a healthy meal. Fish with butter and almonds is always a classic.
—*Bonnie Baumgardner, Sylva, NC*

TAKES: 20 min. • **MAKES:** 2 servings

- 2 Tbsp. cornmeal
- ¼ tsp. salt
- ⅛ tsp. lemon-pepper seasoning
- 2 sole fillets (12 oz. each)
- 2 Tbsp. butter, divided
- ¼ tsp. dill weed
- 3 Tbsp. slivered almonds
  Lemon slices, optional

1. In a shallow dish, combine the first 3 ingredients. Coat both sides of sole fillets with mixture.

2. In a large skillet, melt 1 Tbsp. butter; stir in the dill. Add fillets; cook for 2-3 minutes on each side or until fish flakes easily with a fork. Remove and keep warm.

3. Add almonds and remaining butter to the skillet; cook and stir for 4 minutes or until lightly browned. Sprinkle over fish. Serve with lemon if desired.

1 SERVING: 346 cal., 19g fat (8g sat. fat), 112mg chol., 578mg sod., 9g carb. (1g sugars, 2g fiber), 35g pro.

SALMON SLIDERS WITH
SUN-DRIED TOMATO SPREAD

SALMON SLIDERS WITH SUN-DRIED TOMATO SPREAD

My husband isn't a fan of salmon burgers, but he devoured these! The combination of feta, dill and fresh salmon on the toasted pretzel bun, topped with sun-dried tomato mayonnaise, changed his mind. The pickle adds tartness and crunch to balance the flavors and textures perfectly.
—*Arlene Erlbach, Morton Grove, IL*

PREP: 30 min. + cooling
COOK: 10 min./batch • **MAKES:** 8 servings

- 1 jar (7 oz.) julienned oil-packed sun-dried tomatoes, drained and chopped
- ¼ cup orange juice
- ¾ cup mayonnaise
- 8 oz. crumbled feta cheese
- ⅓ cup crushed saltines
- 1 large egg, lightly beaten
- 3 Tbsp. finely chopped red onion
- 2 Tbsp. snipped fresh dill
- 1 lb. salmon fillet, skin removed, cut into 1-in. cubes
- 2 Tbsp. olive oil
- 8 mini pretzel buns, toasted
- 16 hamburger dill pickle slices

1. Place the tomatoes and orange juice in a small saucepan. Bring to a boil. Reduce heat; simmer, uncovered, until thickened, about 15 minutes. Cool completely. Transfer to a small bowl; stir in mayonnaise. Refrigerate until serving.

2. Meanwhile, in a large bowl, combine the feta, saltines, egg, red onion and dill. Place salmon in a food processor; pulse until coarsely chopped. Add to feta mixture; mix lightly but thoroughly. Shape into eight 1-in.-thick patties.

3. In a large skillet, heat the olive oil over medium-high heat. Add patties in batches; cook until golden brown, 3-4 minutes on each side. Serve on buns with mayonnaise mixture and pickles.

1 SLIDER: 515 cal., 35g fat (8g sat. fat), 68mg chol., 738mg sod., 31g carb. (3g sugars, 4g fiber), 20g pro.

TRUE SHRIMP CREOLE

A true Cajun dish, this recipe is even better if refrigerated overnight to allow all the flavors to blend.
—*Johnnie McLeod, Bastrop, LA*

- -

PREP: 10 min. • **COOK:** 25 min.
MAKES: 6 servings

- ¼ cup all-purpose flour
- ½ cup canola oil
- 1 medium onion, chopped
- 1 medium green pepper, chopped
- 1 celery rib, chopped
- 1 garlic clove, minced
- 1 can (14½ oz.) stewed tomatoes
- 1 can (6 oz.) tomato paste
- 4 bay leaves
- 1 Tbsp. Worcestershire sauce
- ½ tsp. hot pepper sauce
- Salt and pepper to taste
- 2 lbs. fresh or frozen uncooked medium shrimp, peeled and deveined
- Hot cooked rice

1. In a large heavy skillet, combine flour and oil until smooth. Cook and stir over medium heat until flour is a rich deep brown. Add onion, green pepper and celery; cook until vegetables are tender, 5-6 minutes. Add garlic; cook 1 minute longer. Stir in next 6 ingredients. Cover and simmer until heated through, 4-5 minutes.

2. Add shrimp. Simmer, uncovered, until shrimp turn pink, 5-6 minutes. Discard bay leaves. Serve with rice.

1 SERVING: 358 cal., 19g fat (3g sat. fat), 224mg chol., 440mg sod., 20g carb. (10g sugars, 3g fiber), 27g pro.

TRUE SHRIMP CREOLE

LIME-CILANTRO TILAPIA

I have so much fun serving this Mexican-inspired tilapia at summer parties. Finish it off with a side of rice and a salad loaded with sliced avocados and tomatoes.
—*Nadine Mesch, Mount Healthy, OH*

- -

TAKES: 25 min. • **MAKES:** 4 servings

- ⅓ cup all-purpose flour
- ¾ tsp. salt
- ½ tsp. pepper
- ½ tsp. ground cumin, divided
- 4 tilapia fillets (6 oz. each)
- 1 Tbsp. olive oil
- ½ cup reduced-sodium chicken broth
- 2 Tbsp. minced fresh cilantro
- 1 tsp. grated lime zest
- 2 Tbsp. lime juice

1. In a shallow bowl, mix flour, salt, pepper and ¼ tsp. cumin. Dip fillets in flour mixture to coat both sides; shake off excess.

2. In a large nonstick skillet, heat oil over medium heat. Add fillets; cook, uncovered, 3-4 minutes on each side or until fish flakes easily with a fork. Remove and keep warm.

3. To the same pan, add broth, cilantro, lime zest, lime juice and remaining cumin; bring to a boil. Reduce heat; simmer, uncovered, 2-3 minutes or until slightly thickened. Serve with tilapia.

1 FILLET WITH 2 TBSP. SAUCE: 198 cal., 5g fat (1g sat. fat), 83mg chol., 398mg sod., 6g carb. (1g sugars, 0 fiber), 33g pro. **DIABETIC EXCHANGES:** 4 lean meat, ½ starch, ½ fat.

**STEAMED
MUSSELS
WITH
PEPPERS**

PO'BOY TACOS

I intended to make tostadas, but misread a couple of ingredients and had to use what I had on hand. I put my own twist on a po'boy recipe and ended up with something even better than planned.
—*Cynthia Nelson, Saskatoon, , SK*

TAKES: 30 min. • **MAKES:** 4 servings

- ¼ cup mayonnaise
- 2 Tbsp. seafood cocktail sauce
- ½ tsp. Buffalo wing sauce
- ½ medium ripe avocado, peeled
- 1 Tbsp. lime juice
- ½ cup all-purpose flour
- ½ cup cornmeal
- 2 Tbsp. Creole seasoning
- 1 lb. uncooked shrimp (26-30 per lb.), peeled and deveined
- 2 Tbsp. canola oil
- 8 flour tortillas (6 in.)
- 1 medium tomato, chopped
- 2 Tbsp. minced fresh cilantro

1. Combine the mayonnaise, cocktail sauce and wing sauce; set aside. In another bowl, mash avocado and lime juice until combined; set aside.
2. In a shallow bowl, mix flour, cornmeal and Creole seasoning. Add shrimp, a few pieces at a time, and turn to coat; shake off excess. In a large skillet, heat canola oil over medium-high heat. Add shrimp; cook and stir until pink, 4-6 minutes.
3. Spread the reserved avocado mixture over tortillas. Top with shrimp, reserved mayonnaise mixture, tomato and cilantro.
2 TACOS: 551 cal., 29g fat (5g sat. fat), 139mg chol., 977mg sod., 47g carb. (3g sugars, 5g fiber), 25g pro.

TEST KITCHEN TIP

With the crunchy coating on the shrimp, flavorful sauce and rich mashed avocado, this dish tastes like tacos from your favorite food truck.

STEAMED MUSSELS WITH PEPPERS

Use the French bread to soak up the deliciously seasoned broth. If you like food zippy, add the jalapeno seeds.
—*Taste of Home Test Kitchen*

PREP: 30 min. • **COOK:** 10 min.
MAKES: 4 servings

- 2 lbs. fresh mussels, scrubbed and beards removed
- 1 jalapeno pepper, seeded and chopped
- 2 Tbsp. olive oil
- 3 garlic cloves, minced
- 1 bottle (8 oz.) clam juice
- ½ cup white wine or additional clam juice
- ⅓ cup chopped sweet red pepper
- 3 green onions, sliced
- ½ tsp. dried oregano
- 1 bay leaf
- 2 Tbsp. minced fresh parsley
- ¼ tsp. salt
- ¼ tsp. pepper
   French bread baguette, sliced, optional

1. Tap mussels; discard any that do not close. Set aside. In a large skillet, saute jalapeno in oil until tender. Add garlic; cook 1 minute longer. Stir in the clam juice, wine, red pepper, green onions, oregano and bay leaf.
2. Bring to a boil. Reduce heat; add mussels. Cover and simmer for 5-6 minutes or until mussels open. Discard bay leaf and any unopened mussels. Sprinkle with parsley, salt and pepper. Serve with baguette slices if desired.
NOTE: Wear disposable gloves when cutting hot peppers; the oils can burn skin. Avoid touching your face.
ABOUT 1 DOZEN: 293 cal., 12g fat (2g sat. fat), 65mg chol., 931mg sod., 12g carb. (1g sugars, 1g fiber), 28g pro.
STEAMED CLAMS WITH PEPPERS: Substitute clams for the mussels.

PO'BOY TACOS

CURRY SHRIMP LINGUINE

Curry, cilantro and coconut milk make this dish an exciting change of pace. Also try it with rice noodles or spaghetti.
—*Jana Rippee, Casa Grande, AZ*

- -

TAKES: 25 min. • **MAKES:** 6 servings

- 1   pkg. (16 oz.) linguine
- 3   tsp. curry powder
- 1   can (13.66 oz.) light coconut milk
- ½   tsp. salt
- ¼   tsp. pepper
- 1¼ lbs. uncooked medium shrimp, peeled and deveined
- ⅓   cup minced fresh cilantro

1. Cook linguine according to package directions. Meanwhile, in a large skillet over medium heat, toast curry powder for 2 minutes, stirring frequently. Stir in the milk, salt and pepper.

2. Bring to a boil. Add shrimp; cook until shrimp turn pink, 5-6 minutes. Drain linguine; toss with shrimp mixture and cilantro.

1½ CUPS: 406 cal., 8g fat (4g sat. fat), 115mg chol., 313mg sod., 58g carb. (4g sugars, 3g fiber), 26g pro.

TUNA WITH CITRUS PONZU SAUCE

I like this Asian-inspired tuna because it's easy to prepare, delicious and healthy, too. It's a popular dish with my friends.
—*Diane Halferty, Corpus Christi, TX*

- -

TAKES: 20 min. • **MAKES:** 4 servings

- ½   tsp. Chinese five-spice powder
- ¼   tsp. salt
- ¼   tsp. cayenne pepper
- 4   tuna steaks (6 oz. each)
- 1   Tbsp. canola oil
- ¼   cup orange juice
- 2   green onions, thinly sliced
- 1   Tbsp. lemon juice
- 1   Tbsp. reduced-sodium soy sauce
- 2   tsp. rice vinegar
- 1   tsp. brown sugar
- ¼   tsp. minced fresh gingerroot

1. Combine the five-spice powder, salt and cayenne; sprinkle over tuna steaks. In a large skillet, cook tuna in oil over medium heat for 2-3 minutes on each side for medium-rare or until slightly pink in the center; remove and keep warm.

2. Combine the orange juice, onions, lemon juice, soy sauce, vinegar, brown sugar and ginger; pour into skillet. Cook for 1-2 minutes or until slightly thickened. Serve with tuna.

1 TUNA STEAK WITH 1 TBSP. SAUCE: 234 cal., 5g fat (1g sat. fat), 77mg chol., 364mg sod., 5g carb. (3g sugars, 0 fiber), 40g pro. **DIABETIC EXCHANGES:** 5 lean meat, ½ fat.

CURRY SHRIMP LINGUINE

**COD WITH BACON &
BALSAMIC TOMATOES**

TANGY LEMON CATFISH

My husband turns up his nose at any fish dish I prepare, except for this one. In fact, this one makes his eyes light up!
—Carol Mingia, Greensboro, NC

- -

PREP: 10 min. + marinating • **COOK:** 10 min.
MAKES: 2 servings

    2   Tbsp. lemon juice
    1   garlic clove, minced
    ¼   tsp. salt
        Dash dried oregano
    ½   lb. catfish or whitefish fillets
    ¼   cup cornmeal
    2   Tbsp. all-purpose flour
  1½   tsp. canola oil
  1½   tsp. butter
TARTAR SAUCE
    ¼   cup mayonnaise
    1   Tbsp. finely chopped dill pickle
    2   tsp. finely chopped onion
    2   tsp. minced fresh dill or
        ¾ tsp. dill weed

1. In a shallow bowl, combine the lemon juice, garlic, salt and oregano; add fillets and turn to coat. Cover; refrigerate 30-60 minutes, turning fish several times.
2. Drain and discard marinade. In a shallow bowl, combine cornmeal and flour. Coat the fillets with cornmeal mixture. In a skillet, cook fillets in oil and butter for 5 minutes on each side or until fish is golden brown and flakes easily with a fork.
3. Combine the tartar sauce ingredients in a bowl. Serve with fish.
1 SERVING: 287 cal., 10g fat (3g sat. fat), 63mg chol., 717mg sod., 26g carb. (0 sugars, 2g fiber), 22g pro.

COD WITH BACON & BALSAMIC TOMATOES

Let's face it, everything really is better with bacon. I fry it up, add cod fillets to the pan and finish with a big, tomato-y pop.
—Maureen McClanahan, St. Louis, MO

- -

TAKES: 30 min. • **MAKES:** 4 servings

    4   center-cut bacon strips, chopped
    4   cod fillets (5 oz. each)
    ½   tsp. salt
    ¼   tsp. pepper
    2   cups grape tomatoes, halved
    2   Tbsp. balsamic vinegar

1. In a large skillet, cook bacon over medium heat until crisp, stirring occasionally. Remove with a slotted spoon; drain on paper towels.
2. Sprinkle fillets with salt and pepper. Add fillets to the bacon drippings; cook over medium-high heat until fish just begins to flake easily with a fork, 4-6 minutes on each side. Remove and keep warm.

3. Add tomatoes to skillet; cook and stir until tomatoes are softened, 2-4 minutes. Stir in vinegar; reduce heat to medium-low. Cook until sauce is thickened, 1-2 minutes longer. Serve cod with tomato mixture and bacon.
1 FILLET WITH ¼ CUP TOMATO MIXTURE AND 1 TBSP. BACON: 178 cal., 6g fat (2g sat. fat), 64mg chol., 485mg sod., 5g carb. (4g sugars, 1g fiber), 26g pro. **DIABETIC EXCHANGES:** 4 lean meat, 1 vegetable.

DID YOU KNOW?

Balsamic vinegar is made from sweet white grapes and gets its dark color from aging in wooden barrels. The longer it ages, the more thick and sweet it becomes. Highly aged vinegars are expensive and best enjoyed drizzled over cheese or used for dipping with oil and bread. Moderately priced vinegar works fine for preparing sauces and reductions. If needed, add a little sugar to taste.

BREADED SEA SCALLOPS

BREADED SEA SCALLOPS

I never liked seafood until my husband urged me to try scallops, and now I love them. He says my crispy breaded version is the best he's ever had.
—*Martina Preston, Willow Grove, PA*

TAKES: 15 min. • **MAKES:** 2 servings

1 large egg
⅓ cup mashed potato flakes
⅓ cup seasoned bread crumbs
⅛ tsp. salt
⅛ tsp. pepper
6 sea scallops (about ¾ lb.)
2 Tbsp. all-purpose flour
2 Tbsp. butter
1 Tbsp. canola oil

1. In a shallow bowl, lightly beat egg. In another bowl, toss potato flakes and bread crumbs with salt and pepper. In a third bowl, toss scallops with flour to coat lightly. Dip scallops in egg, then in potato mixture, patting to adhere.
2. In a large skillet, heat butter and oil over medium heat. Add the scallops; cook until breading is golden brown and scallops are firm and opaque, 2-3 minutes per side.
3 SCALLOPS: 454 cal., 23g fat (9g sat. fat), 164mg chol., 1262mg sod., 33g carb. (2g sugars, 2g fiber), 28g pro.

DID YOU KNOW?
Farmed scallops are becoming more common. Because scallops are filter feeders that live on plankton, they don't require much feed. Their low environmental impact makes farmed scallops a green choice.

SPEEDY SALMON STIR-FRY

🍎 SPEEDY SALMON STIR-FRY

Salmon is a staple where I live, so I tried it in a stir-fry. My recipe has an orange glaze, but I like it with lime, too.
—*Joni Hilton, Rocklin, CA*

TAKES: 30 min. • **MAKES:** 4 servings

¼ cup reduced-fat honey mustard salad dressing
2 Tbsp. orange juice
1 Tbsp. minced fresh gingerroot
1 Tbsp. reduced-sodium soy sauce
1 Tbsp. molasses
1 tsp. grated orange zest
4 tsp. canola oil, divided
1 lb. salmon fillets, skinned and cut into 1-in. pieces
1 pkg. (16 oz.) frozen stir-fry vegetable blend
2⅔ cups hot cooked brown rice
1 Tbsp. sesame seeds, toasted

1. In a small bowl, whisk first 6 ingredients. In a large skillet, heat 2 tsp. oil over medium-high heat. Add salmon; cook and gently stir 3-4 minutes or until fish just begins to flake easily with a fork. Remove from pan.
2. In same pan, heat remaining oil. Add vegetable blend; stir-fry until crisp-tender. Add salad dressing mixture. Return salmon to skillet. Gently combine; heat through. Serve with rice; sprinkle with sesame seeds.
1 CUP STIR-FRY WITH ⅔ CUP RICE: 498 cal., 19g fat (3g sat. fat), 57mg chol., 394mg sod., 54g carb. (11g sugars, 5g fiber), 26g pro.

SALMON COUSCOUS SUPPER

With its delicate texture and superior flavor, leftover salmon should never go to waste! I use extra portions of couscous and salmon to create this appetizing dish.

—*Jenny Brown, Bloomington, IN*

- -

TAKES: 25 min. • **MAKES:** 2 servings

- ½ cup fresh broccoli florets
- ½ cup sliced fresh carrot
- ½ cup sliced fresh mushrooms
- 2 garlic cloves, minced
- 10 oz. fully cooked salmon, cut into chunks
- ½ cup cooked couscous
- 3 Tbsp. reduced-sodium soy sauce

1. Place broccoli and carrot in a steamer basket; place in a small saucepan over 1 in. of water. Bring to a boil; cover and steam for 6-8 minutes or until crisp-tender.

2. In a large skillet coated with cooking spray, saute mushrooms and garlic for 2 minutes. Add broccoli florets and carrot; saute for 2 minutes longer. Stir in salmon, couscous and soy sauce; heat through.

1¼ CUPS: 345 cal., 16g fat (3g sat. fat), 84mg chol., 1010mg sod., 16g carb. (3g sugars, 2g fiber), 33g pro.

SALMON WITH SPINACH & WHITE BEANS

SALMON WITH SPINACH & WHITE BEANS

My husband, Oscar, is a Southerner at heart. This salmon with garlicky beans and spinach won him over at first bite.

—*Mary Ellen Hofstetter, Brentwood, TN*

- -

TAKES: 15 min. • **MAKES:** 4 servings

- 4 salmon fillets (4 oz. each)
- 2 tsp. plus 1 Tbsp. olive oil, divided
- 1 tsp. seafood seasoning
- 1 garlic clove, minced
- 1 can (15 oz.) cannellini beans, rinsed and drained
- ¼ tsp. salt
- ¼ tsp. pepper
- 1 pkg. (8 oz.) fresh spinach
   Lemon wedges

1. Preheat broiler. Rub fillets with 2 tsp. oil; sprinkle with seafood seasoning. Place on a greased rack of a broiler pan. Broil 5-6 in. from heat 6-8 minutes or until fish just begins to flake easily with a fork.

2. Meanwhile, in a large skillet, heat remaining oil over medium heat. Add garlic; cook 15-30 seconds or until fragrant. Add beans, salt and pepper, stirring to coat beans with garlic oil. Stir in spinach until wilted. Serve salmon with spinach mixture and lemon wedges.

1 FILLET WITH ½ CUP SPINACH MIXTURE: 317 cal., 17g fat (3g sat. fat), 57mg chol., 577mg sod., 16g carb. (0 sugars, 5g fiber), 24g pro. **DIABETIC EXCHANGES:** 3 lean meat, 2 vegetable, 1 fat, ½ starch..

SUMMER FISH SKILLET

On those crazy nights when you have other proverbial fish to fry, this fresh Mediterranean medley will offer the help you need.
—Taste of Home *Test Kitchen*

- -

TAKES: 30 min. • **MAKES:** 4 servings

- 2 pkg. (7.6 oz. each) frozen lemon butter grilled fish fillets
- 1 Tbsp. olive oil
- 2 medium yellow summer squash, halved and sliced
- 2 medium sweet orange peppers, chopped
- ½ cup chopped red onion
- 2 cups fresh salsa, drained
- 4 oz. feta cheese, cubed
- 2 pkg. (8.8 oz. each) ready-to-serve rice pilaf with orzo pasta

1. In a large skillet, cook fish fillets in oil over medium heat for 15-20 minutes, turning once or until fish flakes easily with a fork; remove and keep warm.

2. In the same skillet, saute the squash, peppers and onion until tender. Add salsa; cook 2 minutes longer. Return fish to skillet. Add cheese and heat through.

3. Prepare rice pilaf according to package directions. Serve with fish and vegetables.

1 FISH FILLET WITH 1 CUP VEGETABLES AND 1 CUP RICE: 442 cal., 15g fat (5g sat. fat), 80mg chol., 1828mg sod., 52g carb. (11g sugars, 4g fiber), 25g pro.

SUMMER FISH SKILLET

TUNA NOODLE SKILLET

Enjoy the comforting flavor of tuna noodle casserole in minutes with this creamy stovetop version. It's easy to make with convenient ingredients like frozen peas and jarred Alfredo sauce.
—*Ruth Simon, Buffalo, NY*

- -

TAKES: 30 min. • **MAKES:** 6 servings

- 2 jars (16 oz. each) Alfredo sauce
- 1 can (14½ oz.) chicken broth
- 1 pkg. (16 oz.) wide egg noodles
- 1 pkg. (10 oz.) frozen peas
- ¼ tsp. pepper
- 1 can (12 oz.) albacore white tuna in water

1. In a large skillet over medium heat, bring Alfredo sauce and broth to a boil. Add noodles; cover and cook for 7-8 minutes.

2. Reduce heat; stir in peas and pepper. Cover and cook 4 minutes longer or until noodles are tender. Stir in tuna; heat through.

1⅔ CUPS: 620 cal., 21g fat (12g sat. fat), 131mg chol., 1179mg sod., 73g carb. (4g sugars, 6g fiber), 34g pro.

SALMON WITH PECAN-HONEY SAUCE

If you're looking for an easy dish to serve to company, try this elegant entree. Flaky salmon fillets are draped with a sweet pecan glaze.
—*Buffy Sias, Whitehorse, YT*

- -

TAKES: 30 min. • **MAKES:** 6 servings

- 6 salmon fillets (6 oz. each)
- ¼ tsp. salt
- ¼ tsp. pepper
- ¼ cup canola oil
- 6 Tbsp. butter
- 1 cup chopped pecans
- 1 cup honey

1. Sprinkle salmon with salt and pepper. In a large skillet, cook salmon in oil in batches until fish just begins to flake easily with fork, 10-12 minutes.

2. Meanwhile, in a small saucepan, cook pecans and honey in butter over medium-low heat for 8-10 minutes or until bubbly. Serve with salmon.

1 SERVING: 745 cal., 50g fat (12g sat. fat), 116mg chol., 277mg sod., 49g carb. (47g sugars, 2g fiber), 31g pro.

FOLD-OVER TORTILLA BAKE
PAGE 169

183

194

214

202

Oven Entrees

Three cheers for the classic comfort foods that warm us when there's a chill in the air: cozy casseroles, sizzling entrees and hearty roasts. Turn these pages and discover nearly 100 hot-from-the-oven specialties you'll love. We think you will agree that this book's collection of piping-hot oven dinners saves the best for last.

Beef & Ground Beef

**GROUND BEEF
WELLINGTON**

GROUND BEEF WELLINGTON

Trying new recipes is one of my favorite hobbies. It's also the most gratifying. What could beat the smiles and compliments of the ones you love? This recipe is easy enough for family, yet fancy enough for company.
—*Julie Frankamp, Nicollet, MN*

PREP: 30 min. • **BAKE:** 25 min.
MAKES: 2 servings

- ½ cup chopped fresh mushrooms
- 1 Tbsp. butter
- 2 tsp. all-purpose flour
- ¼ tsp. pepper, divided
- ½ cup half-and-half cream
- 1 large egg yolk
- 2 Tbsp. finely chopped onion
- ¼ tsp. salt
- ½ lb. ground beef
- 1 tube (4 oz.) refrigerated crescent rolls
- 1 tsp. dried parsley flakes
  Large egg, lightly beaten, optional

1. In a saucepan, saute mushrooms in butter until softened. Stir in flour and ⅛ tsp. pepper until blended. Gradually add the cream. Bring to a boil; cook and stir for 2 minutes or until mixture is thickened. Remove from the heat and set aside.

2. In a bowl, combine the egg yolk, onion, 2 Tbsp. mushroom sauce, salt and remaining pepper. Crumble beef over mixture and mix well. Shape into two loaves. Separate the crescent dough into 2 rectangles on a baking sheet. Seal perforations. Place meat loaf on each rectangle. Bring edges together and pinch to seal. If desired, brush with egg wash. Bake at 350° until golden brown and a thermometer inserted into meat loaf reads 160°, 24-28 minutes.

3. Meanwhile, warm remaining sauce over low heat; stir in parsley. Serve sauce with Wellingtons.

1 SERVING: 578 cal., 37g fat (16g sat. fat), 207mg chol., 909mg sod., 28g carb. (7g sugars, 1g fiber), 28g pro.

**MASHED POTATO
MEAT ROLL**

BAKED BARBECUED BEEF BRISKET

My tasty barbecued brisket conveniently bakes for hours, allowing me lots of time to prepare the rest of the meal. Leftover brisket makes delicious sandwiches.
—*Martha Lewis, Glen Allen, VA*

PREP: 30 min. + chilling
BAKE: 2½ hours + standing
MAKES: 12 servings

- 1 tsp. garlic powder
- ½ tsp. onion salt
- ½ tsp. celery salt
- 1 fresh beef brisket (4 lbs.)
- 3 to 4 tsp. liquid smoke, optional
- 3 cups water, divided
- 1 cup ketchup
- ½ cup chopped onion
- 6 Tbsp. Worcestershire sauce, divided
- ¼ cup packed brown sugar
- ¼ cup cider vinegar
- 1 tsp. celery seed
- 1 tsp. pepper
- ½ tsp. salt

1. Combine the garlic powder, onion salt and celery salt; rub over brisket. Place in a large shallow bowl; sprinkle brisket with liquid smoke if desired. Turn to coat; cover and refrigerate overnight.
2. For sauce, in a large saucepan, combine 2 cups water, ketchup, onion, 4 Tbsp. Worcestershire sauce, brown sugar, vinegar, celery seed, pepper and salt. Bring to a boil. Reduce heat; cover and simmer 15 minutes, stirring occasionally. Cool the mixture; cover and refrigerate.
3. Place the brisket in a Dutch oven; add remaining water and Worcestershire sauce to pan. Cover pan tightly. Bake at 325° for 1½ hours; drain.
4. Baste with sauce. Bake, uncovered, until meat is tender, 1-2 hours longer. Let stand for 20 minutes; thinly slice across the grain.
NOTE: This is a fresh beef brisket, not corned beef.
4 OZ. COOKED BEEF: 239 cal., 7g fat (2g sat. fat), 64mg chol., 625mg sod., 13g carb. (11g sugars, 0 fiber), 31g pro. **DIABETIC EXCHANGES:** 4 lean meat, 1 starch.

MASHED POTATO MEAT ROLL

This family favorite is requested often for special occasions. We got the recipe from a fellow faculty member when my husband and I were in our first years of teaching.
—*Judy Knaupp, Rickreall, OR*

PREP: 30 min. + chilling • **BAKE:** 30 min.
MAKES: 6 servings

- 2 cups mashed potatoes (with added milk and butter)
- 2 hard-boiled large eggs, chopped
- ½ cup Miracle Whip
- ⅓ cup grated Parmesan cheese
- ¼ cup chopped celery
- 1 green onion, chopped
- ¼ tsp. salt
- ¼ tsp. ground mustard
- ¼ tsp. pepper

MEAT LOAF
- 1 large egg, lightly beaten
- ¼ cup dry bread crumbs
- 1 tsp. salt
- 1¼ lbs. ground beef

SAUCE
- ½ cup Miracle Whip
- ¼ cup 2% milk
- 1 green onion, sliced

1. For filling, mix first 9 ingredients. In a large bowl, combine beaten egg, bread crumbs and salt. Add beef; mix lightly but thoroughly. On a large piece of heavy-duty foil, pat the mixture into a 14x8-in. rectangle. Spread filling over top to within 1 in. of edges. Roll up jelly-roll style, starting with a short side, removing foil as you roll. Seal seam and ends; place on a large plate. Refrigerate, covered, overnight.
2. Preheat oven to 350°. Cut roll into 6 slices. Place on rack in a broiler pan, cut side up. Bake until a thermometer reads 160°, 30-35 minutes. Mix sauce ingredients; serve with meat loaf.
1 SLICE WITH 4 TSP. SAUCE: 439 cal., 28g fat (9g sat. fat), 167mg chol., 1187mg sod., 20g carb. (5g sugars, 1g fiber), 24g pro.

STEAK & ONION PIE

This hearty main dish has been a favorite in our family for at least 30 years. Our three sons are now grown and on their own, but they always come home when they hear I have this in the oven!

—Ardis Wirtz, Newburgh, IN

- -

PREP: 1¾ hours • **BAKE:** 25 min.
MAKES: 6 servings

- 1 large onion, sliced
- 3 Tbsp. canola oil
- ⅓ cup all-purpose flour
- 1½ tsp. ground allspice
- 1 tsp. salt
- 1 tsp. pepper
- ½ tsp. ground ginger
- 1½ lbs. beef top round steak, cut into 1-in. cubes
- 2 cups boiling water
- 1½ cups diced peeled potatoes
- 1 cup diced carrots
- 1 cup frozen peas
- 1 sheet refrigerated pie crust

1. In a Dutch oven, lightly brown onion in oil. Meanwhile, combine the flour, allspice, salt, pepper and ginger in a large shallow bowl, Add meat cubes to the bowl, a few pieces at a time, and toss to coat.

2. Remove onion and set aside. Brown beef on all sides. Add water; cover and simmer for 1 hour or until meat is tender, stirring occasionally.

3. Add the potatoes, carrots and reserved onions; cover and cook for 10 minutes. Stir in the peas; cook for 10 minutes or until all vegetables are tender.

4. Spoon meat mixture into an 8-in. square baking dish. Roll crust out to a 9-in. square; place over meat mixture and seal edges to pan. Cut several small steam vents in crust. Bake at 450° for 25-30 minutes or until pastry is browned.

1 SERVING: 460 cal., 20g fat (6g sat. fat), 70mg chol., 601mg sod., 39g carb. (5g sugars, 3g fiber), 30g pro.

TOMATO-FRENCH BREAD LASAGNA

For a big hearty meal, I make this recipe as a side dish to go with veal cutlets or a roast. But you could also serve the beefy lasagna as a main dish. Just pair it with a tossed green salad and loaf of garlic bread.

—Patricia Collins, Imbler, OR

- -

PREP: 30 min. • **BAKE:** 40 min.
MAKES: 10 servings

- 1 lb. ground beef
- ⅓ cup chopped onion
- ⅓ cup chopped celery
- 2 garlic cloves, minced
- 14 slices French bread (½ in. thick)
- 4 large tomatoes, sliced ½ in. thick
- 1 tsp. dried basil
- 1 tsp. dried parsley flakes
- 1 tsp. dried oregano
- 1 tsp. dried rosemary, crushed
- 1 tsp. garlic powder
- ¾ tsp. salt
- ½ tsp. pepper
- 2 tsp. olive oil, divided
- 3 Tbsp. butter
- 3 Tbsp. all-purpose flour
- 1½ cups whole milk
- ⅓ cup grated Parmesan cheese
- 2 cups shredded mozzarella cheese

1. In a skillet, cook beef, onion, celery and garlic over medium heat until beef is no longer pink; drain and set aside. Toast bread; line the bottom of an ungreased 13x9-in. baking dish with 10 slices. Top with half of the meat mixture and half of the tomatoes.

2. Combine seasonings; sprinkle half over tomatoes. Drizzle with 1 tsp. oil. Crumble remaining bread over top. Repeat layers of meat, tomatoes, seasonings and oil.

3. In a saucepan over medium heat, melt the butter; stir in flour until smooth. Gradually stir in milk; bring to a boil. Cook and stir until thickened and bubbly, about 2 minutes. Remove from the heat; stir in Parmesan. Pour over casserole. Top with mozzarella. Bake, uncovered, at 350° for 40-45 minutes or until bubbly and cheese is golden brown.

1 PIECE: 280 cal., 16g fat (8g sat. fat), 56mg chol., 500mg sod., 17g carb. (4g sugars, 2g fiber), 17g pro.

TOMATO-FRENCH BREAD LASAGNA

BLUE RIBBON BEEF BURRITOS

FREEZE OPTION: Cool filling before making burritos. After wrapping burritos in foil, freeze in freezer container. To use, partially thaw overnight in refrigerator. Reheat foil-wrapped burritos on a baking sheet in a preheated 350° oven 25-30 minutes or until heated through. Or, to reheat 1 burrito, remove foil and rewrap burrito in paper towel; place on a microwave-safe plate. Microwave on high for 3-4 minutes or until heated through, turning once. Let stand 20 seconds.

1 BURRITO: 682 cal., 37g fat (17g sat. fat), 103mg chol., 1166mg sod., 44g carb. (2g sugars, 7g fiber), 34g pro.

POOR MAN'S FILET MIGNON

Kansas is a leading beef producer, so this is a fitting recipe for our state. Our entire family, including the grandchildren, loves this hearty main dish.
—*Gayle Mollenkamp, Russell Springs, KS*

- -

PREP: 20 min. • **BAKE:** 50 min.
MAKES: 12 servings

4 slices bread, crumbled
2 large eggs, lightly beaten
½ cup whole milk
2 tsp. salt
1 Tbsp. finely chopped onion
2 tsp. dried celery flakes
½ tsp. chili powder
1 bottle (18 oz.) hickory smoke-flavored barbecue sauce, divided
2 lbs. lean ground beef
12 bacon strips

1. In a large bowl, combine the first 7 ingredients and 2 Tbsp. barbecue sauce. Crumble beef over mixture and mix well. Form into 12 patties. Wrap a bacon slice around the sides of each patty and secure with a toothpick.

2. Place on a greased rack in a shallow baking pan. Bake at 350° for 50-60 minutes or until meat is no longer pink, basting frequently with remaining barbecue sauce during the last 30 minutes.

1 SERVING: 314 cal., 21g fat (8g sat. fat), 98mg chol., 1000mg sod., 10g carb. (6g sugars, 1g fiber), 19g pro.

BLUE RIBBON BEEF BURRITOS

I have a son who lives in Mexico, so we don't see him very often. Whenever I make these burritos, it feels as if he is right there at the table with us, inhaling them.
—*Marina Castle Kelley, Canyon Country, CA*

- -

PREP: 40 min. • **BAKE:** 15 min.
MAKES: 8 servings

1½ lbs. ground beef
1 bottle (8 oz.) taco sauce
1 Tbsp. Worcestershire sauce
1½ tsp. onion powder
1 tsp. paprika
½ tsp. garlic powder
½ tsp. salt, divided
¼ tsp. pepper
Juice of ½ lemon
1 can (2¼ oz.) sliced ripe olives, drained, optional

Oil for frying
¾ lb. potatoes (about 2 medium), peeled and cut into ½-in. cubes
8 flour tortillas (10 in.), warmed
4 cups shredded Mexican cheese blend

1. Preheat oven to 400°. In a large skillet, cook beef over medium heat 8-10 minutes or until no longer pink, breaking into crumbles; drain. Stir in taco sauce, Worcestershire sauce, onion powder, paprika, garlic powder, ¼ tsp. salt and pepper. Add lemon juice and, if desired, olives.

2. In an electric skillet, heat 1 in. of oil to 375°. Working in batches, fry potatoes 3-4 minutes or until golden brown, stirring occasionally. Remove with a slotted spoon; drain on paper towels. Sprinkle with remaining salt.

3. Stir potatoes into meat mixture. Place ⅔ cup mixture in the center of each tortilla; top with ½ cup cheese. Fold bottom and sides of tortilla over filling and roll up.

4. Wrap each burrito in foil; place on a baking sheet. Bake burritos 15-18 minutes or until heated through.

MEATY MANICOTTI

SOUR CREAM SWISS STEAK

I spent a year searching for new and different beef recipes. This is the dish that my family raves about, and they agree that it's a nice change from regular Swiss steak.
—*Barb Benting, Grand Rapids, MI*

PREP: 50 min. • **BAKE:** 1½ hours
MAKES: 8 servings

- ⅓ cup all-purpose flour
- 1½ tsp. each salt, pepper, paprika and ground mustard
- 3 lbs. beef top round steak, cut into serving-size pieces
- 3 Tbsp. canola oil
- 3 Tbsp. butter
- 1½ cups water
- 1½ cups sour cream
- 1 cup finely chopped onion
- 2 garlic cloves, minced
- ⅓ cup soy sauce
- ¼ to ⅓ cup packed brown sugar
- 3 Tbsp. all-purpose flour
  Additional paprika, optional

1. In a shallow bowl, combine flour, salt, pepper, paprika and ground mustard; dredge the steak.
2. In a large skillet, heat oil and butter. Cook steak on both sides until browned. Carefully add water; cover and simmer for 30 minutes.
3. In a bowl, combine the sour cream, onion, garlic, soy sauce, brown sugar and flour; stir until smooth. Transfer steaks to a greased 2½-qt. baking dish; add sour cream mixture.
4. Cover and bake at 325° for 1½ hours or until tender. Sprinkle with paprika if desired.
1 SERVING: 460 cal., 23g fat (10g sat. fat), 137mg chol., 1173mg sod., 17g carb. (10g sugars, 1g fiber), 43g pro.

MEATY MANICOTTI

This simple dish has been very popular at family gatherings and potlucks. You can assemble it ahead of time.
—*Lori Thompson, New London, TX*

PREP: 20 min. + cooling • **BAKE:** 45 min.
MAKES: 7 servings

- 14 uncooked manicotti shells
- 1 lb. bulk Italian sausage
- ¾ lb. ground beef
- 2 garlic cloves, minced
- 2 cups shredded part-skim mozzarella cheese
- 3 oz. cream cheese, cubed
- ¼ tsp. salt
- 4 cups meatless spaghetti sauce, divided
- ¼ cup grated Parmesan cheese

1. Cook manicotti shells according to package directions. Meanwhile, in a large skillet, cook sausage and beef over medium heat until meat is no longer pink. Add garlic; cook 1 minute longer. Drain. Remove from the heat. Cool for 10 minutes.

2. Drain shells and rinse in cold water. Stir the mozzarella cheese, cream cheese and salt into meat mixture. Spread 2 cups spaghetti sauce in a greased 13x9-in. baking dish.
3. Stuff each shell with about ¼ cup meat mixture; arrange over sauce. Pour remaining sauce over top. Sprinkle with Parmesan cheese.
4. Cover and bake at 350° for 40 minutes. Uncover; bake 5-10 minutes longer or until bubbly and heated through.
FREEZE OPTION: Cover and freeze unbaked casserole. To use, partially thaw in refrigerator overnight. Remove from the refrigerator 30 minutes before baking. Preheat oven to 350°. Bake casserole as directed, increasing time as necessary to heat through and for a thermometer inserted in center to read 165°.
2 MANICOTTI: 507 cal., 26g fat (13g sat. fat), 90mg chol., 1265mg sod., 39g carb. (11g sugars, 3g fiber), 30g pro.

SOUR CREAM SWISS STEAK

BAKED BEEF TACOS

BAKED BEEF TACOS

We give tacos a fresh approach by baking the shells upright in refried beans and tomatoes. The bottoms get soft, and the tops stay crispy and crunchy.

—*Patricia Stagich, Elizabeth, NJ*

- -

PREP: 15 min. • **BAKE:** 20 min.
MAKES: 12 servings

1½ lbs. ground beef
1   envelope taco seasoning
2   cans (10 oz. each) diced tomatoes
    and green chiles, divided
1   can (16 oz.) refried beans
2   cups shredded Mexican
    cheese blend, divided
¼   cup chopped fresh cilantro
1   tsp. hot pepper sauce, optional
12 taco shells
    Chopped green onions

1. Preheat oven to 425°. In a large skillet, cook beef over medium heat 6-8 minutes or until no longer pink, breaking into crumbles; drain. Stir in taco seasoning and 1 can of undrained tomatoes; heat through.
2. Meanwhile, in a bowl, mix beans, ½ cup cheese, cilantro, remaining can of undrained tomatoes and, if desired, pepper sauce. Spread onto bottom of a greased 13x9-in. baking dish.
3. Stand taco shells upright over bean mixture. Fill each with 1 Tbsp. cheese and about ⅓ cup beef mixture. Bake, covered, 15 minutes.
4. Uncover; sprinkle with remaining cheese. Bake, uncovered, 5-7 minutes or until cheese is melted and shells are lightly browned. Sprinkle with green onions.

1 TACO WITH ¼ CUP BEAN MIXTURE:
277 cal., 15g fat (7g sat. fat), 52mg chol., 836mg sod., 17g carb. (0 sugars, 3g fiber), 17g pro.

DRESSED-UP STEAK SALAD

The sirloin in this salad tastes wonderful paired with tomato, red onion and avocado. Steak sauce makes the dressing deliciously different. To complete the meal, serve soft breadsticks and lemon sherbet.
—Taste of Home *Test Kitchen*

PREP: 15 min. + marinating • **BROIL:** 5 min.
MAKES: 2 servings

⅓ cup canola oil
2 Tbsp. lime juice
1 Tbsp. steak sauce
1 Tbsp. red wine vinegar
½ tsp. Dijon mustard
¼ tsp. salt
MARINADE
2 Tbsp. steak sauce
1 tsp. canola oil
1 tsp. lime juice
⅛ to ¼ tsp. hot pepper sauce

SALAD
½ lb. boneless beef sirloin steak
3 cups torn mixed salad greens
1 medium tomato, cut into wedges
1 small ripe avocado, peeled and cubed
2 slices red onion, separated into rings

1. In a jar with a tight-fitting lid, combine the first 6 ingredients; shake well. Refrigerate until serving.
2. In a small bowl, combine the marinade ingredients. Brush on both sides of steak; let stand for 30 minutes. Broil steak 4 in. from the heat until meat reaches desired doneness, 5-6 minutes on each side.
3. Meanwhile, on 2 plates, arrange salad greens, tomato wedges, avocado and onion. Thinly slice steak; place on top of salads. Serve with dressing.
1 SERVING: 696 cal., 59g fat (9g sat. fat), 64mg chol., 834mg sod., 19g carb. (8g sugars, 7g fiber), 26g pro.

MARMALADE-GLAZED STEAKS

Marmalade and mustard? They may sound like strange bedfellows, but this tasty main course proves they're a match made in dinnertime heaven.
—*Mike Tchou, Pepper Pike, OH*

TAKES: 20 min. • **MAKES:** 4 servings

½ cup orange marmalade
2 Tbsp. spicy brown mustard
2 Tbsp. cold butter
1 beef top sirloin steak (1¼ lbs.), cut into four steaks
2 green onions, chopped

1. In a small saucepan, heat marmalade and mustard over low heat. Whisk in butter until melted. Set aside ¼ cup glaze for serving.
2. Broil steaks 4 in. from the heat for 5-7 minutes on each side or until meat reaches desired doneness (for medium-rare, a thermometer should read 135°; medium, 140°; medium-well, 145°), basting steaks occasionally with remaining glaze.
3. Spoon reserved glaze over steaks; sprinkle with onions.
1 SERVING: 338 cal., 11g fat (6g sat. fat), 72mg chol., 225mg sod., 27g carb. (24g sugars, 0 fiber), 31g pro.

TEST KITCHEN TIP
A good way to estimate your daily protein need is to multiply your weight in pounds by 0.4 gram. A 150-lb. person needs about 60 grams of protein daily. Four oz. of uncooked beef sirloin, pork loin, tuna, chicken or turkey breast (or 3 oz. cooked, about the size of a deck of playing cards) provides about 25 grams of protein.

DRESSED-UP STEAK SALAD

**FOLD-OVER
TORTILLA BAKE**

FOLD-OVER TORTILLA BAKE

Here's something a little different from the usual tacos. It's special enough for potlucks or dinner guests.
—*Deborah Smith, DeWitt, NE*

PREP: 20 min. • **BAKE:** 20 min.
MAKES: 6 servings

1   lb. ground beef
1   cup chopped onion
2   cans (14½ oz. each) stewed tomatoes
1   cup enchilada sauce
1   to 2 tsp. ground cumin
½   tsp. salt
¼   tsp. pepper
12 flour or corn tortillas (6 in.)
6   oz. cream cheese, softened
1   can (4 oz.) chopped green chiles, drained
1   cup shredded Monterey Jack cheese
    Minced fresh cilantro, optional

1. In a large skillet, cook ground beef and onion until beef is no longer pink; drain. Stir in the tomatoes, enchilada sauce and seasonings. Bring to a boil. Reduce heat and simmer, covered, for 5 minutes. Pour half of the meat sauce into a 13x9-in. baking dish. Set aside.

2. Wrap the stack of tortillas in foil; warm at 350° for 8-10 minutes. Spread warm tortillas with cream cheese and top with chiles. Fold tortillas in half. Arrange folded tortillas over meat sauce; pour remaining sauce over top.

3. Cover and bake at 350° for 15 minutes. Sprinkle with cheese; bake until cheese is melted, about 5 minutes longer. If desired, top with cilantro.

1 SERVING: 473 cal., 25g fat (10g sat. fat), 69mg chol., 1138mg sod., 38g carb. (7g sugars, 2g fiber), 27g pro.

BALSAMIC-SEASONED STEAK

BALSAMIC-SEASONED STEAK

This simple recipe ensures a tender steak without a long marinating time. Steak sauce and balsamic vinegar are a great team, and you can't go wrong with melty Swiss on top.
—*Peggy Woodward, Shullsburg, WI*

TAKES: 25 min. • **MAKES:** 4 servings

1   beef top sirloin steak (¾ in. thick and 1 lb.)
¼   tsp. coarsely ground pepper
2   Tbsp. balsamic vinegar
2   tsp. steak sauce
2   oz. sliced reduced-fat Swiss cheese, cut into thin strips

1. Preheat broiler. Place steak on a broiler pan; sprinkle with pepper. Broil 4 in. from heat 7 minutes. Meanwhile, mix vinegar and steak sauce.

2. Turn steak; drizzle with 1 Tbsp. of the vinegar mixture. Broil just until meat reaches desired doneness (for medium-rare, a thermometer should read 135°; medium, 140°; medium-well, 145°), 4-6 minutes.

3. Remove steak to a cutting board; let stand 5 minutes. Cut steak into ¼-in. slices; return to broiler pan, arranging slices close together. Drizzle slices with remaining vinegar mixture; top with cheese. Broil just until cheese is melted, 30-60 seconds.

3 OZ. COOKED BEEF WITH ½ OZ. CHEESE: 188 cal., 8g fat (3g sat. fat), 70mg chol., 116mg sod., 2g carb. (1g sugars, 0 fiber), 26g pro. **DIABETIC EXCHANGES:** 3 lean meat, ½ fat.

CRESCENT CHEESEBURGER PIE

My mother gave me this recipe just before my wedding. Now, 32 years later, my husband, six children and nine grandchildren still enjoy it!

—*Elinore Dumont, Drumheller, AB*

PREP: 30 min. • **BAKE:** 40 min. + standing
MAKES: 6 servings

- 1 lb. ground beef
- ½ cup chopped onion
- 1 can (8 oz.) tomato sauce
- 1 can (4 oz.) mushroom stems and pieces, drained
- ¼ cup minced fresh parsley
- ¼ tsp. salt
- ¼ tsp. dried oregano
- ⅛ tsp. pepper
- 2 tubes (8 oz. each) refrigerated crescent rolls
- 2 large eggs
- 1 large egg, separated
- 6 slices process American cheese
- 1 Tbsp. water

1. Preheat oven to 350°. In a large skillet, cook beef and onion over medium heat until the meat is no longer pink; drain. Stir in tomato sauce, mushrooms, parsley, salt, oregano and pepper; set aside.

2. Unroll 1 tube of crescent dough; separate dough into 8 triangles. Arrange in a single layer in a lightly greased 9-in. pie plate. Press into dish to form a crust and seal seams. In a small bowl, whisk eggs and 1 egg white.

3. Pour half of beaten egg mixture over pie shell. Spoon meat mixture into shell; arrange cheese slices on top. Spread with remaining beaten egg. Mix water and remaining egg yolk; set aside.

4. Unroll second tube of crescent dough; place 4 sections of dough together to form a 12x6-in. rectangle. Press perforations to seal; roll dough into a 12-in. square.

5. Brush edges of bottom crust with some of the egg yolk mixture; place dough on top of filling. Trim, seal and flute edges. Cut slits in top. Brush top crust with the remaining egg yolk mixture.

6. Bake for 40 minutes, tenting with foil after 15 minutes if necessary. Let stand 10 minutes before serving.

1 PIECE: 418 cal., 24g fat (11g sat. fat), 164mg chol., 1110mg sod., 22g carb. (6g sugars, 1g fiber), 26g pro.

STUFFED PEPPERS FOR TWO

My husband likes stuffed peppers, but my old recipe made too much. I devised this recipe to accommodate just the two of us. It helps to use a smaller casserole so the peppers won't tip over while baking. For color, I serve steamed carrots with the peppers, rounding out the meal perfectly.

—*Elaine Carpenter, Horseshoe Bay, TX*

PREP: 20 min. • **BAKE:** 50 min.
MAKES: 2 servings

- 2 medium green peppers
- ½ lb. ground beef
- 1 can (8 oz.) tomato sauce, divided
- ¼ cup uncooked instant rice
- 3 Tbsp. shredded cheddar cheese, divided
- 1 Tbsp. chopped onion
- ½ tsp. Worcestershire sauce
- ½ tsp. salt
- ¼ tsp. pepper
- 1 large egg, beaten

Cut tops off peppers and discard; remove seeds. Blanch peppers in boiling water for 5 minutes. Drain and rinse in cold water; set aside. In a bowl, combine beef, ¼ cup tomato sauce, instant rice, 2 Tbsp. cheese, onion, Worcestershire sauce, salt, pepper and egg; mix well. Stuff peppers; place in an ungreased 1½-qt. baking dish. Pour remaining tomato sauce over peppers. Cover and bake at 350° for 45-60 minutes or until meat is no longer pink and peppers are tender. Sprinkle with remaining cheese; return to the oven for 5 minutes or until cheese is melted.

1 SERVING: 405 cal., 20g fat (9g sat. fat), 193mg chol., 1277mg sod., 25g carb. (6g sugars, 3g fiber), 32g pro.

STUFFED PEPPERS FOR TWO

**HEARTY BAKED
BEEF STEW**

ITALIAN BEEF KABOBS

Balsamic vinegar and fresh herbs combine in a marinade that gives great flavor to the tender cubes of steak on these shish kabobs. Along with the beef, I skewer mushrooms, zucchini and cherry tomatoes for an easy, well-balanced meal.
—*Joyce Triggs, Thibodaux, LA*

PREP: 20 min. • **BROIL:** 10 min.
MAKES: 4 servings

- ½ cup balsamic vinegar
- ½ cup water
- 1 Tbsp. olive oil
- 4 garlic cloves, minced
- 2 Tbsp. minced fresh oregano
  or 2 tsp. dried oregano
- 1 Tbsp. minced fresh marjoram
  or 1 tsp. dried marjoram
- 2 tsp. sugar
- 1¼ lbs. beef top sirloin steak,
  cut into 1-in. cubes
- 3 medium zucchini, cut into ½-in. slices
- 32 small fresh mushrooms
- ½ tsp. salt
- 8 cherry tomatoes

1. In a small bowl, combine first 7 ingredients. Pour ⅔ cup marinade into a large shallow bowl. Add beef and turn to coat; cover and refrigerate for 4 hours. Cover and refrigerate remaining marinade for basting.
2. Drain and discard marinade from beef. On 4 metal or soaked wooden skewers, alternately thread the beef, zucchini and mushrooms. Spoon over uncooked kabobs with reserved marinade; sprinkle with salt. Broil 4 in. from heat for 5 minutes on each side or until meat reaches desired doneness, basting frequently with reserved marinade. Place a cherry tomato on the end of each skewer before serving.
2 EACH: 315 cal., 13g fat (4g sat. fat), 96mg chol., 379mg sod., 14g carb. (0 sugars, 3g fiber), 37g pro. **DIABETIC EXCHANGES:** 4 lean meat, 2 vegetable, 1 fat.

HEARTY BAKED BEEF STEW

This is such an easy way to make a wonderful beef stew. You don't need to brown the meat first—just combine it with hearty chunks of carrots, potatoes and celery, and let it all cook together in a flavorful gravy. My daughter Karen came up with the recipe for her busy family, and we love it.
—*Doris Sleeth, Naples, FL*

PREP: 15 min. • **BAKE:** 1¾ hours
MAKES: 8 servings

- 1 can (14½ oz.) diced
  tomatoes, undrained
- 1 cup water
- 3 Tbsp. quick-cooking tapioca
- 2 tsp. sugar
- 1½ tsp. salt
- ½ tsp. pepper
- 2 lbs. beef stew meat, cut
  into 1-in. cubes
- 4 medium carrots, cut into 1-in. chunks
- 3 medium potatoes, peeled
  and quartered
- 2 celery ribs, cut into ¾-in. chunks
- 1 medium onion, cut into chunks
- 1 slice bread, cubed

1. In a large bowl, combine the tomatoes, water, tapioca, sugar, salt and pepper. Stir in the remaining ingredients.
2. Pour into a greased 13x9-in. or 3-qt. baking dish. Cover and bake at 375° until meat and vegetables are tender, 1¾-2 hours. Serve stew in bowls.
1 CUP: 300 cal., 8g fat (3g sat. fat), 70mg chol., 628mg sod., 31g carb. (7g sugars, 4g fiber), 25g pro. **DIABETIC EXCHANGES:**
3 lean meat, 2 starch.

**PEPPERCORN
BEEF ROAST**

PEPPERCORN BEEF ROAST

A savory red wine sauce complements the caramelized brown sugar crust of this special roast. It's the ultimate entree for a special family occasion.
—Taste of Home *Test Kitchen*

PREP: 30 min. • **BAKE:** 1 hour + standing
MAKES: 10 servings (1½ cups sauce)

- 1 beef top round roast (4 lbs.)
- ⅓ cup packed brown sugar
- 3 Tbsp. whole peppercorns, crushed
- 4 garlic cloves, minced
- ¾ tsp. salt
- 1 large onion, finely chopped
- 1 Tbsp. olive oil
- 2 Tbsp. tomato paste
- 2 tsp. Worcestershire sauce
- 1½ cups port wine
- 1½ cups dry red wine

1. Preheat oven to 325° Trim fat from roast. If desired, tie roast with kitchen twine every 1½ to 2 in. to help beef maintain shape while cooking. In a small bowl, combine brown sugar, peppercorns, garlic and salt. Rub over meat. Place in a shallow roasting pan.

2. Bake until meat reaches desired doneness (for medium-rare, a thermometer should read 135°; medium, 140°; medium-well, 145°), 1-1½ hours. Remove from oven, tent and let stand 15 minutes before slicing.

3. Meanwhile, in a large saucepan, saute onion in oil until tender. Stir in tomato paste and Worcestershire sauce until blended. Add wines. Bring to a boil; cook until liquid is reduced to about 1½ cups. Serve with roast.

5 OZ. COOKED BEEF: 444 cal., 26g fat (10g sat. fat), 99mg chol., 275mg sod., 12g carb. (9g sugars, 0 fiber), 32g pro.

"It was great to find a flavorful low-sodium option for my father-in-law. I even used a little less salt than the recipe calls for. I made this to replace the high-sodium lunch meat he usually has for lunch."
—SHERRI DURAN, TASTEOFHOME.COM

ZUCCHINI BOATS

ZUCCHINI BOATS

After working hard and raising a family, we're now enjoying a simpler, slower-paced life. Getting back to the basics means enjoying old-fashioned comfort foods like this.
—*Mrs. C. Thon, Atlin, BC*

PREP: 35 min. • **BAKE:** 25 min.
MAKES: 4 servings

- 2 medium zucchini (about 8 in.)
- ¾ lb. ground beef
- 1 small onion, chopped
- ½ cup chopped fresh mushrooms
- ½ cup chopped sweet red pepper
- ½ cup chopped green pepper
- 1 cup shredded cheddar cheese, divided
- 2 Tbsp. ketchup
  Salt and pepper to taste

1. Trim the ends off zucchini. Cut zucchini in half lengthwise; scoop out pulp, leaving ½-in. shells. Finely chop pulp.

2. In a skillet, cook beef, zucchini pulp, onion, mushrooms and peppers over medium heat until meat is no longer pink; drain. Remove from the heat. Add ½ cup cheese, ketchup, salt and pepper; mix well. Spoon into the zucchini shells. Place in a greased 13x9-in. baking dish. Sprinkle with remaining cheese.

3. Bake, uncovered, at 350° until zucchini is tender, 25-30 minutes.

1 STUFFED ZUCCHINI HALF: 312 cal., 20g fat (9g sat. fat), 81mg chol., 337mg sod., 10g carb. (6g sugars, 2g fiber), 24g pro.

MEAT LOAF CORDON BLEU

BASIL-BUTTER STEAKS WITH ROASTED POTATOES

A few ingredients and 30 minutes are all you'll need for this incredibly satisfying meal. A simple basil butter gives these steaks a special taste.
—Taste of Home *Test Kitchen*

TAKES: 30 min. • **MAKES:** 4 servings

- 1 pkg. (15 oz.) frozen Parmesan and roasted garlic red potato wedges
- 4 beef tenderloin steaks (1¼ in. thick and 6 oz. each)
- ½ tsp. salt
- ½ tsp. pepper
- 5 Tbsp. butter, divided
- 2 cups grape tomatoes
- 1 Tbsp. minced fresh basil

1. Bake the potato wedges according to package directions.
2. Meanwhile, sprinkle steaks with salt and pepper. In a 10-in. cast-iron or other ovenproof skillet, brown steaks in 2 Tbsp. butter. Add tomatoes to skillet. Bake, uncovered, at 425° until meat reaches desired doneness, 15-20 minutes (for medium-rare, a thermometer should read 135°; medium, 140°; medium-well, 145°).
3. In a small bowl, combine basil and remaining butter. Spoon over steaks and serve with potatoes.
1 SERVING: 538 cal., 29g fat (13g sat. fat), 112mg chol., 740mg sod., 27g carb. (2g sugars, 3g fiber), 41g pro.

TEST KITCHEN TIP
Don't feel like potatoes? Add any side dish you like to the skillet beef and tomatoes. Green beans, spinach salad and cooked orzo are all good options.

MEAT LOAF CORDON BLEU

I'm a school counselor and mother of one young child. Even with my busy schedule, I can make this in the morning and pop it into the oven when I get home.
—Barb Jacobsen, Campbell, NE

PREP: 15 min. • **BAKE:** 1¼ hours
MAKES: 10 servings

- 1 large egg, beaten
- 1 envelope meat loaf seasoning mix
- ½ cup tomato sauce
- 2 cups soft bread crumbs
- 2 lbs. lean ground beef
- 8 thin slices fully cooked ham
- 8 thin slices Swiss cheese
- 1 can (4 oz.) sliced mushrooms

In a large bowl, mix together egg, meat loaf seasoning, tomato sauce and bread crumbs. Add ground beef; mix well. On a piece of waxed paper, pat meat mixture into an 18x9-in. rectangle. Top with layers of ham, cheese and mushrooms. Roll rectangle, jelly-roll style, starting from narrow end. Pinch edges to seal. Place seam side down in a shallow baking pan. Bake at 350° until no pink remains, about 1¼ hours. Let stand several minutes before slicing.

FREEZE OPTION: Securely wrap and freeze cooled meat loaf in foil. To use, partially thaw in refrigerator overnight. Unwrap meat loaf; reheat on a greased 15x10x1-in. baking pan in a preheated 350° oven until heated through and a thermometer inserted in center reads 165°.
1 SERVING: 287 cal., 14g fat (7g sat. fat), 105mg chol., 659mg sod., 10g carb. (1g sugars, 1g fiber), 28g pro.

BASIL-BUTTER STEAKS WITH ROASTED POTATOES

MEXICAN-STYLE MEAT LOAVES

On a vacation to Arizona, I fell in love with *albondigas*, Latin American meatballs. After playing with a number of spices, I came up with a version that's amazing as a meat loaf.
—*James Schend, Pleasant Prairie, WI*

PREP: 20 min. • **BAKE:** 50 min. + standing
MAKES: 2 loaves (8 servings each)

- 3 large eggs, lightly beaten
- ⅔ cup 2% milk
- ⅔ cup thick and zesty tomato sauce
- 2 Tbsp. Worcestershire sauce
- 1 large onion, finely chopped
- 2 cans (2¼ oz. each) sliced ripe olives, drained
- ¾ cup dry bread crumbs
- ⅓ cup minced fresh cilantro
- 2½ tsp. ground cumin
- 2½ tsp. chili powder
- 1 tsp. salt
- 1 tsp. pepper
- 3 lbs. lean ground beef (90% lean)
  Salsa and additional cilantro, optional

1. Preheat oven to 350°. In a large bowl, combine the first 12 ingredients. Add beef; mix lightly but thoroughly. Transfer to 2 greased 9x5-in. loaf pans.
2. Bake meat loaves 50-55 minutes or until a thermometer reads 160°. Let stand 10 minutes before slicing. If desired, top with salsa and cilantro.
FREEZE OPTION: Shape meat loaves in plastic wrap-lined loaf pans; cover and freeze until firm. Remove from pans and wrap securely in foil; return to freezer. To use, unwrap and bake meat loaves in pans as directed, until a thermometer inserted in center reads 160°, 1¼-1½ hours.
1 SLICE: 196 cal., 10g fat (3g sat. fat), 89mg chol., 453mg sod., 7g carb. (2g sugars, 1g fiber), 19g pro. **DIABETIC EXCHANGES:** 3 lean meat, ½ starch.

FLANK STEAK WITH COUSCOUS

It takes just minutes to broil this nicely seasoned flank steak. Slice the meat on an angle across the grain for the most tender results. You can substitute a pound of sirloin steak for the flank steak if you prefer.
—Taste of Home *Test Kitchen*

TAKES: 25 min. • **MAKES:** 4 servings

- 1 garlic clove, minced
- 1 tsp. olive oil
- ½ tsp. Italian seasoning
- ¼ tsp. pepper
- ⅛ tsp. salt
- 1 beef flank steak (1 lb.)
- 2 pkg. (5.8 oz. each) roasted garlic and olive oil couscous
- ¾ cup diced roasted sweet red pepper, drained
- ½ cup Italian salad dressing

1. Preheat broiler. Mix first 5 ingredients; rub over steak. Place on a broiler pan.
2. Broil 2-3 in. from heat until meat reaches desired doneness (for medium-rare, a thermometer should read 135°), 6-8 minutes per side. Let stand 5 minutes.
3. Meanwhile, cook couscous according to package directions. Stir in red pepper. Slice steak thinly across the grain; drizzle with dressing. Serve with couscous.
1 SERVING: 587 cal., 21g fat (5g sat. fat), 54mg chol., 1445mg sod., 61g carb. (5g sugars, 3g fiber), 34g pro.

TEST KITCHEN TIP
Nix the couscous mix to cut almost 750 milligrams of sodium per serving. Instead, cook plain couscous in water, then add roasted garlic and a drizzle of olive oil.

FLANK STEAK WITH COUSCOUS

3. Return ribs to pan; add water, if necessary, to cover. Bake, covered, until meat is tender, 2½-3 hours. Remove from oven; drain, reserving juices. When cool enough to handle, remove ribs from pan and remove meat from bones; discard bones. Shred meat with 2 forks. Skim fat from reserved juices. Return meat and juices to Dutch oven; heat through. Serve on tortillas with pico de gallo and queso fresco.

2 TACOS: 508 cal., 26g fat (9g sat. fat), 97mg chol., 557mg sod., 32g carb. (4g sugars, 6g fiber), 37g pro.

VEAL CUTLETS SUPREME

This dish has been in the family for years and is still one of our favorites. Guests love it and usually ask for the recipe.
—*Irene Bruntz, Grand Rapids, MI*

- -

PREP: 35 min. • **BAKE:** 25 min.
MAKES: 6 servings

6	veal cutlets (½ in. thick)
2	garlic cloves, minced
1	tsp. salt, divided
¼	tsp. pepper
4	Tbsp. butter, divided
2	medium onions, chopped
¾	lb. sliced fresh mushrooms
3	Tbsp. crushed butter-flavored crackers
1	cup heavy whipping cream
¾	cup dry white wine or chicken broth
2	Tbsp. minced fresh parsley
¾	cup shredded cheddar cheese

1. Preheat oven to 350°. Sprinkle veal with garlic, ½ tsp. salt and pepper. In a large skillet, brown veal in 2 Tbsp. butter on both sides. Transfer to a greased 13x9-in. baking dish.
2. In the same skillet, saute onions and mushrooms in remaining butter until tender. Stir in cracker crumbs, cream, wine or broth and remaining salt; cook and stir until mixture comes to a boil. Stir in parsley; pour over veal.
3. Cover and bake 20 minutes. Uncover; sprinkle with cheese. Bake 5 minutes or until cheese is melted.

1 SERVING: 551 cal., 41g fat (22g sat. fat), 184mg chol., 664mg sod., 11g carb. (5g sugars, 2g fiber), 31g pro.

SHORT RIB TACOS

When we go to Houston to visit family, we like to track down *cabeza*. It's cow's head, cooked very slowly, and it makes an excellent, tender taco filling. Cabeza is hard to find in Seattle, so I use short ribs to replicate the texture. I like corn tortillas for these tacos and a quick pico de gallo to add freshness to the rich, flavorful meat.
—*Anai Yost, Bothell, WA*

- -

PREP: 40 min. • **BAKE:** 2½ hours
MAKES: 6 servings

2	Tbsp. canola oil
6	bone-in beef short ribs
¼	tsp. salt
¼	tsp. pepper
2	medium carrots, finely chopped
1	small yellow onion, finely chopped
2	Tbsp. baking cocoa
1	can (15 oz.) tomato sauce
1	bottle (12 oz.) dark beer or beef broth
	Water, optional
12	corn tortillas (6 in.), warmed
¾	cup pico de gallo
¾	cup queso fresco or crumbled feta cheese

1. Preheat oven to 325°. In an ovenproof Dutch oven, heat oil over medium-high heat. Sprinkle beef with salt and pepper; brown in batches. Remove with tongs.
2. Reduce heat to medium. Add carrots and onion to drippings; cook, stirring frequently, until starting to brown, 3-5 minutes. Add baking cocoa; toast, stirring frequently, until aromatic, 1-2 minutes. Add tomato sauce and beer, stirring to loosen browned bits from pan. Bring to a boil; simmer 2-3 minutes.

SHORT RIB TACOS

**SALSA STEAK
GARLIC TOASTS**

SALSA STEAK GARLIC TOASTS

These open-faced steak sandwiches play up the popular combo of steak and garlic bread. The salsa, sour cream and garnish elevate it into a quick, satisfying meal. Substitute chopped green onions or chives for the cilantro if desired.
—*Arlene Erlbach, Morton Grove, IL*

TAKES: 25 min. • **MAKES:** 4 servings

4 slices frozen garlic Texas toast
1 Tbsp. olive oil
1 beef top sirloin steak
   (1 lb.), thinly sliced
1½ cups salsa
   Sour cream and chopped fresh
   cilantro

1. Prepare garlic toast according to the package directions.
2. Meanwhile, in a large skillet, heat oil over medium heat. Saute steak until no longer pink, 3-5 minutes; drain. Stir in salsa; cook and stir until heated through. Serve over toast. Top with sour cream and cilantro.
1 GARLIC TOAST WITH ¾ CUP STEAK MIXTURE: 375 cal., 16g fat (4g sat. fat), 52mg chol., 721mg sod., 27g carb. (5g sugars, 1g fiber), 29g pro.

TEST KITCHEN TIP
You can use a less expensive olive oil than virgin or extra virgin for cooking. The higher grades have a more delicate flavor that shines in salads and uncooked foods, but is generally lost in recipes that require cooking. Pure olive oil works fine—and sometimes even better—for cooked recipes.

FAST PHILLY CHEESESTEAK PIZZA

FAST PHILLY CHEESESTEAK PIZZA

Cheesesteaks and pizza are such favorites, I just had to combine them. We top a pizza crust with roast beef, cheese, onions and peppers for a handheld feast.
—*Jackie Hannahs, Cedar Springs, MI*

TAKES: 30 min. • **MAKES:** 6 slices

1 tube (13.8 oz.) refrigerated
   pizza crust
2 cups frozen pepper and
   onion stir-fry blend
2 Tbsp. Dijon-mayonnaise blend
½ lb. thinly sliced deli roast
   beef, cut into wide strips
1½ cups shredded cheddar cheese

1. Preheat oven to 425°. Grease a 12-in. pizza pan. Unroll and press dough to fit prepared pan. Pinch edge to form a rim. Bake for 8-10 minutes or until edge is lightly browned.
2. Meanwhile, place a large nonstick skillet coated with cooking spray over medium-high heat. Add stir-fry blend; cook and stir for 3-5 minutes or until heated through.
3. Spread mayonnaise blend over crust; top with roast beef and vegetables. Sprinkle with cheddar cheese. Bake 10-15 minutes or until the cheese is melted.
1 SLICE: 330 cal., 13g fat (7g sat. fat), 51mg chol., 983mg sod., 34g carb. (6g sugars, 1g fiber), 20g pro.

Poultry

ARTICHOKE ROSEMARY CHICKEN

ARTICHOKE ROSEMARY CHICKEN

Rosemary, mushrooms and artichokes combine to give chicken a wonderful savory flavor. I've served this dish for a large group by doubling the recipe. It's always a big hit with everyone—especially my family!
—*Ruth Stenson, Santa Ana, CA*

PREP: 15 min. • **BAKE:** 50 min.
MAKES: 8 servings

- 8 boneless skinless chicken breast halves (4 oz. each)
- 2 Tbsp. butter
- 2 jars (6 oz. each) marinated quartered artichoke hearts, drained
- 1 jar (4½ oz.) whole mushrooms, drained
- ½ cup chopped onion
- ⅓ cup all-purpose flour
- 1½ tsp. dried rosemary, crushed
- ¾ tsp. salt
- ¼ tsp. pepper
- 2 cups chicken broth or 1 cup broth and 1 cup dry white wine
    Hot cooked noodles
    Minced fresh parsley

1. In a large skillet, brown chicken in butter. Remove chicken to an ungreased 13x9-in. baking dish. Arrange the artichokes and mushrooms on top of chicken; set aside.
2. Saute onion in pan juices until crisp-tender. Combine the flour, dried rosemary, salt and pepper. Stir into the pan until blended. Add chicken broth. Bring to a boil; cook and stir until thickened and bubbly, about 2 minutes. Spoon over chicken.
3. Bake, uncovered, at 350° for 40 minutes or until a thermometer inserted in the chicken reads 165°. Serve with noodles and sprinkle with parsley.

FREEZE OPTION: Cool unbaked casserole; cover and freeze. To use, partially thaw in refrigerator overnight. Remove from the refrigerator 30 minutes before baking. Preheat oven to 350°. Bake casserole as directed, increasing time as necessary to heat through and for a thermometer inserted in the chicken to read 165°.

1 SERVING: 232 cal., 9g fat (3g sat. fat), 81mg chol., 752mg sod., 7g carb. (1g sugars, 1g fiber), 28g pro. **DIABETIC EXCHANGES:** 4 lean meat, 1½ fat, ½ starch.

TURKEY ALFREDO PIZZA

GINGERED CHICKEN THIGHS

This recipe was born from my desire to develop a timesaving Asian entree that's easy on the budget. It's a favorite at the girls' camp where I am the head cook. I usually serve it with rice prepared with coconut milk.
—*Debbie Fleenor, Monterey, TN*

- -

PREP: 20 min. + marinating • **BAKE:** 20 min.
MAKES: 6 servings

   2 Tbsp. ground ginger
   2 Tbsp. orange juice
   2 Tbsp. honey
   2 Tbsp. reduced-sodium soy sauce
   2 tsp. curry powder
   2 garlic cloves, minced
  ½ tsp. crushed red pepper flakes
   6 boneless skinless chicken thighs (about 1½ lbs.)

PEANUT SAUCE

   2 Tbsp. chicken broth
   2 Tbsp. orange juice
   1 Tbsp. reduced-fat creamy peanut butter
  ½ tsp. ground ginger

1. In a large shallow dish, combine the first 7 ingredients; add the chicken. Turn to coat; cover and refrigerate for up to 4 hours.
2. Drain chicken, discarding marinade. In a large skillet coated with cooking spray, brown chicken on each side. Transfer to an 11x7-in. baking dish coated with cooking spray. In a small bowl, whisk sauce ingredients; pour over chicken. Bake, uncovered, at 350° for 20-25 minutes or until no longer pink.

1 CHICKEN THIGH: 201 cal., 9g fat (2g sat. fat), 76mg chol., 196mg sod., 6g carb. (4g sugars, 1g fiber), 22g pro. **DIABETIC EXCHANGES:** 3 lean meat.

TURKEY ALFREDO PIZZA

A longtime family favorite, this pizza is packed with rich flavor, good-for-you spinach and satisfying protein—and it's an excellent way to use up leftover turkey.
—*Edie DeSpain, Logan, UT*

- -

TAKES: 25 min. • **MAKES:** 6 servings

   1 prebaked 12-in. thin pizza crust
   1 garlic clove, peeled and halved
  ¾ cup reduced-fat Alfredo sauce, divided
   1 pkg. (10 oz.) frozen chopped spinach, thawed and squeezed dry
   2 tsp. lemon juice
  ¼ tsp. salt
  ⅛ tsp. pepper
   2 cups shredded cooked turkey breast
  ¾ cup shredded Parmesan cheese
  ½ tsp. crushed red pepper flakes

1. Place the crust on a baking sheet; rub with cut sides of garlic. Discard the garlic. Spread ½ cup Alfredo sauce over crust.
2. In a small bowl, combine the spinach, lemon juice, salt and pepper; spoon evenly over sauce. Top with the turkey; drizzle with remaining the Alfredo sauce. Sprinkle with Parmesan cheese and pepper flakes.
3. Bake at 425° until heated through and cheese is melted, 11-13 minutes.

1 PIECE: 300 cal., 9g fat (4g sat. fat), 60mg chol., 823mg sod., 27g carb. (2g sugars, 2g fiber), 25g pro. **DIABETIC EXCHANGES:** 3 lean meat, 2 starch, ½ fat.

**CHICKEN
PROVOLONE**

CHICKEN PROVOLONE

Though one of my simplest dishes, this is also one of my husband's favorites. It's quick to prepare and looks fancy served on a dark plate with a garnish of fresh parsley or basil.
—*Dawn E. Bryant, Thedford, NE*

- -

TAKES: 25 min. • **MAKES:** 4 servings

- 4   boneless skinless chicken breast halves (4 oz. each)
- ¼   tsp. pepper
- 8   fresh basil leaves
-      Butter-flavored cooking spray
- 4   thin slices prosciutto or deli ham
- 4   slices provolone cheese

1. Sprinkle the chicken with pepper. In a large skillet coated with cooking spray, cook the chicken over medium heat until a thermometer reads 165°, 4-5 minutes on each side.

2. Transfer to an ungreased baking sheet; top with the basil, prosciutto and cheese. Broil 6-8 in. from the heat until cheese is melted, 1-2 minutes.

1 CHICKEN BREAST HALF: 236 cal., 11g fat (6g sat. fat), 89mg chol., 435mg sod., 1g carb. (0 sugars, 0 fiber), 33g pro.

"Really good. Quick and easy, too. Love that. I added more seasoning and had the hubby grill it."
— ROBBIE JACKSON, TASTEOFHOME.COM

BLACK BEAN & CHICKEN ENCHILADA LASAGNA

BLACK BEAN & CHICKEN ENCHILADA LASAGNA

Twice a month I make chicken enchiladas, lasagna-style. It's a regular with us because assembly is easy and my whole family gives it a thumbs-up.
—*Cheryl Snavely, Hagerstown, MD*

- -

PREP: 30 min. • **BAKE:** 25 min. + standing
MAKES: 8 servings

- 2   cans (10 oz. each) enchilada sauce
- 12   corn tortillas (6 in.)
- 2   cups coarsely shredded rotisserie chicken
- 1   small onion, chopped
- 1   can (15 oz.) black beans, rinsed and drained
- 3   cans (4 oz. each) whole green chiles, drained and coarsely chopped
- 3   cups crumbled queso fresco or shredded Mexican cheese blend
- 2   medium ripe avocados
- 2   Tbsp. sour cream
- 2   Tbsp. lime juice
- ½   tsp. salt
-      Chopped fresh tomatoes and cilantro

1. Preheat oven to 350°. Spread ½ cup enchilada sauce into a greased 13x9-in. baking dish; top with 4 tortillas, 1 cup chicken, ¼ cup onion, ¼ cup beans, ⅓ cup green chiles and 1 cup cheese. Repeat layers. Drizzle with ½ cup enchilada sauce; top with the remaining tortillas, onion, beans, chiles, sauce and cheese.

2. Bake, uncovered, 25-30 minutes or until bubbly and cheese is melted. Let stand for 10 minutes before serving.

3. Meanwhile, quarter, peel and pit 1 of the avocados; place in a food processor. Add sour cream, lime juice and salt; process until smooth. Peel, pit and cut remaining avocado into small cubes.

4. Top lasagna with tomatoes, cilantro and cubed avocado. Serve with avocado sauce.

1 PIECE WITH 1 TBSP. SAUCE: 407 cal., 18g fat (7g sat. fat), 64mg chol., 857mg sod., 39g carb. (4g sugars, 8g fiber), 28g pro.

CHICKEN RANCH
FLATBREADS

CHICKEN RANCH FLATBREADS

To get my son to try new things, I revamped this mini pizza. Mr. Picky ate it, so it's definitely kid-friendly. This is one of those meals you can make in a hurry with hardly any prep work.
—Jenny Dubinsky, Inwood, WV

TAKES: 25 min. • **MAKES:** 4 servings

- 4   whole wheat or white pita breads (6 in.)
- 2   cups chopped cooked chicken breast
- ¼   cup reduced-fat ranch salad dressing
- 2   plum tomatoes, thinly sliced
- 1   cup shredded part-skim mozzarella cheese
- 4   bacon strips, cooked and crumbled
- 1   tsp. dried oregano

1. Preheat oven to 400°. Place pita breads on a large baking sheet; bake 10-12 minutes or until lightly browned. Meanwhile, in a bowl, toss chicken with dressing.

2. Top pitas with tomatoes and chicken mixture; sprinkle with cheese, bacon and oregano. Bake 8-10 minutes or until cheese is melted.

1 PITA PIZZA: 448 cal., 16g fat (6g sat. fat), 86mg chol., 888mg sod., 42g carb. (3g sugars, 5g fiber), 37g pro.

DIJON CHICKEN

This is one of easiest recipes I have! The Dijon mustard adds so much flavor, and the dish comes together so quickly.
—Carol Roberts, Dumas, TX

PREP: 15 min. • **BAKE:** 1 hour
MAKES: 6 servings

- ½   cup Dijon mustard
- ½   cup water
- 1   broiler/fryer chicken (3 to 4 lbs.), cut up
- 4½   cups herb-seasoned stuffing, crushed

1. In a shallow bowl, combine mustard and water; dip the chicken pieces, then roll in stuffing. Place in a greased 13x9-in. baking pan. Sprinkle with the remaining stuffing.
2. Bake, uncovered, at 350° for 1 hour or until juices run clear.

5 OZ. COOKED CHICKEN: 414 cal., 17g fat (4g sat. fat), 88mg chol., 1122mg sod., 31g carb. (2g sugars, 2g fiber), 33g pro.

"This is really tasty and easy to put together. It is pretty high in sodium, though. Next time I make it, I think I'll use cornflake crumbs instead of stuffing. The Dijon mustard is so flavorful that I don't anticipate it being bland."
—NEBRASKAGIRL, TASTEOFHOME.COM

BARBECUE SHEPHERD'S PIE

Have a wholesome home-cooked meal even on hectic nights. I like to add leftover veggies, such as green beans, sweet potatoes or corn, and zip it up with chipotle powder.
—*Angela Buchanan, Longmont, CO*

- -

PREP: 15 min. • **BAKE:** 30 min.
MAKES: 6 servings

- 1 Tbsp. olive oil
- 1 lb. ground turkey
- 1 medium onion, chopped
- 2 medium carrots, thinly sliced
- ½ cup frozen peas
- ½ cup honey barbecue sauce
- ⅓ cup ketchup
- 1 pkg. (24 oz.) refrigerated mashed potatoes
- ½ tsp. paprika

1. Preheat oven to 350°. In a large skillet, heat oil over medium heat. Add turkey and onion; cook 6-8 minutes or until turkey is no longer pink, breaking up the turkey into crumbles; drain. Stir in carrots, peas, barbecue sauce and ketchup.

2. Transfer to a greased 1½-qt. baking dish. Spread mashed potatoes over top; sprinkle with paprika. Bake, uncovered, 30-35 minutes or until filling is bubbly.

FREEZE OPTION: Cool unbaked casserole; cover and freeze. To use, partially thaw in refrigerator overnight. Remove from the refrigerator 30 minutes before baking. Preheat oven to 350°. Bake casserole as directed, increasing time as necessary to heat through and for a thermometer inserted in center to read 165°.

1 SERVING: 405 cal., 21g fat (10g sat. fat), 63mg chol., 870mg sod., 39g carb. (16g sugars, 4g fiber), 16g pro.

GARLIC-HERB ROASTED CHICKEN

Since the garlic and herbs make this roasted chicken so flavorful, you can eliminate the salt from the recipe if you'd like.
—*Cindy Steffen, Cedarburg, WI*

- -

PREP: 20 min. • **BAKE:** 1½ hours + standing
MAKES: 8 servings

- 1 roasting chicken (4 to 5 lbs.)
- 2 tsp. each minced fresh parsley, rosemary, sage and thyme
- ¾ tsp. salt
- ¼ tsp. pepper
- 20 garlic cloves, peeled and sliced
- 1 medium lemon, halved
- 1 large whole garlic bulb
- 1 sprig each fresh parsley, rosemary, sage and thyme

1. With fingers, carefully loosen skin around the chicken breast, leg and thigh. Combine minced parsley, rosemary, sage, thyme, salt and pepper; rub half under skin. Place sliced garlic cloves under skin. Squeeze half of the lemon into the cavity and place the squeezed half in the cavity.

2. Remove papery outer skin from whole garlic bulb (do not peel or separate cloves). Cut top off garlic bulb. Place garlic bulb and herb sprigs in the cavity. Skewer the chicken openings; tie the drumsticks together with kitchen string.

3. Place chicken breast side up on a rack in a roasting pan. Squeeze the remaining lemon half over chicken; rub remaining herb mixture over chicken.

4. Bake chicken, uncovered, at 350° until a thermometer inserted in thickest part of thigh reads 170°-175°, 1½-1¾ hours (cover loosely with foil if browning too quickly). If desired, baste with pan drippings.

5. Cover and let stand 15 minutes. Remove and discard garlic, lemon and herbs from cavity before carving.

5 OZ. COOKED CHICKEN: 163 cal., 6g fat (2g sat. fat), 67mg chol., 289mg sod., 3g carb. (0 sugars, 0 fiber), 23g pro. **DIABETIC EXCHANGES:** 3 lean meat.

BARBECUE SHEPHERD'S PIE

TURKEY BUNDLES

SKILLET-ROASTED LEMON CHICKEN WITH POTATOES

This is a meal I have my students make in our nutrition unit. It has a delicious lemon-herb flavor and is simple to make.
—*Mindy Rottmund, Lancaster, PA*

- -

PREP: 20 min. • **BAKE:** 25 min.
MAKES: 4 servings

   1   Tbsp. olive oil, divided
   1   medium lemon, thinly sliced
   4   garlic cloves, minced and divided
   ¼   tsp. grated lemon zest
   ½   tsp. salt, divided
   ¼   tsp. pepper, divided
   8   boneless skinless chicken
        thighs (4 oz. each)
   ¼   tsp. dried rosemary, crushed
   1   lb. fingerling potatoes,
        halved lengthwise
   8   cherry tomatoes
        Minced fresh parsley, optional

1. Preheat oven to 450°. Grease a 10-in. cast-iron or other ovenproof skillet with 1 tsp. oil. Arrange lemon slices in a single layer in skillet.
2. Combine 1 tsp. oil, 2 minced garlic cloves, lemon zest, ¼ tsp. salt and ⅛ tsp. pepper; rub over chicken. Place over lemon.
3. In a large bowl, combine rosemary and the remaining oil, garlic, salt and pepper. Add the potatoes and tomatoes; toss to coat. Arrange over chicken. Bake, uncovered, until chicken is no longer pink and potatoes are tender, 25-30 minutes. Before serving, sprinkle with minced parsley if desired.
2 CHICKEN THIGHS WITH 4 OZ. POTATOES AND 2 TOMATOES: 446 cal., 20g fat (5g sat. fat), 151mg chol., 429mg sod., 18g carb. (2g sugars, 3g fiber), 45g pro.

DID YOU KNOW?
Yes, you can cook acidic ingredients such as lemon in a cast-iron skillet. Just be sure to use a well-used, well-seasoned one. Use a little oil to help protect the pan's finish.

TURKEY BUNDLES

This recipe is a must-try. Crescent roll dough is wrapped around creamy turkey filling to form cute bundles. I usually double the recipe so I have extras for lunch the next day.
—*Lydia Garrod, Tacoma, WA*

- -

TAKES: 30 min. • **MAKES:** 6 servings

   4   oz. cream cheese, softened
   2   Tbsp. whole milk
   ½   tsp. dill weed
   ¼   tsp. celery salt
   ¼   tsp. pepper
   2   cups cubed cooked turkey
   ¼   cup chopped water chestnuts
   1   green onion, chopped
   2   tubes (one 8 oz., one 4 oz.)
        refrigerated crescent rolls
   2   Tbsp. butter, melted
   2   Tbsp. seasoned bread crumbs

1. Preheat oven to 375°. In a large bowl, beat the first 5 ingredients until smooth. Stir in turkey, water chestnuts and green onion.
2. Unroll both tubes of crescent dough and separate the dough into 6 rectangles; press the perforations to seal. Place ⅓ cup turkey mixture in center of each rectangle. Bring 4 corners of dough together above filling; twist and pinch seams to seal.
3. Place on an ungreased baking sheet. Brush tops with butter; sprinkle with bread crumbs. Bake 15-20 minutes or until golden brown.
1 BUNDLE: 418 cal., 25g fat (10g sat. fat), 67mg chol., 674mg sod., 26g carb. (5g sugars, 0 fiber), 20g pro.

SKILLET-ROASTED LEMON CHICKEN WITH POTATOES

CHICKEN & RICE CASSEROLE

CHICKEN & RICE CASSEROLE

Everyone loves this casserole because it's a tasty combination of hearty and crunchy ingredients mixed in a creamy sauce. It's a time-tested classic.
—*Myrtle Matthews, Marietta, GA*

PREP: 15 min. • **BAKE:** 1 hour
MAKES: 12 servings

- 4 cups cooked white rice or a combination of wild and white rice
- 4 cups diced cooked chicken
- ½ cup slivered almonds
- 1 small onion, chopped
- 1 can (8 oz.) sliced water chestnuts, drained
- 1 pkg. (10 oz.) frozen peas, thawed
- ¾ cup chopped celery
- 1 can (10¾ oz.) condensed cream of celery soup, undiluted
- 1 can (10¾ oz.) condensed cream of chicken soup, undiluted
- 1 cup mayonnaise
- 2 tsp. lemon juice
- 1 tsp. salt
- 2 cups crushed potato chips
  Paprika

1. Preheat oven to 350°. In a greased 13x9-in. baking dish, combine first 7 ingredients. In a large bowl, combine the soups, mayonnaise, lemon juice and salt. Pour over the chicken mixture and toss to coat.
2. Sprinkle with potato chips and paprika. Bake until heated through, about 1 hour.
1 CUP: 439 cal., 26g fat (5g sat. fat), 51mg chol., 804mg sod., 31g carb. (3g sugars, 3g fiber), 19g pro.

TEST KITCHEN TIP
This is a great recipe for using up leftover chicken or even a rotisserie chicken!

TURKEY CORDON BLEU WITH ALFREDO SAUCE

TURKEY CORDON BLEU WITH ALFREDO SAUCE

For our annual Kentucky Derby party, I wanted to create a twist on a traditional Kentucky hot brown sandwich. The turkey here is tender and flavorful, filled with smoky ham and melted cheese. But the crispy bacon is what really sets the dish off.
—*Sandy Komisarek, Swanton, OH*

PREP: 30 min. • **BAKE:** 20 min.
MAKES: 8 servings

- 8 slices part-skim mozzarella cheese
- 8 thin slices deli honey ham
- 8 turkey breast cutlets
- 2 cups panko (Japanese) bread crumbs
- 2 large eggs, lightly beaten
- ½ cup all-purpose flour
- ½ tsp. salt
- ¼ tsp. pepper
- ¼ cup canola oil
- 1 jar (15 oz.) Alfredo sauce, warmed
- 8 bacon strips, cooked and crumbled
- ¼ cup grated Parmesan cheese

1. Preheat oven to 350°. Place 1 slice of mozzarella cheese and ham on each cutlet. Roll up each from a short side and secure with toothpicks.
2. Place bread crumbs and eggs in separate shallow bowls. In another shallow bowl, combine flour, salt and pepper. Dip turkey in flour mixture, eggs, then bread crumbs.
3. In a large skillet, brown the turkey in oil in batches. Place in a greased 13x9-in. baking dish. Bake, uncovered, until turkey juices run clear, 20-25 minutes. Discard toothpicks.
4. Spoon Alfredo sauce over turkey. Sprinkle with bacon and Parmesan cheese.
1 TURKEY ROLL-UP WITH ABOUT 3 TBSP. SAUCE: 455 cal., 24g fat (10g sat. fat), 147mg chol., 910mg sod., 18g carb. (1g sugars, 1g fiber), 39g pro.

TEXAN RANCH CHICKEN CASSEROLE

I'm so happy this Texas-style recipe was passed down to me. It's easy to make and freezes well. If your family likes a little spice, this would be good topped with jalapenos.
—*Kendra Doss, Colorado Springs, CO*

- -

PREP: 25 min. • **BAKE:** 30 min.
MAKES: 8 servings

- 1 large onion, finely chopped
- 2 celery ribs, finely chopped
- 1 medium green pepper, finely chopped
- 1 medium sweet red pepper, finely chopped
- 1 Tbsp. canola oil
- 1 garlic clove, minced
- 3 cups cubed cooked chicken breast
- 1 can (10¾ oz.) reduced-fat reduced-sodium condensed cream of celery soup, undiluted
- 1 can (10¾ oz.) reduced-fat reduced-sodium condensed cream of chicken soup, undiluted
- 1 can (10 oz.) diced tomatoes and green chiles, undrained
- 1 Tbsp. chili powder
- 12 corn tortillas (6 in.), cut into 1-in. strips
- 2 cups shredded reduced-fat cheddar cheese, divided

1. In a large skillet coated with cooking spray, saute the onion, celery and peppers in oil until crisp-tender. Add garlic; cook 1 minute longer. Stir in the chicken, soups, tomatoes and chili powder.

2. Line the bottom of a 3-qt. baking dish with half of the tortilla strips; top with half of the chicken mixture and 1 cup cheese. Repeat layers. Bake, uncovered, at 350° until bubbly, 30-35 minutes.

1 CUP: 329 cal., 12g fat (5g sat. fat), 65mg chol., 719mg sod., 31g carb. (4g sugars, 3g fiber), 26g pro. **DIABETIC EXCHANGES:** 3 lean meat, 1½ starch, 1 vegetable, 1 fat.

ENCHILADA STUFFED SHELLS

I served this pasta entree to my husband, my sister and her husband, and received many compliments. My brother-in-law is difficult to please when it comes to food, so when he said he loved it, I was thrilled. He even took some leftovers for lunch the next day. I'll definitely be making this again!
—*Rebecca Stout, Conroe, TX*

- -

PREP: 20 min. • **BAKE:** 30 min.
MAKES: 5 servings

- 15 uncooked jumbo pasta shells
- 1 lb. lean ground turkey
- 1 can (10 oz.) enchilada sauce
- ½ tsp. dried minced onion
- ¼ tsp. dried basil
- ¼ tsp. dried oregano
- ¼ tsp. ground cumin
- ½ cup fat-free refried beans
- 1 cup shredded reduced-fat cheddar cheese

1. Cook pasta according to the package directions; drain and rinse in cold water. In a nonstick skillet, cook turkey over medium heat until no longer pink; drain. Stir in the enchilada sauce and seasonings; set aside.

2. Place a rounded teaspoonful of refried beans in each pasta shell, then fill with turkey mixture. Place shells in an 11x7-in. baking dish coated with cooking spray.

3. Cover and bake at 350° for 25 minutes. Uncover; sprinkle with cheese. Bake until cheese is melted, about 5 minutes longer.

3 STUFFED SHELLS: 345 cal., 13g fat (5g sat. fat), 79mg chol., 622mg sod., 30g carb. (2g sugars, 3g fiber), 31g pro. **DIABETIC EXCHANGES:** 2 starch, 3 lean meat, 1 fat.

ENCHILADA STUFFED SHELLS

TERRIFIC TURKEY MEAT LOAF

ITALIAN TURKEY TENDERS

Delicious and crispy, this healthier version of a kids' favorite should delight the whole family. Seasoned bread crumbs or ranch dressing would make tasty variations.
—*Mary Shivers, Ada, OK*

- -

PREP: 25 min. • **BAKE:** 20 min.
MAKES: 6 servings

- 1 large egg, beaten
- ½ cup fat-free Italian salad dressing
- ½ cup all-purpose flour
- 1¼ cups dry bread crumbs
- 1 tsp. dried parsley flakes
- 1 tsp. Italian seasoning
- ¾ tsp. salt
- ½ tsp. onion powder
- ½ tsp. garlic powder
- ½ tsp. dried oregano
- ½ tsp. pepper
- 2 lbs. boneless skinless turkey breast half, cut into 1-in. strips
  Cooking spray

1. In a shallow bowl, whisk the egg and salad dressing. Place flour in another shallow bowl. In a third shallow bowl, combine the bread crumbs and seasonings. Coat turkey with flour, then dip in egg mixture and coat with bread crumb mixture.
2. Place on baking sheets coated with cooking spray. Spritz turkey with cooking spray. Bake at 375° until no longer pink, 20-25 minutes, turning once.
1 SERVING: 309 cal., 5g fat (1g sat. fat), 117mg chol., 870mg sod., 22g carb. (3g sugars, 1g fiber), 40g pro.

TEST KITCHEN TIP
No Italian seasoning on hand? No worries. Just mix an equal amount of basil, thyme, rosemary and oregano to create your own seasoning blend.

TERRIFIC TURKEY MEAT LOAF

We love this moist, tender entree that's loaded with flavor but low in carbohydrates and saturated fat. It's a tasty way to eat right on busy weeknights.
—*Wanda Bannister, New Bern, NC*

- -

PREP: 15 min. • **BAKE:** 50 min.
MAKES: 4 servings

- 1 large egg white, lightly beaten
- ½ cup oat bran
- ½ cup chopped green pepper
- ¼ cup finely chopped onion
- 3 Tbsp. ketchup
- 2 Tbsp. chopped ripe olives
- 1 Tbsp. Worcestershire sauce
- 1 garlic clove, minced
- ½ tsp. Dijon mustard
- ¼ tsp. celery salt
- ¼ tsp. dried marjoram
- ¼ tsp. rubbed sage
- ¼ tsp. pepper
- 1 lb. ground turkey

1. Preheat oven to 375°. In a large bowl, combine all ingredients except turkey. Add turkey; mix lightly but thoroughly. Pat into a loaf in an 11x7-in. baking dish coated with cooking spray.
2. Bake, uncovered, until a thermometer reads 165°, 50-60 minutes.
1 SLICE: 253 cal., 12g fat (3g sat. fat), 82mg chol., 421mg sod., 14g carb. (3g sugars, 3g fiber), 26g pro. **DIABETIC EXCHANGES:** 3 lean meat, 1 starch.

3. Preheat oven to 375°. Place bottom buns in a greased 13x9-in. baking dish. Place half a slice of cheese on each of the buns; spoon chicken mixture on top of cheese. Top with remaining cheese slices and bun tops. Stir together remaining olive oil, honey and pepper flakes. Brush over bun tops. Sprinkle with the coarse salt, if desired.

4. Bake until tops are golden and cheese has melted, 10-15 minutes. Garnish with chopped green onions.

5. For sauce, stir together all ingredients. Serve alongside sliders.

1 SLIDER: 516 cal., 26g fat (7g sat. fat), 100mg chol., 892mg sod., 40g carb. (18g sugars, 1g fiber), 31g pro.

SO-SIMPLE TURKEY BREAST

My family always requests this turkey at family gatherings. The Italian dressing adds zip that you don't find in other recipes. If you'd like, you can make a flavorful gravy from the pan drippings.
—*Cindy Carlson, Ingleside, TX*

- -

PREP: 10 min. • **BAKE:** 2 hours + standing
MAKES: 14 servings

- 1 bone-in turkey breast (about 7 lbs.)
- 1 tsp. garlic powder
- ½ tsp. onion powder
- ½ tsp. salt
- ¼ tsp. pepper
- 1½ cups Italian dressing

1. Place turkey breast in a greased 13x9-in. baking dish. Combine the seasonings; sprinkle over turkey. Pour dressing over the top.

2. Cover and bake turkey at 325° until a thermometer reads 170°, 2-2½ hours, basting occasionally with pan drippings. Let stand for 10 minutes before slicing.

6 OZ. COOKED TURKEY: 406 cal., 22g fat (5g sat. fat), 122mg chol., 621mg sod., 2g carb. (1g sugars, 0 fiber), 47g pro.

ROASTED TURKEY: Combine 1¾ tsp. garlic powder, ¾ tsp. each onion powder and salt, and ½ tsp. pepper; sprinkle over a 12- to 14-pound turkey. Place in a roasting pan; top with 2½ cups Italian dressing. Cover and bake at 325° for 3-3½ hours or until a thermometer inserted in the thigh reads 180°, basting occasionally with pan drippings. Let stand for 20 minutes before carving.

JIMMY'S BANG BANG CHICKEN SLIDERS

JIMMY'S BANG BANG CHICKEN SLIDERS

I simmer chicken thighs in a spicy-sweet sauce, shred it and pile it high on pretzel buns to create an incredibly addictive party food.
—*James Schend, Pleasant Prairie, WI*

- -

PREP: 20 min. • **BAKE:** 45 min.
MAKES: 1 dozen

- 3 lbs. boneless skinless chicken thighs
- 3 Tbsp. olive oil, divided
- ½ cup ketchup
- ½ cup Sriracha chili sauce
- ½ cup plus 2 Tbsp. honey, divided
- ½ cup water
- 3 Tbsp. lime juice
- 2 tsp. grated lime zest
- 2 tsp. minced garlic
- 1 tsp. ground ginger
- ¼ tsp. pepper
- 12 mini pretzel buns, split

- 12 slices part-skim mozzarella cheese, halved
- ¼ to ½ tsp. crushed red pepper flakes
   Coarse salt, optional

SRIRACHA-LIME DIPPING SAUCE
- 1 cup reduced-fat mayonnaise
- 2 Tbsp. Sriracha chili sauce
- 2 Tbsp. lime juice
- 2 tsp. grated lime zest
- 2 green onions, chopped

1. In a Dutch oven over medium heat, brown chicken in 1 Tbsp. olive oil, about 5 minutes.
2. Meanwhile, stir together ketchup, chili sauce, ½ cup honey, water, lime juice and zest, garlic, ginger and pepper. Pour over browned chicken and bring to a boil. Reduce the heat to low and cook, covered, stirring occasionally, 25-30 minutes or until chicken is tender. Remove chicken and bring sauce back to a simmer; cook until thick, about 5 minutes. Shred chicken with 2 forks; toss with reduced sauce.

SO-SIMPLE TURKEY BREAST

BUFFALO CHICKEN PASTA BAKE

Sure, 10-cent wing night at your local pub is a blast. But a night at home with a clever casserole can't be beat. If you're not fond of blue cheese, use ranch salad dressing instead.
—Lindsay Sprunk, Brooklyn, NY

PREP: 30 min. • **BAKE:** 25 min.
MAKES: 8 servings

- 1 pkg. (16 oz.) penne pasta
- 1 lb. boneless skinless chicken breasts, cubed
- ⅛ tsp. salt
- ⅛ tsp. pepper
- 2 Tbsp. olive oil, divided
- 2 medium carrots, finely chopped
- 2 celery ribs, finely chopped
- ¾ cup finely chopped red onion
- 4 garlic cloves, minced
- ¾ cup blue cheese salad dressing
- ¾ cup mayonnaise
- ½ cup Louisiana-style hot sauce
- 1½ cups shredded Swiss cheese
- ½ cup dry bread crumbs
- 3 Tbsp. butter, melted

1. Cook penne pasta according to the package directions.
2. Meanwhile, sprinkle chicken with salt and pepper. In a large skillet, saute the chicken in 1 Tbsp. oil until no longer pink. Remove from skillet. In same skillet, saute carrots, celery and onion in remaining oil until tender. Add garlic; cook 1 minute longer. Remove from the heat.
3. Preheat oven to 350°. Stir in salad dressing, mayonnaise and hot sauce into skillet. Drain pasta. Add pasta and chicken to skillet; toss to coat. Transfer to a greased 13x9-in. baking dish. Sprinkle with cheese and bread crumbs. Drizzle with butter.
4. Bake, uncovered, 25-30 minutes or until heated through and cheese is melted.
1½ CUPS: 719 cal., 45g fat (12g sat. fat), 73mg chol., 586mg sod., 53g carb. (6g sugars, 3g fiber), 27g pro.

LEEK & HERB STUFFED CHICKEN

LEEK & HERB STUFFED CHICKEN

You're likely to find a lot of herb-stuffed chicken breast recipes out there, but this one is unique. It makes great use of leeks, an aromatic vegetable that's uncommon on the dinner table, but easy to find.
—Shirley Glaab, Hattiesburg, MS

PREP: 30 min. • **BAKE:** 35 min.
MAKES: 4 servings

- 3 medium leeks (white and light green portions only), cleaned and chopped
- 1 Tbsp. olive oil
- ½ tsp. dried rosemary, crushed
- ½ tsp. dried thyme
- ¼ tsp. salt
- ¼ tsp. pepper
- 4 boneless skinless chicken breast halves (6 oz. each)

PECAN CRUST
- ¼ cup finely chopped pecans
- ¼ cup dry bread crumbs
- ¼ tsp. dried rosemary, crushed
- ¼ tsp. dried thyme
- ½ tsp. salt
- ¼ tsp. pepper
- ¼ cup Dijon mustard
- 1 Tbsp. olive oil

1. In a small skillet, saute the leeks in oil until almost tender. Add the rosemary, thyme, salt and pepper; saute 1 minute longer. Remove from the heat; cool.
2. Flatten each chicken breast half to ¼-in. thickness; top with leek mixture. Roll up and secure with toothpicks.
3. In a small shallow bowl, combine the pecans, bread crumbs, rosemary, thyme, salt and pepper. Brush the mustard over chicken, then coat with pecan mixture. Place seam side down in a greased 11x7-in. baking dish. Drizzle with oil.
4. Bake, uncovered, at 375° until the chicken is no longer pink, 35-40 minutes. Discard the toothpicks.
1 CHICKEN BREAST HALF: 333 cal., 15g fat (2g sat. fat), 73mg chol., 929mg sod., 16g carb. (3g sugars, 2g fiber), 29g pro.

MOM'S TURKEY TETRAZZINI

If you're looking for stick-to-your-ribs comfort food, this hearty dish will meet your needs.

—*Judy Batson, Tampa, FL*

PREP: 25 min. • **BAKE:** 25 min. + standing
MAKES: 6 servings

- 1 pkg. (12 oz.) fettuccine
- ½ lb. sliced fresh mushrooms
- 1 medium onion, chopped
- ¼ cup butter, cubed
- 3 Tbsp. all-purpose flour
- 1 cup white wine or chicken broth
- 3 cups 2% milk
- 3 cups cubed cooked turkey
- ¾ tsp. salt
- ½ tsp. pepper
- ½ tsp. hot pepper sauce
- ½ cup shredded Parmesan cheese
  Paprika, optional

1. Preheat oven to 375°. Cook fettuccine according to package directions.
2. Meanwhile, in a large skillet, saute the mushrooms and onion in butter until tender. Stir in flour until blended; whisk in wine until smooth, about 2 minutes. Slowly whisk in milk. Bring to a boil; cook and stir until thickened. Stir in turkey, salt, pepper and pepper sauce.
3. Drain the fettuccine. Layer half of the fettuccine, turkey mixture and cheese in a greased 13x9-in. baking dish. Repeat layers. Sprinkle with paprika if desired.
4. Cover and bake for 25-30 minutes or until heated through. Let stand for 10 minutes before serving.
1 CUP: 516 cal., 17g fat (9g sat. fat), 87mg chol., 596mg sod., 53g carb. (10g sugars, 4g fiber), 37g pro.

TEXAS TOAST TURKEY MELTS

Strips of bacon and warm cheese sauce turn these open-faced sandwiches into a quick, satisfying lunch. These are just as good made with ham instead of turkey.

—*Karen Gentry, Eubank, NY*

TAKES: 10 min. • **MAKES:** 6 servings

- 6 Tbsp. butter, softened
- 6 thick slices white bread
- ½ lb. thinly sliced deli turkey
- 18 bacon strips, cooked
- 1 cup process cheese sauce

1. Butter 1 side of each slice of bread; place buttered side up on a baking sheet. Broil 5 in. from the heat for 3 minutes or until lightly toasted. Top with the turkey; broil for 2 minutes or until heated through. Top each with 3 strips of bacon.
2. Place cheese sauce in a microwave-safe dish. Microwave on high for 45 seconds; stir. Microwave 45 seconds longer or until heated through. Pour over sandwiches.
1 OPEN-FACED SANDWICH: 437 cal., 32g fat (18g sat. fat), 91mg chol., 1732mg sod., 18g carb. (2g sugars, 1g fiber), 19g pro.

TEST KITCHEN TIP
This recipe is drizzled with warm Cheez Whiz. For a bit of heat, stir in minced chipotle peppers or sprinkle sandwiches with cayenne.

MOM'S TURKEY TETRAZZINI

CHICKEN FLORENTINE CASSEROLE

CHICKEN FLORENTINE CASSEROLE

Creamy and comforting, this chicken and spinach bake is sure to be a hit at dinnertime. The toasty bread crumb topping delivers a bit of a crunch.
—*Dori Jackson, Gulf Breeze, FL*

- -

PREP: 20 min. • **BAKE:** 40 min.
MAKES: 6 servings

- 2 cups uncooked elbow macaroni
- 3 cups shredded cooked chicken
- 1 can (10¾ oz.) condensed cream of mushroom soup, undiluted
- 2 cups shredded Swiss cheese
- 1 pkg. (10 oz.) frozen creamed spinach, thawed
- ½ cup mayonnaise
- ¼ cup loosely packed minced fresh basil
- 1 tsp. garlic powder
- ½ tsp. dried thyme
- ½ tsp. pepper
- ½ cup seasoned bread crumbs
- 2 Tbsp. butter, melted

1. Preheat oven to 350°. Cook macaroni according to package directions.
2. Meanwhile, in a large bowl, combine chicken, soup, cheese, spinach, mayonnaise, basil, garlic powder, thyme and pepper.
3. Drain macaroni; gently stir into chicken mixture. Transfer to an ungreased 2½-qt. baking dish. Toss bread crumbs and butter; sprinkle over casserole.
4. Bake casserole, uncovered, 40-45 minutes or until bubbly.

1½ CUPS: 539 cal., 36g fat (13g sat. fat), 111mg chol., 1006mg sod., 17g carb. (4g sugars, 2g fiber), 36g pro.

CHICKEN VEGGIE PACKETS

CHICKEN VEGGIE PACKETS

People think I went to a lot of trouble when I serve these packets. Individual aluminum foil pouches hold the juices in during baking to keep the herbed chicken moist and tender. It saves time and makes cleanup a breeze.
—*Edna Shaffer, Beulah, MI*

- -

TAKES: 30 min. • **MAKES:** 4 servings

- 4 boneless skinless chicken breast halves (4 oz. each)
- ½ lb. sliced fresh mushrooms
- 1½ cups fresh baby carrots
- 1 cup pearl onions
- ½ cup julienned sweet red pepper
- ¼ tsp. pepper
- 3 tsp. minced fresh thyme
- ½ tsp. salt, optional
  Lemon wedges, optional

1. Flatten chicken breasts to ½-in. thickness; place each on a piece of heavy-duty foil (about 12-in. square). Layer the mushrooms, carrots, onions and red pepper over chicken; sprinkle with pepper, minced thyme and, if desired, salt.
2. Fold foil around the chicken and vegetables and seal tightly. Place on a baking sheet. Bake at 375° for 30 minutes or until chicken juices run clear. Serve with lemon wedges if desired.
1 SERVING: 175 cal., 3g fat (1g sat. fat), 63mg chol., 100mg sod., 11g carb. (6g sugars, 2g fiber), 25g pro. **DIABETIC EXCHANGES:** 3 lean meat, 2 vegetable.

Pork

BACON-WRAPPED PESTO PORK TENDERLOIN

I love to serve this favorite tenderloin—maybe because of the compliments that always come with it! When the weather warms up, we like to grill it instead.
—*Megan Riofski, Frankfort, IL*

PREP: 30 min. • **BAKE:** 20 min.
MAKES: 4 servings

- 10 bacon strips
- 1 pork tenderloin (1 lb.)
- ¼ tsp. pepper
- ⅓ cup prepared pesto
- 1 cup shredded Italian cheese blend
- 1 cup fresh baby spinach

1. Preheat oven to 425°. Arrange bacon strips lengthwise in a foil-lined 15x10x1-in. pan, overlapping slightly.
2. Cut tenderloin lengthwise through the center to within ½ in. of bottom. Open tenderloin flat and pound with a meat mallet to ½-in. thickness. Place tenderloin on center of bacon, perpendicular to strips.
3. Sprinkle pepper over pork. Spread with pesto; layer with cheese and spinach. Close tenderloin; wrap with bacon, overlapping ends. Tie with kitchen string at 3-in. intervals. Secure ends with toothpicks.
4. In a 12-in. skillet, brown roast on all sides, about 8 minutes. Return to baking pan; roast in oven until a thermometer inserted in pork reads 145°, 17-20 minutes. Remove string and toothpicks; let stand 5 minutes before slicing.
1 SERVING: 402 cal., 25g fat (9g sat. fat), 104mg chol., 864mg sod., 4g carb. (1g sugars, 1g fiber), 37g pro.

BACON-WRAPPED PESTO PORK TENDERLOIN

**PORK &
CABBAGE
POCKETS**

PORK & CABBAGE POCKETS

I like to welcome my family home on fall days to the aroma of these hearty pork pie pockets. I sometimes double the recipe so I can have leftovers for busy-day dinners.
—*Jan Smith, Kalispell, MT*

- -

PREP: 25 min. + rising • **BAKE:** 25 min.
MAKES: 8 servings

1 pkg. (¼ oz.) active dry yeast
1 cup warm water (110° to 115°)
¼ cup shortening
¼ cup sugar
1 large egg
1 tsp. salt, divided
3 to 3¾ cups all-purpose flour
1 lb. bulk pork sausage
3 cups shredded cabbage
1 medium onion, chopped
¼ cup water
1½ tsp. dried oregano
1½ tsp. ground cumin
¼ tsp. pepper
1 Tbsp. butter, melted

1. In a large bowl, dissolve yeast in water. Add shortening, sugar, egg, ½ tsp. salt and 2 cups flour; beat until smooth. Add enough remaining flour to form a soft dough. Turn onto a floured surface; knead until smooth and elastic, 6-8 minutes. Place in a greased bowl, turning once to grease top. Cover and let rise in a warm place until doubled, about 1 hour.
2. Meanwhile, in a large skillet, cook pork sausage until no longer pink; drain. Add cabbage, onion, water, oregano, cumin, pepper and remaining salt. Cook, uncovered, until vegetables are tender and no liquid remains, about 15 minutes. Cool mixture to room temperature.
3. Punch dough down. Roll into a 24x12-in. rectangle; cut into eight 6-in. squares. Spoon ⅓ cup filling into the center of each square. Bring corners to the center and pinch to seal; pinch seams together. Place on greased baking sheets. Cover and let rise 30 minutes.
4. Brush with melted butter. Bake at 375° until golden brown, 25-30 minutes.
1 POCKET: 405 cal., 19g fat (6g sat. fat), 51mg chol., 558mg sod., 47g carb. (10g sugars, 3g fiber), 11g pro.

SUNDAY SUPPER SANDWICHES

Here's a great way to put a traditional dinner on the table with very little hands-on time. You can cook the meat in a slow cooker as well. Put the ingredients in a 4-quart slow cooker, cover and cook on low for 8-10 hours or until meat is tender.
—*Elizabeth Godecke, Chicago, IL*

- -

PREP: 25 min. • **BAKE:** 2½ hours
MAKES: 8 servings

1 can (14 oz.) sauerkraut, rinsed and well drained
1 boneless pork shoulder butt roast (2½ to 3 lbs.)
½ tsp. salt
¼ tsp. pepper
¼ cup stone-ground mustard, divided
1 cup apple cider or unsweetened apple juice
¼ cup sweetened applesauce
8 slices rye bread, toasted
1 cup shredded Swiss cheese

1. Place sauerkraut in an ovenproof Dutch oven. Sprinkle pork with salt and pepper; brush with 2 Tbsp. mustard. Place over sauerkraut. Add cider and applesauce.
2. Cover and bake at 325° for 2½-3 hours or until pork is tender. Remove roast; cool slightly. Drain sauerkraut mixture; set aside. Shred pork with 2 forks.
3. Place rye toast on an ungreased baking sheet. Spread with remaining mustard. Top with pork, then sauerkraut mixture; sprinkle with cheese. Broil 4-6 in. from the heat for 2-3 minutes or until cheese is melted.
1 SANDWICH: 403 cal., 20g fat (8g sat. fat), 96mg chol., 966mg sod., 25g carb. (8g sugars, 4g fiber), 31g pro.

TEST KITCHEN TIP
Pork shoulder is a flavorful cut with plenty of fatty marbling throughout. Trim any excess fat before cooking. The meat needs a long cook time to become tender.

OLD-WORLD PORK CHOPS

Years ago, a relative ran a restaurant in downtown Milwaukee, long known for its German restaurants. This is one of the recipes she developed. The savory stuffing and juicy pork chops are always a hit.
—*Jeanne Schuyler, Wauwatosa, WI*

PREP: 15 min. • **BAKE:** 45 min.
MAKES: 4 servings

- 2 Tbsp. canola oil
- 4 bone-in pork loin chops (8 oz. each)
   Salt and pepper to taste
- 3 cups dry unseasoned bread cubes
- 1 can (14¾ oz.) cream-style corn
- 1 large egg, lightly beaten
- 1 Tbsp. grated onion
- ½ tsp. rubbed sage
- ½ tsp. dried basil
- ½ tsp. salt
- ¼ tsp. pepper

In a large skillet, heat oil over medium heat. Sprinkle pork chops with salt and pepper; brown on both sides. Meanwhile, in a bowl, combine remaining ingredients. Alternately arrange stuffing and pork chops lengthwise across a greased 3-qt. baking dish. Bake, uncovered, at 350° until a thermometer reads 145°, 45 minutes. Let stand 5 minutes before serving.

1 PORK CHOP: 591 cal., 25g fat (8g sat. fat), 158mg chol., 995mg sod., 50g carb. (6g sugars, 3g fiber), 45g pro.

TEST KITCHEN TIP
Skip dirtying your grater and cutting board with a smart substitution. Instead of grated onion, use ¼ tsp. of onion powder, or 1 tsp. of dried minced onion.

TANGY SPARERIBS

TANGY SPARERIBS

I still remember coming home from church to the smell of these ribs baking in the oven alongside baked potatoes. They have an old-fashioned homemade barbecue sauce that clings to every morsel.
—*Judy Clark, Elkhart, IN*

PREP: 30 min. • **BAKE:** 1½ hours
MAKES: 6 servings

- 4 to 5 lbs. pork spareribs
- 2 Tbsp. butter
- 1 medium onion, finely chopped
- ½ cup finely chopped celery
- 1 cup water
- 1 cup ketchup
- ⅓ cup lemon juice
- 2 Tbsp. brown sugar
- 2 Tbsp. white vinegar
- 1 Tbsp. Worcestershire sauce
- ½ tsp. ground mustard
- ⅛ tsp. pepper
- ⅛ tsp. chili powder

1. Cut ribs into serving-size pieces; place in a shallow roasting pan, bone side down. Bake, uncovered, at 350° for 45 minutes.
2. Meanwhile, in a large saucepan, heat butter over medium-high heat. Add onion and celery; cook and stir for 4-5 minutes or until tender. Stir in the remaining ingredients. Bring to a boil; reduce heat. Simmer about 10 minutes or until slightly thickened, stirring occasionally; remove from the heat.
3. Drain fat from roasting pan. Pour sauce over ribs. Bake 45-60 minutes longer or until ribs are tender.

1 SERVING: 318 cal., 17g fat (7g sat. fat), 94mg chol., 478mg sod., 15g carb. (8g sugars, 1g fiber), 27g pro.

MAPLE-GLAZED PORK TENDERLOIN

I got this recipe from a friend after we enjoyed it for dinner at their house. My husband says it tastes like a fancy restaurant dish. Maple is a terrific accent to pork tenderloin, perfect for fall veggies like squash or Brussels sprouts.
—Colleen Mercier, Salmon Arm, BC

TAKES: 30 min. • **MAKES:** 4 servings

- ¾ tsp. salt
- ¾ tsp. rubbed sage
- ½ tsp. pepper
- 2 pork tenderloins (¾ lb. each)
- 1 tsp. butter
- ¼ cup maple syrup
- 3 Tbsp. cider vinegar
- 1¾ tsp. Dijon mustard

1. Preheat oven to 425°. Mix seasonings; sprinkle over pork. In a large nonstick skillet, heat butter over medium heat; brown the tenderloins on all sides. Transfer to foil-lined 15x10x1-in. pan. Roast 10 minutes.
2. Meanwhile, for glaze, in same skillet, mix the syrup, vinegar and mustard; bring to a boil, stirring to loosen browned bits from pan. Cook and stir until slightly thickened, 1-2 minutes; remove from heat.
3. Brush 1 Tbsp. glaze over pork; continue roasting until a thermometer inserted in pork reads 145°, 7-10 minutes, brushing halfway through with remaining glaze. Let stand for 5 minutes before slicing.
5 OZ. COOKED PORK: 264 cal., 7g fat (3g sat. fat), 98mg chol., 573mg sod., 14g carb. (12g sugars, 0 fiber), 34g pro. **DIABETIC EXCHANGES:** 5 lean meat, 1 starch.

SAUSAGE LASAGNA

The idea for my sausage lasagna recipe comes from my mother-in-law, who always makes it for my three boys on special holidays. I've put my own easy twist on Carole's classic dish and it's become one of my go-to dinners as well!
—Blair Lonergan, Rochelle, VA

PREP: 45 min. • **BAKE:** 35 min. + standing
MAKES: 12 servings

- 1 lb. bulk Italian sausage
- 1 medium onion, chopped
- 2 garlic cloves, minced
- 1 can (6 oz.) tomato paste
- 1 can (28 oz.) crushed tomatoes
- 1 can (8 oz.) tomato sauce
- 3 tsp. dried basil
- ¾ tsp. pepper, divided
- ¼ tsp. salt
- 1 large egg, lightly beaten
- 1 carton (15 oz.) whole-milk ricotta cheese
- 1½ cups grated Parmesan cheese, divided
- 12 no-cook lasagna noodles
- 4 cups shredded part-skim mozzarella cheese

1. Preheat oven to 400°. In a large skillet, cook and crumble sausage with onion over medium heat until no longer pink, 5-7 minutes; drain. Add garlic and tomato paste; cook and stir 1 minute.
2. Stir in the tomatoes, tomato sauce, basil, ½ tsp. pepper and salt; bring to a boil. Reduce the heat; simmer, uncovered, until slightly thickened, 10-15 minutes.
3. In a bowl, mix egg, ricotta cheese, 1¼ cups Parmesan cheese and the remaining pepper. Spread 1½ cups meat sauce into a greased 13x9-in. baking dish. Layer with 4 noodles, 1½ cups ricotta cheese mixture, 1½ cups mozzarella cheese and 1½ cups sauce. Repeat layers. Top with remaining noodles, sauce, mozzarella and Parmesan cheeses.
4. Cover with greased foil; bake 30 minutes. Uncover; bake until lightly browned and heated through, 5-10 minutes. Let stand 15 minutes before serving.
1 PIECE: 416 cal., 23g fat (11g sat. fat), 83mg chol., 978mg sod., 29g carb. (8g sugars, 3g fiber), 25g pro.

MAPLE-GLAZED PORK TENDERLOIN

PEPPER-STUFFED PORK TENDERLOIN

PEPPER-STUFFED PORK TENDERLOIN

Our New Year's tradition includes eating black-eyed peas and collard greens for good fortune, along with this elegantly simple pork tenderloin.

—*Margaret Allen, Abingdon, VA*

- -

PREP: 40 min. • **BAKE:** 45 min. + standing
MAKES: 8 servings

- 2   Tbsp. canola oil
- 3   small sweet red peppers, finely chopped
- 1   large onion, finely chopped
- 2   small celery ribs, finely chopped
- 1½ tsp. dried thyme
- ¾   tsp. garlic salt
- ¾   tsp. paprika
- ½   tsp. cayenne pepper
- 3   pork tenderloins (¾ lb. each)
- 4   tsp. lemon-pepper seasoning
- 4   tsp. fennel seed, crushed

1. Preheat oven to 325°. In a large skillet, heat oil over medium-high heat. Add red peppers, onion and celery; saute until tender, 3-4 minutes. Add thyme, garlic salt, paprika and cayenne; saute 1 minute longer. Remove from heat; set aside.

2. Make a lengthwise slit down the center of each tenderloin to within ½ in. of bottom. Open tenderloins so they lie flat. With a meat mallet, flatten pork to ½-in. thickness. Fill with vegetable stuffing mixture. Close the tenderloins; tie at 2-in. intervals with kitchen string, securing ends with toothpicks.

3. Place on a rack in a shallow baking pan coated with cooking spray. Combine lemon pepper and fennel; rub over tenderloins.

4. Bake until a thermometer inserted into pork reads 145°, 45-55 minutes. Remove tenderloins from oven; let stand 5 minutes. Discard toothpicks and string. Cut each tenderloin into 8 slices.

3 SLICES: 201 cal., 8g fat (2g sat. fat), 71mg chol., 492mg sod., 5g carb. (2g sugars, 2g fiber), 26g pro. **DIABETIC EXCHANGES:** 4 lean meat, ½ fat.

LEMON-DIJON PORK SHEET-PAN SUPPER

Most nights, I need something on the table with minimal effort and maximum results. This sheet-pan supper has become a favorite, not only because of its bright fall flavors, but also because of its speedy cleanup time!

—*Elisabeth Larsen, Pleasant Grove, UT*

- -

PREP: 20 min. • **BAKE:** 20 min.
MAKES: 4 servings

- 4   tsp. Dijon mustard
- 2   tsp. grated lemon zest
- 1   garlic clove, minced
- ½   tsp. salt
- 2   Tbsp. canola oil
- 1½ lbs. sweet potatoes (about 3 medium), cut into ½-in. cubes
- 1   lb. fresh Brussels sprouts (about 4 cups), quartered
- 4   boneless pork loin chops (6 oz. each)
      Coarsely ground pepper, optional

1. Preheat oven to 425°. In a large bowl, mix first 4 ingredients; gradually whisk in oil. Remove 1 Tbsp. mixture for brushing pork. Add vegetables to remaining mixture; toss to coat.

2. Place pork chops and vegetables in a 15x10x1-in. pan coated with cooking spray. Brush chops with reserved mustard mixture. Roast 10 minutes.

3. Turn chops and stir vegetables; roast until a thermometer inserted in pork reads 145° and vegetables are tender, 10-15 minutes. If desired, sprinkle with pepper. Let stand 5 minutes before serving.

1 PORK CHOP WITH 1¼ CUPS VEGETABLES: 516 cal., 17g fat (4g sat. fat), 82mg chol., 505mg sod., 51g carb. (19g sugars, 9g fiber), 39g pro. **DIABETIC EXCHANGES:** 5 lean meat, 3 starch, 1½ fat, 1 vegetable.

**LEMON-DIJON PORK
SHEET-PAN SUPPER**

GREEK PORK CUTLETS

Serve succulent slices of pork rich with Mediterranean flair. The garden-fresh cucumber sauce pairs perfectly with the herb-seasoned entree.
—Taste of Home *Test Kitchen*

PREP: 15 min. + marinating • **COOK:** 15 min.
MAKES: 4 servings

- 1 pork tenderloin (1 lb.)
- 1 small onion, chopped
- 2 Tbsp. lemon juice
- 1 Tbsp. minced fresh parsley
- 2 garlic cloves, minced
- ¾ tsp. dried thyme
- ⅛ tsp. pepper

CUCUMBER SAUCE

- 1 small tomato, seeded and chopped
- ⅔ cup reduced-fat plain yogurt
- ½ cup chopped seeded cucumber
- 1 Tbsp. finely chopped onion
- ½ tsp. lemon juice
- ⅛ tsp. garlic powder

1. Cut pork into 8 slices; flatten to ½-in. thickness. In a large shallow dish, combine the onion, lemon juice, parsley, garlic, thyme and pepper. Add pork and toss to coat; cover and refrigerate for 4 hours or overnight. In a small bowl, combine the cucumber sauce ingredients. Cover and refrigerate until serving.

2. Drain pork and discard marinade. Place on a broiler pan coated with cooking spray. Broil 4 in. from the heat for 6-8 minutes on each side or until juices run clear. Serve with cucumber sauce.

1 SERVING: 177 cal., 5g fat (2g sat. fat), 66mg chol., 77mg sod., 8g carb. (5g sugars, 1g fiber), 25g pro. **DIABETIC EXCHANGES:** 3 lean meat, 1 vegetable.

DIJON-RUBBED PORK WITH RHUBARB SAUCE

This moist and tender pork loin roast is served with a rhubarb sauce that's just delicious! It's an excellent choice for company and makes a special meal.
—Marilyn Rodriguez, Sparks, NV

PREP: 15 min. • **BAKE:** 1 hour + standing
MAKES: 12 servings (1½ cups sauce)

- 1 boneless pork loin roast (3 lbs.)
- ¼ cup Dijon mustard
- 6 garlic cloves, minced
- 1 Tbsp. minced fresh rosemary or 1 tsp. dried rosemary, crushed
- ¾ tsp. salt
- ½ tsp. pepper

SAUCE

- 3 cups sliced fresh or frozen rhubarb
- ⅓ cup orange juice
- ⅓ cup sugar
- 1 Tbsp. cider vinegar

1. Score the surface of the pork, making diamond shapes ¼ in. deep. In a small bowl, combine the mustard, garlic, rosemary, salt and pepper; rub over pork.

2. Coat a roasting pan and rack with cooking spray; place seasoned pork roast on rack in pan. Bake, uncovered, at 350° for 1 hour or until a thermometer reads 145°. Let stand for 10 minutes before slicing.

3. In a small saucepan, bring the sauce ingredients to a boil. Reduce heat; cover and simmer for 8-12 minutes or until the rhubarb is tender. Serve warm with pork.

NOTE: If using frozen rhubarb, measure rhubarb while still frozen, then thaw completely. Drain in a colander, but do not press liquid out.

3 OZ. COOKED PORK: 181 cal., 6g fat (2g sat. fat), 56mg chol., 308mg sod., 9g carb. (7g sugars, 1g fiber), 23g pro. **DIABETIC EXCHANGES:** 3 lean meat, ½ starch.

DIJON-RUBBED PORK WITH RHUBARB SAUCE

PORK SPANISH RICE

HAM & SWISS-TOPPED POTATOES

This is one of husband's favorite recipes. I often double the sauce to make sure I have some left over. It reheats easily to top a microwaved potato for a quick lunch.
—*Jill Hayes, Westerville, OH*

- -

PREP: 10 min. • **BAKE:** 1¼ hours
MAKES: 6 servings

3	large baking potatoes (12 oz. each)
2	Tbsp. cornstarch
2	cups fat-free milk
1	Tbsp. Dijon mustard
½	tsp. pepper
½	cup shredded reduced-fat Swiss cheese
2	cups cubed fully cooked ham
2	cups steamed cut fresh asparagus

1. Bake potatoes at 375° for 1 hour or until tender.
2. Meanwhile, in a saucepan, combine cornstarch and milk until smooth. Bring to a boil over medium heat; cook and stir for 2 minutes or until thickened. Reduce heat; add mustard, pepper and Swiss cheese. Cook and stir until cheese is melted.
3. Add ham and asparagus; heat through. Cut potatoes in half lengthwise; place cut side up and fluff the pulp with a fork. Spoon ⅔ cup sauce over each half.
1 SERVING: 269 cal., 3g fat (1g sat. fat), 33mg chol., 692mg sod., 41g carb. (0 sugars, 5g fiber), 21g pro. **DIABETIC EXCHANGES:** 3 lean meat, 2 starch, ½ fat-free milk.

TEST KITCHEN TIP

Asparagus season runs February through June. The most tender, prized stalks have a small diameter and bits of purple on the tips. They're usually the first of the season. Since asparagus is part of the lily family, it's a perennial plant that comes back year after year.

PORK SPANISH RICE

My family wasn't fond of pork until I used it in this yummy recipe that tastes like it came from a restaurant.
—*Betty Unrau, MacGregor, MB*

- -

PREP: 20 min. • **BAKE:** 20 min.
MAKES: 4 servings

1	medium green pepper, chopped
1	small onion, chopped
2	Tbsp. butter
1	can (14½ oz.) diced tomatoes, drained
1	cup chicken broth
½	tsp. salt
¼	tsp. pepper
1¾	cups cubed cooked pork
1	cup uncooked instant rice
	Limes and minced cilantro, optional

1. In a large skillet, saute green pepper and onion in butter until tender. Stir in the tomatoes, broth, salt and pepper. Bring to a boil; stir in pork and rice.
2. Transfer to a greased 2-qt. baking dish. Cover and bake at 350° until rice is tender and liquid is absorbed, 20-25 minutes. Stir before serving. If desired, serve with lime wedges and top with minced cilantro.
1 CUP: 304 cal., 12g fat (6g sat. fat), 71mg chol., 756mg sod., 29g carb. (5g sugars, 3g fiber), 21g pro. **DIABETIC EXCHANGES:** 3 lean meat, 2 starch, 1½ fat.

DOUBLE JACK MAC

This recipe came about when I asked my two sisters what they would like to add to mac and cheese to make it special. One said pepper jack cheese and the other said black beans. I liked both of the ideas and this is the result. The black beans add color and nutrition. The pepper jack cheese adds zip and fun.
—Andrea Johnson, Freeport, IL

- -

PREP: 25 min. • **BAKE:** 25 min.
MAKES: 6 servings

- 1   lb. small pasta shells
- ¼   cup chopped onion
- ¼   cup butter, cubed
- 2   garlic cloves, minced
- ¼   cup all-purpose flour
- 2½ cups 2% milk
- 4   oz. cream cheese, cubed
- 1   cup shredded Monterey Jack cheese
- 1   cup shredded pepper jack cheese
- 1   cup shredded sharp cheddar cheese
- 1   tsp. salt
- 1   tsp. ground cumin
- ⅛   tsp. pepper
- 1   can (15 oz.) black beans, rinsed and drained
- 8   bacon strips, cooked and crumbled
- 2   Tbsp. minced fresh cilantro
- ½   cup shredded Mexican cheese blend
      Additional minced fresh cilantro

1. Cook pasta shells according to the package directions.
2. Meanwhile, in a Dutch oven, saute onion in butter. Add garlic; cook 1 minute longer. Stir in flour until blended; gradually add milk. Bring to a boil; cook and stir for 2 minutes or until thickened.
3. Add the cream cheese, Monterey Jack cheese, pepper jack cheese, cheddar cheese, salt, cumin and pepper; cook and stir until cheese is melted.
4. Drain pasta. Add beans, bacon, cilantro and pasta to cheese sauce. Transfer to a greased 13x9-in. baking dish. Sprinkle with Mexican cheese blend.
5. Bake, uncovered, at 375° until bubbly and golden brown, 25-30 minutes. Garnish with additional cilantro.
1½ CUPS: 837 cal., 41g fat (24g sat. fat), 123mg chol., 1283mg sod., 79g carb. (8g sugars, 6g fiber), 37g pro.

PLEASING POTATO PIZZA

PLEASING POTATO PIZZA

I first heard of this distinctive pizza after a friend tried it at a restaurant. It inspired me to come up with my own recipe. The way the slices disappear, there's no doubt about this pizza's potatoey goodness.
—Barbara Zimmer, Wanless, MB

- -

PREP: 30 min. • **BAKE:** 30 min.
MAKES: 8 servings

- 1   lb. bacon strips, chopped
- 1   large onion, chopped
- ½   cup chopped sweet red pepper
- 2   lbs. potatoes (about 3 large), peeled and cut into 1-in. cubes
- 1   tube (13.8 oz.) refrigerated pizza crust
- ¼   cup 2% milk
- ¼   tsp. salt
- 1½   cups shredded cheddar cheese
- 1½   cups shredded part-skim mozzarella cheese
       Minced fresh chives and sour cream, optional

1. Preheat oven to 350°. In a large skillet, cook bacon over medium heat until partially cooked but not crisp, stirring occasionally. Add onion and pepper; cook and stir until bacon is crisp. Drain well.
2. Place potatoes and water to cover in a large saucepan; bring to a boil. Reduce heat; cook, uncovered, until tender, 10-15 minutes.
3. Meanwhile, unroll and press pizza crust onto an ungreased 14-in. pizza pan; prick several times with a fork. Bake until lightly browned, about 15 minutes. Increase oven setting to 375°.
4. Drain potatoes; return to pan. Mash potatoes, gradually adding milk and salt. Spread over crust. Top with bacon mixture and cheeses.
5. Bake until cheese is melted, 15-20 minutes. If desired, sprinkle with chives and serve with sour cream.
1 SLICE: 456 cal., 22g fat (10g sat. fat), 51mg chol., 1012mg sod., 43g carb. (6g sugars, 2g fiber), 21g pro.

DOUBLE
JACK MAC

**PECAN
PORK CHOPS**

PECAN PORK CHOPS

A delicate butter and brown sugar glaze is a tasty topping for these broiled pork chops.
—Taste of Home *Test Kitchen*

- -

TAKES: 15 min. • **MAKES:** 8 servings

8	boneless pork loin chops (4 oz. each)
¼	cup packed brown sugar
2	Tbsp. cornstarch
¼	tsp. salt
⅛	tsp. ground mustard
2	Tbsp. butter, softened
2	tsp. cider vinegar
3	Tbsp. chopped pecans

1. Broil chops 4-5 in. from the heat for 4 minutes. Meanwhile, in a small bowl, combine the sugar, cornstarch, salt and mustard. Stir in the butter and vinegar until smooth.

2. Turn chops over and broil for 2 minutes longer. Spoon about 2 tsp. sugar mixture over top of each chop. Broil 2-3 minutes longer or until a thermometer reads 145°. Top each chop with 1 tsp. pecans. Broil until pecans are toasted, about 1 minute longer. Let stand for 5 minutes before serving.

1 PORK CHOP: 229 cal., 11g fat (4g sat. fat), 62mg chol., 130mg sod., 9g carb. (7g sugars, 0 fiber), 22g pro.

HERBED PORK ROAST

This recipe deliciously proves that pork roasts don't have to be loaded with fat and calories to be satisfying. Even folks not on restricted diets will find this roast appealing.
—*Dianne Bettin, Truman, MN*

- -

PREP: 5 min. • **BAKE:** 1 hour + standing
MAKES: 6 servings

3	Tbsp. finely chopped fresh parsley, divided
2	tsp. paprika
2	tsp. dried basil
1½	tsp. salt
1	tsp. pepper
1	tsp. garlic powder
1	tsp. dried oregano
½	tsp. crushed fennel seed
½	tsp. dried thyme
1	boneless pork loin roast (2 lbs.)

Combine half the parsley with the herb and seasonings. Rub over roast. Place in shallow pan; cover with remaining parsley. Roast, uncovered, at 325° until a thermometer reads 145°, 60-70 minutes. Remove roast from oven; tent with foil. Let stand for 10 minutes before slicing.

4 OZ. COOKED PORK: 195 cal., 7g fat (3g sat. fat), 75mg chol., 636mg sod., 2g carb. (0 sugars, 1g fiber), 30g pro. **DIABETIC EXCHANGES:** 4 lean meat.

PINEAPPLE HAM CASSEROLE

Living in Hawaii, I wanted to share a recipe which features pineapple. It's our most important fruit crop, and it really shines in this dish.
—*Marsha Fleming, Kula, HI*

- -

PREP: 15 min. • **BAKE:** 30 min.
MAKES: 4 servings

- 2 cups uncooked wide egg noodles
- ½ cup chopped celery
- 2 Tbsp. butter, divided
- 1 pkg. (8 oz.) cream cheese, cubed
- ¾ cup whole milk
- 2 cups cubed fully cooked ham
- 2 cans (8 oz. each) crushed pineapple, drained
- 2 tsp. Worcestershire sauce
- ½ tsp. salt
  Dash pepper
- ¼ cup dry bread crumbs

1. Cook egg noodles according to package directions; drain. In a large skillet, saute celery in 1 Tbsp. butter until tender. Stir in cream cheese and milk; cook and stir until cheese is melted. Add the noodles, ham, pineapple, Worcestershire sauce, salt and pepper.
2. Transfer to an ungreased 1½-qt. baking dish. Melt remaining 1 Tbsp. butter; toss with bread crumbs. Sprinkle over the top. Bake, uncovered, at 350° for 30-35 minutes or until heated through.
1 SERVING: 527 cal., 34g fat (19g sat. fat), 139mg chol., 1541mg sod., 34g carb. (11g sugars, 1g fiber), 22g pro.

ZUCCHINI PORK CHOP SUPPER

My mom gave me a recipe for zucchini casserole and I added the meat because I was trying to make a one-dish supper. I look forward to fresh zucchini now.
—*Linda Martin, Rhinebeck, NY*

- -

PREP: 20 min. • **BAKE:** 1 hour
MAKES: 6 servings

- 1 pkg. (14 oz.) seasoned cubed stuffing mix, divided
- ¼ cup butter, melted
- 2 lbs. zucchini, cut into ½-in. pieces
- ½ cup grated carrots
- 1 can (10½ oz.) condensed cream of celery soup, undiluted
- ½ cup whole milk
- 1 cup sour cream
- 1 Tbsp. chopped fresh parsley or 1 tsp. dried parsley flakes
- ½ tsp. pepper
- 6 pork loin chops (1 in. thick and 8 oz. each)
  Water or additional milk

1. In a large bowl, combine two-thirds of the stuffing mix with butter; place half in a greased 13x9-in. baking dish. In another large bowl, combine the zucchini, carrots, soup, milk, sour cream, parsley and pepper; spoon over stuffing. Sprinkle remaining buttered stuffing on top.
2. Crush remaining stuffing mix; place in a shallow bowl. Place water or milk in another shallow bowl. Dip pork chops in water or milk, then roll in stuffing crumbs.
3. Place pork on top of stuffing mixture. Bake, uncovered, at 350° for 1 hour or until pork chops are tender.
1 SERVING: 559 cal., 27g fat (12g sat. fat), 70mg chol., 1583mg sod., 57g carb. (13g sugars, 4g fiber), 18g pro.

PINEAPPLE HAM CASSEROLE

GLAZED SMOKED CHOPS WITH PEARS

GLAZED SMOKED CHOPS WITH PEARS

My husband would eat pork chops every day if he could. Luckily, they're good all sorts of ways, including with pears.
—*Lynn Moretti, Oconomowoc, WI*

TAKES: 30 min. • **MAKES:** 4 servings

- 4   smoked boneless pork chops
- 1   Tbsp. olive oil
- 1   large sweet onion, cut into thin wedges
- ½   cup dry red wine or reduced-sodium chicken broth
- 2   Tbsp. balsamic vinegar
- 2   Tbsp. honey
- 2   large ripe pears, cut into 1-in. wedges

1. Preheat oven to 350°. In an ovenproof skillet over medium-high heat, brown pork chops on both sides; remove from pan.
2. In same pan, heat oil over medium heat; saute onion until tender, 3-5 minutes. Add the wine, vinegar and honey; bring to a boil, stirring to loosen browned bits from pan. Reduce heat; simmer, uncovered, until glaze is slightly thickened, about 5 minutes, stirring occasionally.
3. Return pork chops to pan; top with pears. Transfer to oven; bake until pears are tender, 10-15 minutes.
1 SERVING: 313 cal., 4g fat (6g sat. fat), 41mg chol., 1056mg sod., 34g carb. (26g sugars, 4g fiber), 22g pro.

TEST KITCHEN TIP
Sweet onions are typically available in just the spring and summer months. Some South American varieties, such as the Oso Sweet, arrive in large North American markets in winter. If you can't find sweet onions such as Vidalia (from Georgia), Walla Walla (from Washington) or Hawaii's Maui onion, red onion is always a good substitute.

BAKED LASAGNA ROLL-UPS

BAKED LASAGNA ROLL-UPS

Move over, store-bought lasagna. Ham and spinach combine here for absolutely fabulous flavor.
—*Delia Kennedy, Deer Park, WA*

PREP: 20 min. • **BAKE:** 40 min. + standing
MAKES: 4 servings

- 1   pkg. (10 oz.) frozen spinach, thawed and squeezed dry
- 1   large egg, beaten
- 1¾ cups ricotta cheese
- 4   Tbsp. grated Parmesan cheese, divided
- ½   tsp. salt
- ¼   tsp. pepper
- ⅛   tsp. ground nutmeg
- 8   thin slices deli ham, halved lengthwise
- 8   lasagna noodles, cooked and drained
- 1   jar (14 oz.) spaghetti sauce

1. In a bowl, combine the spinach, egg, ricotta cheese, 2 Tbsp. Parmesan cheese, salt, pepper and nutmeg. Place 2 pieces of ham on each noodle. Spread with ⅓ cup spinach mixture. Roll up and place seam side down in a greased 13 x9-in. baking dish. Top with spaghetti sauce.
2. Cover and bake at 350° for 40-45 minutes or until heated through. Uncover; sprinkle with remaining Parmesan. Let stand for 15 minutes before cutting.
2 ROLL-UPS: 710 cal., 31g fat (14g sat. fat), 181mg chol., 3047mg sod., 57g carb. (14g sugars, 5g fiber), 53g pro.

DIJON PORK CHOPS WITH CABBAGE & FENNEL

While living in Switzerland for a few years, I discovered an area renowned for its cabbage, pork and potato dishes. I decided to try a cabbage-fennel combination and believe they complement each other well. The juniper berries are a special addition that I learned after many years of cooking this recipe.
—*Grace Voltolina, Westport, CT*

- -

PREP: 35 min. • **BAKE:** 55 min.
MAKES: 6 servings

- 1 small head green cabbage (about 1½ lbs.)
- 1 small head red cabbage (about 1½ lbs.)
- 4 Tbsp. whole grain Dijon mustard, divided
- 2 Tbsp. light brown sugar
- 3 tsp. kosher salt, divided
- 2½ tsp. pepper, divided
- 3 cups chicken stock
- 2 Tbsp. olive oil, divided
- 1 large onion, halved and thinly sliced
- 4 garlic cloves, thinly sliced
- 3 large Granny Smith apples, quartered
- 1 fennel bulb, cored and cut into ¼-in. slices
- 3 tsp. rubbed sage
- 6 center-cut pork rib chops (1 in. thick and 8 oz. each)
- 2 Tbsp. all-purpose flour

1. Preheat oven to 375°. Core cabbages and cut each into 6 wedges. In a bowl, mix 2 Tbsp. mustard, brown sugar, 1½ tsp. salt, 1 tsp. pepper and stock.
2. In a large Dutch oven, heat 1 Tbsp. oil over medium-high heat; saute onion until lightly browned, 4-6 minutes. Add garlic; cook and stir 1 minute. Remove from heat; add apples, fennel and cabbage. Pour mustard mixture over top. Bake, covered, until cabbage is tender, 45-60 minutes.
3. Meanwhile, mix sage and the remaining salt and pepper; rub onto both sides of chops. Dust with flour; shake off excess. In a large skillet, heat the remaining oil over medium-high heat. Brown chops in batches, 4-6 minutes per side; remove from pan.
4. Spread tops of pork chops with the remaining mustard; place over vegetables in Dutch oven. Bake, uncovered, until a thermometer inserted in pork reads 145°, 8-10 minutes.

1 PORK CHOP WITH 2 CUPS VEGETABLES:
435 cal., 16g fat (5g sat. fat), 72mg chol., 1533mg sod., 42g carb. (25g sugars, 10g fiber), 36g pro.

HOISIN PORK TENDERLOIN

Ramen noodles graduate from college-casual when served with saucy pork tenderloin. Our guests appreciate sitting down to this Asian-style meal.
—*Connie Keller, Lake Ozark, MO*

- -

TAKES: 30 min. • **MAKES:** 4 servings

- ⅓ cup hoisin sauce
- 3 Tbsp. reduced-sodium soy sauce
- 3 Tbsp. sugar
- 3 garlic cloves, minced
  Dash crushed red pepper flakes
- 1 pork tenderloin (1 lb.)
- ¼ cup water
- 2 Tbsp. butter
- 2 pkg. (3 oz. each) ramen noodles or 2 cups hot cooked rice
  Sliced green onions

1. Preheat oven to 475°. Off the heat, mix first 5 ingredients in a small saucepan. Place tenderloin on a greased rack in a foil-lined 15x10x1-in. pan; brush with ¼ cup hoisin mixture. Roast until a thermometer reads 145°, 15-20 minutes.
2. Stir water into remaining hoisin mixture; bring to a boil. Reduce the heat; simmer, uncovered, to allow flavors to blend, about 5 minutes, stirring occasionally. Remove from heat; stir in butter. Keep warm.
3. Remove pork tenderloin from oven; let stand 5 minutes before slicing. Cook noodles according to package directions, omitting seasoning packets; drain. Serve with pork; top with sauce and green onions.

3 OZ. COOKED PORK WITH ½ CUP NOODLES AND 2 TBSP. SAUCE: 458 cal., 17g fat (9g sat. fat), 80mg chol., 1010mg sod., 45g carb. (15g sugars, 1g fiber), 28g pro.

HOISIN PORK TENDERLOIN

HAWAIIAN PORK ROAST

HAWAIIAN PORK ROAST

Bananas, liquid smoke and soy sauce flavor this fall-apart-tender pork roast just like the specialty I enjoyed so much at the luaus I went to in Hawaii.
—*Mary Gaylord, Balsam Lake, WI*

- -

PREP: 10 min. + marinating • **BAKE:** 4½ hours
MAKES: 10 servings

- 1 boneless pork shoulder
  butt roast (3 to 4 lbs.)
- 4 tsp. liquid smoke
- 4 tsp. soy sauce
- 2 unpeeled ripe bananas
- ½ cup water

1. Place the roast on a 22x18-in. piece of heavy-duty foil; sprinkle with liquid smoke and soy sauce. Wash bananas and place at the base of each side of roast. Pull sides of foil up round meat; add water. Seal foil tightly; wrap again with another large piece of foil. Place in a shallow baking pan; refrigerate overnight, turning several times.
2. Place foil-wrapped meat in a roasting pan. Bake at 400° for 1 hour. Reduce heat to 325°; continue baking for 3½ hours. Drain; discard bananas and liquid. Shred meat with a fork.
FREEZE OPTION: Freeze cooled meat with some of the cooking juices in freezer containers. To use, partially thaw in the refrigerator overnight. Heat through in a saucepan, stirring occasionally and adding a little water if necessary.
3 OZ. COOKED PORK: 222 cal., 14g fat (5g sat. fat), 81mg chol., 207mg sod., 0 carb. (0 sugars, 0 fiber), 23g pro.

WILD RICE HAM ROLLS

Need a simple buffet or brunch entree? Roll up these individual portions and let guests serve themselves. It's equally simple to put it together ahead of time.
—*Becky Carcich, Littleton, CO*

- -

PREP: 15 min. • **BAKE:** 25 min.
MAKES: 12 servings

- 1 medium onion, chopped
- ½ cup butter
- ½ cup all-purpose flour
- 1 tsp. dill weed
- ½ tsp. garlic salt
- ½ tsp. pepper
- 1 can (14½ oz.) chicken broth
- 1½ cups half-and-half cream
- 1 Tbsp. Dijon mustard
- 3 cups cooked wild rice
- 1 can (8 oz.) mushroom stems
  and pieces, drained
- 12 thin slices fully cooked
  ham (about ¾ lb.)
- ½ cup shredded cheddar cheese
  Minced fresh parsley

1. In a large saucepan, saute onion in butter until tender. Stir in flour, dill, garlic salt and pepper until smooth and bubbly. Gradually add the broth, cream and mustard; cook until thickened.
2. Pour 1 cup into an ungreased 13x9-in. baking pan; reserve another cup for topping. To the remaining sauce, add wild rice and mushrooms; spoon ⅓ cup onto each ham slice. Roll up and place with seam side down over sauce in pan. Top with reserved sauce.
3. Bake, uncovered, at 350° until heated through, 25-30 minutes. Sprinkle with cheese and parsley; serve immediately.
1 ROLL: 227 cal., 13g fat (8g sat. fat), 53mg chol., 688mg sod., 16g carb. (3g sugars, 1g fiber), 10g pro.

Fish & Seafood

**KOREAN SALMON
SKEWERS WITH RICE SLAW**

KOREAN SALMON SKEWERS WITH RICE SLAW

This easy dinner is light and lovely, with so many delicious flavors and textures in one stunning dish. It's so impressive that I often serve it to guests.
—*Janice Elder, Charlotte, NC*

TAKES: 30 min. • **MAKES:** 4 servings

- 1 can (20 oz.) unsweetened pineapple chunks
- 3 Tbsp. honey
- 2 Tbsp. gochujang (Korean red pepper paste), divided
- 2 cups broccoli coleslaw mix
- 2 cups hot cooked brown rice
- ¼ cup dried cranberries
- ¼ cup slivered almonds, toasted
- 1 lb. salmon fillet, skin removed, cut into 1-in. cubes

1. Preheat broiler. Drain pineapple chunks, reserving juice. For glaze, whisk together honey, 1 Tbsp. gochujang and ½ cup of the pineapple juice. For slaw, mix the remaining pineapple juice and gochujang until smooth; toss with coleslaw mix, rice, cranberries and almonds. Let stand, covered, until serving.
2. On metal or soaked wooden skewers, alternately thread salmon and pineapple chunks. Place on a foil-lined 15x10x1-in. pan.
3. Broil kabobs 4-5 in. from heat until fish just begins to flake easily with a fork, 5-6 minutes; brush frequently with glaze during the last 2 minutes. Brush the kabobs with remaining glaze; serve with slaw.
1 SERVING: 533 cal., 15g fat (3g sat. fat), 57mg chol., 310mg sod., 74g carb. (42g sugars, 6g fiber), 26g pro.

BAKED TILAPIA

SOY-GLAZED SCALLOPS

Two thumbs-ups for scallops—an amazing dinner option and an excellent source of vitamin B-12 and heart-healthy minerals such as magnesium.
—*April Korando, Ava, IL*

- -

PREP: 25 min. + marinating • **BROIL:** 5 min.
MAKES: 4 servings

¼ cup lemon juice
2 Tbsp. canola oil
2 Tbsp. reduced-sodium soy sauce
2 Tbsp. honey
2 garlic cloves, minced
½ tsp. ground ginger
12 sea scallops (about 1½ lbs.)

1. In a small bowl, combine the first 6 ingredients. Pour ⅓ cup marinade into a bowl or dish. Add the scallops and turn to coat. Cover and refrigerate 20 minutes.
2. Place remaining marinade in a small saucepan. Bring to a boil. Reduce heat; simmer, uncovered, for 8-10 minutes or until slightly thickened.
3. Drain and discard marinade. Thread scallops onto 4 metal or soaked wooden skewers. Broil 4 in. from the heat for 2-4 minutes on each side or until scallops are firm and opaque, basting occasionally with remaining marinade.
3 SCALLOPS: 250 cal., 8g fat (1g sat. fat), 54mg chol., 567mg sod., 15g carb. (9g sugars, 0 fiber), 28g pro. **DIABETIC EXCHANGES:** 4 lean meat, 1 fat, ½ starch.

BAKED TILAPIA

I've decided to cook healthier for my family, and that includes having more fish at home. This is a tasty recipe, and it's fast, too!
—*Hope Stewart, Raleigh, NC*

- -

TAKES: 20 min. • **MAKES:** 4 servings

4 tilapia fillets (6 oz. each)
3 Tbsp. butter, melted
3 Tbsp. lemon juice
1½ tsp. garlic powder
⅛ tsp. salt
2 Tbsp. capers, drained
½ tsp. dried oregano
⅛ tsp. paprika

1. Place tilapia in an ungreased 13x9-in. baking dish. In a small bowl, combine the butter, lemon juice, garlic powder and salt; pour over the fillets. Sprinkle with capers, oregano and paprika.
2. Bake, uncovered, at 425° for 10-15 minutes or until fish flakes easily with a fork.
1 FILLET: 224 cal., 10g fat (6g sat. fat), 106mg chol., 304mg sod., 2g carb. (0 sugars, 0 fiber), 32g pro.

DID YOU KNOW?

Capers are the flower buds of a small bush from the Mediterranean and Middle East. The smallest capers, French nonpareils, are considered the finest. Caper berries, from Spain, are the olive-size fruit of the caper shrub. Rinse capers well before using to remove excess salt.

BAKED LOBSTER TAILS

Lobster tails always make a rich and special entree, especially when served alongside steak. In this recipe, three lobster tails are cut in half to serve six people. Here's a good, simple dish to break out for New Year's Eve or Mother's Day.
—Taste of Home *Test Kitchen*

PREP: 15 min. • **BAKE:** 20 min.
MAKES: 6 servings

- 3 lobster tails (8 to 10 oz. each)
- 1 cup water
- 1 Tbsp. minced fresh parsley
- ⅛ tsp. salt
  Dash pepper
- 1 Tbsp. butter, melted
- 2 Tbsp. lemon juice
  Lemon wedges and additional melted butter, optional

1. Split lobster tails in half lengthwise. With cut side up and using scissors, cut along the edge of shell to loosen the cartilage covering the tail meat from the shell; remove and discard cartilage.

2. Pour water into a 13x9-in. baking dish; place lobster tails in dish. Combine parsley, salt and pepper; sprinkle over lobster. Drizzle with butter and lemon juice.

3. Bake, uncovered, at 375° until meat is firm and opaque, 20-25 minutes. Serve with lemon wedges and melted butter if desired.

1 SERVING: 120 cal., 3g fat (1g sat. fat), 113mg chol., 405mg sod., 1g carb. (0 sugars, 0 fiber), 21g pro. **DIABETIC EXCHANGES:** 3 very lean meat, ½ fat.

DAD'S FAMOUS STUFFIES

The third of July is almost as important as the Fourth in my family. We make these stuffed clams on the third every year, and it's an event in and of itself!
—*Karen Barros, Bristol, RI*

PREP: 1¼ hours • **BAKE:** 20 min.
MAKES: 10 servings (3 clams each)

- 20 fresh large quahog clams (about 10 lbs.)
- 1 lb. hot chourico or linguica (smoked Portuguese sausage) or fully cooked Spanish chorizo

DAD'S FAMOUS STUFFIES

- 1 large onion, chopped (about 2 cups)
- 3 tsp. seafood seasoning
- 1 pkg. (14 oz.) herb stuffing cubes
- 1 cup water
  Lemon wedges, optional
  Hot pepper sauce, optional

1. Add 2 in. of water to a stockpot. Add clams and chourico; bring to a boil. Cover and steam 15-20 minutes or until clams open.

2. Remove clams and sausage from pot, reserving 2 cups cooking liquid; cool slightly. Discard any unopened clams.

3. Preheat oven to 350°. Remove clam meat from shells. Separate shells; reserve 30 half shells for stuffing. Place clam meat in a food processor; process until finely chopped. Transfer to a large bowl.

4. Remove casings from sausage; cut sausage into 1½-in. pieces. Place in a food processor; process until finely chopped. Add sausage, onion and seafood seasoning to chopped clams. Stir in stuffing cubes. Add reserved

cooking liquid and enough water to reach desired moistness, about 1 cup.

5. Spoon clam mixture into reserved shells. Place in 15x10x1-in. baking pans. Bake until heated through, 15-20 minutes. Preheat the broiler.

6. Broil clams 4-6 in. from heat 4-5 minutes or until golden brown. If desired, serve with lemon wedges and pepper sauce.

FREEZE OPTION: Cover and freeze unbaked stuffed clams in a 15x10x1-in. baking pan until firm. Transfer to freezer containers; return to freezer. To use, place 3 stuffed clams on a microwave-safe plate. Cover with a paper towel; microwave on high until heated through, 3-4 minutes. Serve as directed.

NOTE: Hot chourico is available from *michaelsprovision.com* and *gasparssausage.com.*

3 STUFFED CLAMS: 296 cal., 11g fat (3g sat. fat), 71mg chol., 1188mg sod., 34g carb. (3g sugars, 2g fiber), 18g pro.

HOMEMADE FISH STICKS

I'm a nutritionist and needed a healthy fish fix. Moist inside and crunchy outside, these are great with oven fries or roasted veggies and low-fat homemade tartar sauce.
—*Jennifer Rowland, Elizabethtown, KY*

- -

TAKES: 25 min. • **MAKES:** 2 servings

- ½ cup dry bread crumbs
- ½ tsp. salt
- ½ tsp. paprika
- ½ tsp. lemon-pepper seasoning
- ½ cup all-purpose flour
- 1 large egg, beaten
- ¾ lb. cod fillets, cut into 1-in. strips
   Butter-flavored cooking spray

1. Preheat oven to 400°. In a shallow bowl, mix bread crumbs and seasonings. Place flour and egg in separate shallow bowls. Dip fish in flour to coat both sides; shake off excess. Dip in egg, then in crumb mixture, patting to help coating adhere.

2. Place on a baking sheet coated with cooking spray; spritz with butter-flavored cooking spray. Bake 10-12 minutes or until fish just begins to flake easily with a fork, turning once.

1 SERVING: 278 cal., 4g fat (1g sat. fat), 129mg chol., 718mg sod., 25g carb. (2g sugars, 1g fiber), 33g pro. **DIABETIC EXCHANGES:** 4 lean meat, 1½ starch.

ZIPPY TOMATO-TOPPED SNAPPER

Seafood fans will be delighted with this pleasantly zesty entree for two. Serve the fish fillets with a salad and baked potato, and it's a balanced, healthy meal.
—*Mary Anne Zimmerman, Silver Springs, FL*

- -

PREP: 10 min. • **BAKE:** 25 min.
MAKES: 2 servings

- 1 red snapper fillet (¾ lb.), cut in half
- ¾ tsp. lemon-pepper seasoning
- ⅛ tsp. salt
- ½ cup canned diced tomatoes and green chiles
- 2 Tbsp. chopped onion
- 2 Tbsp. chopped celery
- 1 Tbsp. minced fresh parsley
- ⅛ tsp. celery seed

1. Sprinkle both sides of red snapper with lemon-pepper and salt. Place in a greased 11x7-in. baking dish.

2. Combine the tomatoes, onion, celery, parsley and celery seed; spoon over snapper.

3. Cover and bake at 350° for 25-30 minutes or until fish flakes easily with a fork.

1 SERVING: 179 cal., 2g fat (0 sat. fat), 60mg chol., 643mg sod., 4g carb. (1g sugars, 1g fiber), 34g pro. **DIABETIC EXCHANGES:** 5 lean meat.

DID YOU KNOW?

You can keep parsley and cilantro fresh for up to a month with the following technique. Trim the stems with sharp kitchen scissors and place the herb bunch in a short tumbler containing an inch or two of water. Remove any loose leaves so only the stems (and no greenery) are in contact with the water. Loosely tie a produce bag around the tumbler to trap humidity around the leaves and pop the tumbler in the fridge. Each time you use the herbs, change the water. Turn the produce bag inside out so any excess moisture that has built up inside of the bag can evaporate.

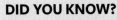

HOMEMADE FISH STICKS

GREEK TILAPIA

GREEK TILAPIA

While on a trip through the Greek islands, my husband and I had a dish that we loved. I tried to duplicate it by combining several different recipes and came up with this.
—Sally Jean Burrell, Idaho Falls, ID

PREP: 30 min. • **BAKE:** 10 min.
MAKES: 4 servings

- 4   tilapia fillets (4 oz. each)
- 4   tsp. butter
- 1   large egg
- ¾   cup crumbled tomato and basil feta cheese
- ¼   cup fat-free milk
- ¼   tsp. cayenne pepper
- 1   large tomato, seeded and chopped
- ¼   cup chopped ripe olives
- ¼   cup pine nuts, toasted
- 1   Tbsp. minced fresh parsley
- 1   Tbsp. lemon juice
- ⅛   tsp. pepper

1. In a large cast-iron or other ovenproof skillet, brown tilapia fillets in butter.
2. In a small bowl, combine the egg, cheese, milk and cayenne; spoon over fish. Sprinkle with tomato, olives and toasted pine nuts. Bake, uncovered, at 425° until fish just begins to flake easily with a fork, 10-15 minutes.
3. In a small bowl, combine parsley, lemon juice and pepper; drizzle over fish.
1 FILLET: 279 cal., 16g fat (6g sat. fat), 123mg chol., 362mg sod., 5g carb. (2g sugars, 2g fiber), 29g pro.

"First saw this recipe in Taste of Home *magazine. Made it and loved it! It's so easy and full of flavor. Even my husband went back for seconds! I used toasted almonds instead of pine nuts. Have made it twice already and added it to my favorites. Also a great recipe for those on the South Beach Diet."*
—WRITER2, TASTEOFHOME.COM

SHRIMP & CRAB CASSEROLE

SHRIMP & CRAB CASSEROLE

This quick, easy recipe is truly delicious. The succulent, melt-in-your-mouth seafood flavors and textures make for elegant comfort food. To make ahead, just assemble, cover and refrigerate, then bake when ready.
—Jan Bartley, Evergreen, NC

PREP: 25 min. • **BAKE:** 40 min.
MAKES: 8 servings

- 2   pkg. (8.8 oz. each) ready-to-serve long grain and wild rice
- ¼   cup butter, cubed
- 2   celery ribs, chopped
- 1   medium onion, chopped
- 3   Tbsp. all-purpose flour
- 1½ cups half-and-half cream
- 1   tsp. seafood seasoning
- ¾   tsp. salt
- ½   tsp. hot pepper sauce
- ¼   tsp. pepper
- 1½ lbs. uncooked shrimp (31-40 per lb.), peeled and deveined
- 2   cans (6 oz. each) lump crabmeat, drained
- 1   cup shredded Colby-Monterey Jack cheese

1. Preheat oven to 350°. Spread rice into a greased 13x9-in. baking dish. In a large skillet, heat butter over medium-high heat. Add the celery and onion; cook and stir until tender, 6-8 minutes. Stir in flour until blended; gradually whisk in cream. Bring to a boil, stirring constantly; cook and stir until thickened, 1-2 minutes.
2. Stir in seafood seasoning, salt, pepper sauce and pepper. Fold in shrimp and crab. Spoon over rice. Sprinkle with shredded cheese. Bake, covered until shrimp turn pink, 40-45 minutes. Let stand 5 minutes.
To Make Ahead: Prepare recipe as directed, cooling sauce slightly before adding shrimp and crab. Cover and refrigerate overnight. Remove from the refrigerator 30 minutes before baking. Bake as directed.
1 SERVING: 376 cal., 17g fat (10g sat. fat), 195mg chol., 1127mg sod., 24g carb. (3g sugars, 1g fiber), 29g pro.

CHEESY SEAFOOD ENCHILADAS

Quick-cooking seafood and mildly spicy chile peppers and salsa make this dish a flavor adventure that my family loves. I've made it with chicken instead of fish, too. Just saute until done.
—Trisha Kruse, Eagle, ID

- -

PREP: 30 min. • **BAKE:** 20 min.
MAKES: 6 servings

- 1 Tbsp. butter
- 1 small onion, chopped
- ½ lb. uncooked shrimp (31-40 per lb.), peeled, deveined and chopped
- ½ lb. red snapper fillet or other firm white fish, cut into 1-in. chunks
- 1½ cups salsa verde
- 1 pkg. (8 oz.) cream cheese, cubed
- 1 can (4 oz.) chopped green chiles
- ½ tsp. salt
- 2 cups shredded Monterey Jack cheese, divided
- 12 corn tortillas (6 in.)
     Fresh cilantro leaves or jalapeno pepper slices

1. Preheat oven to 350°. In a large skillet, heat butter over medium-high heat. Add onion; cook and stir until crisp-tender, 3-4 minutes. Add shrimp and snapper; cook until shrimp turn pink, 5-7 minutes. Remove from pan.
2. In the same pan, cook and stir salsa, cream cheese, chiles and salt over medium heat just until cream cheese is melted. Stir in 1 cup shredded cheese; remove from heat.
3. Spread 1 cup cheese sauce into a greased 13x9-in. baking dish. Gently stir remaining cheese sauce into shrimp mixture. Place ⅓ cup shrimp mixture off center on each tortilla. Roll up and place in prepared dish, seam side down. Sprinkle with remaining shredded cheese.

4. Cover and bake until heated through and cheese is melted, 20-25 minutes. Sprinkle with cilantro before serving.
2 ENCHILADAS: 481 cal., 29g fat (16g sat. fat), 136mg chol., 1055mg sod., 30g carb. (5g sugars, 4g fiber), 28g pro.

🍎

CRUMB-TOPPED SOLE

Looking for a low-carb supper that's ready in a pinch? Then this buttery sole entree is for you! The moist fillets are covered with golden bread crumbs and topped with a rich sauce.
—Taste of Home *Test Kitchen*

- -

TAKES: 15 min. • **MAKES:** 4 servings

- 3 Tbsp. reduced-fat mayonnaise
- 3 Tbsp. grated Parmesan cheese, divided
- 2 tsp. mustard seed
- ¼ tsp. pepper
- 4 sole fillets (6 oz. each)
- 1 cup soft bread crumbs
- 1 green onion, finely chopped
- ½ tsp. ground mustard
- 2 tsp. butter, melted
     Thinly sliced green onions, optional

1. Combine the mayonnaise, 2 Tbsp. cheese, mustard seed and pepper; spread over tops of fillets. Place on a broiler pan coated with cooking spray. Broil 4 in. from the heat until fish flakes easily with a fork, 3-5 minutes.
2. Meanwhile, in a small bowl, combine the bread crumbs, onion, ground mustard and remaining cheese; stir in butter. Spoon over the fillets; spritz topping with cooking spray. Broil until golden brown, 1-2 minutes longer. Sprinkle with green onions, if desired.
1 FILLET: 267 cal., 10g fat (3g sat. fat), 94mg chol., 378mg sod., 8g carb. (1g sugars, 1g fiber), 35g pro. **DIABETIC EXCHANGES:** 5 lean meat, 1 fat, ½ starch.

CRUMB-TOPPED SOLE

HERBED SEAFOOD CASSEROLE

HERBED SEAFOOD CASSEROLE

When I wanted a seafood dish for my annual Christmas Eve buffet, my friend gave me a wonderful recipe. It's a rich, creamy casserole loaded with shrimp, scallops and crab.
—Donna Schmuland, Wetaskiwin, AB

- -

PREP: 40 min. • **BAKE:** 50 min. + standing
MAKES: 12 servings

1½ cups uncooked long grain rice
2 Tbsp. butter
3 celery ribs, thinly sliced
1 medium onion, finely chopped
1 medium carrot, shredded
3 garlic cloves, minced
½ tsp. salt
¼ tsp. pepper
2 Tbsp. minced fresh parsley
1½ tsp. snipped fresh dill
or ½ tsp. dill weed
SEAFOOD
1 lb. uncooked medium shrimp, peeled and deveined
1 lb. bay scallops
1 can (16 oz.) crabmeat, drained, flaked and cartilage removed
5 Tbsp. butter, cubed
¼ cup all-purpose flour
1½ cups half-and-half cream
1 pkg. (8 oz.) cream cheese, cubed
1½ tsp. snipped fresh dill
or ½ tsp. dill weed
½ tsp. salt
¼ tsp. pepper
¼ tsp. dried thyme
TOPPING
1½ cups soft bread crumbs
2 Tbsp. butter, melted

1. Preheat oven to 325°. Cook rice according to package directions. Meanwhile, in a large skillet, heat butter over medium-high heat. Add celery, onion and carrot; cook and stir until crisp-tender. Add garlic, salt and pepper; cook 1 minute longer.
2. Add to cooked rice. Stir in parsley and dill. Transfer to a greased 13x9-in. baking dish.
3. Fill a large saucepan two-thirds full with water; bring to a boil. Reduce heat to medium. Add shrimp; simmer, uncovered, 30 seconds. Add scallops; cook 2-3 minutes longer or just until shrimp turn pink and scallops are firm and opaque. Drain cooking liquid, reserving 1 cup. Place seafood in a large bowl; stir in crab.
4. In a small saucepan, melt butter over medium heat. Stir in flour until blended; gradually stir in cream and reserved cooking liquid. Bring to a boil; cook and stir 2 minutes or until thickened and bubbly. Reduce heat. Stir in cream cheese, dill and seasonings until smooth. Stir into seafood mixture.
5. Pour over rice mixture. Toss bread crumbs with melted butter; sprinkle over top. Bake, uncovered, 50-55 minutes or until golden brown. Let stand 10 minutes before serving.
1 CUP: 404 cal., 20g fat (12g sat. fat), 150mg chol., 616mg sod., 29g carb. (3g sugars, 1g fiber), 26g pro.

GARLIC-LIME SEA BASS

I was a chef on a dive boat, and this was one of my favorite ways to serve our fresh catch.
—Peg Nelson, Islamorada, FL

- -

PREP: 45 min. • **BAKE:** 30 min.
MAKES: 4 servings

1 whole garlic bulb
1 tsp. olive oil
¼ cup butter, cubed
1 large onion, chopped
2 to 3 Tbsp. lime juice
1 Tbsp. spicy brown mustard
¼ tsp. salt
¼ tsp. pepper
4 sea bass or grouper fillets (8 oz. each)

1. Remove the papery outer skin from garlic (do not peel or separate cloves). Cut top off of bulb. Brush with oil. Wrap in heavy-duty foil. Bake at 425° for 30-35 minutes or until softened. Cool for 10-15 minutes.
2. Reduce heat to 350°. In a small saucepan, melt butter. Squeeze softened garlic into pan. Stir in the onion, lime juice, mustard, salt and pepper. Cook and stir over medium heat until onion is tender.
3. Arrange the fillets in an ungreased 11x7-in. baking dish; top with onion mixture. Bake, uncovered, for 30-35 minutes or until fish flakes easily with a fork.
1 SERVING: 198 cal., 14g fat (8g sat. fat), 54mg chol., 353mg sod., 7g carb. (3g sugars, 1g fiber), 12g pro.

PECAN-CRUSTED SALMON

PECAN-CRUSTED SALMON

These delicious salmon fillets are wonderful for company because they take only a few minutes to prepare, yet they taste like you care. I receive requests for the recipe every time I serve them.
—*Kara Cook, Elk Ridge, UT*

- -

PREP: 15 min. + standing • **BAKE:** 10 min.
MAKES: 4 servings

- 4   salmon fillets (about 6 oz. each)
- 1   cup 2% milk
- 1   cup finely chopped pecans
- ¼   cup all-purpose flour
- 2   Tbsp. packed brown sugar
- 1   tsp. seasoned salt
- 1   tsp. pepper
- 3   Tbsp. canola oil

1. Place salmon fillets in a shallow dish; add milk. Turn to coat. Let stand for 10 minutes; drain milk.
2. Meanwhile, in a shallow bowl, combine the pecans, flour, brown sugar, seasoned salt and pepper. Coat fillets with the pecan mixture, gently pressing into the fish.
3. In a large cast-iron or other ovenproof skillet, brown salmon over medium-high heat in oil. Bake at 400° until fish just begins to flake easily with fork, 8-10 minutes.

1 FILLET: 523 cal., 40g fat (5g sat. fat), 86mg chol., 375mg sod., 11g carb. (6g sugars, 2g fiber), 31g pro.

WHITE SEAFOOD LASAGNA

We make lasagna with shrimp and scallops as part of the traditional Italian Feast of the Seven Fishes. Every bite delivers a tasty jewel from the sea.
—*Joe Colamonico, North Charleston, SC*

- -

PREP: 1 hour • **BAKE:** 40 min. + standing
MAKES: 12 servings

- 9   uncooked lasagna noodles
- 1   Tbsp. butter
- 1   lb. uncooked shrimp (31 to 40 per lb.), peeled and deveined
- 1   lb. bay scallops
- 5   garlic cloves, minced
- ¼   cup white wine
- 1   Tbsp. lemon juice
- 1   lb. fresh crabmeat

CHEESE SAUCE
- ¼   cup butter, cubed
- ¼   cup all-purpose flour
- 3   cups 2% milk
- 1   cup shredded part-skim mozzarella cheese
- ½   cup grated Parmesan cheese
- ½   tsp. salt

- ¼   tsp. pepper
     Dash ground nutmeg

RICOTTA MIXTURE
- 1   carton (15 oz.) part-skim ricotta cheese
- 1   pkg. (10 oz.) frozen chopped spinach, thawed and squeezed dry
- 1   cup shredded part-skim mozzarella cheese
- ½   cup grated Parmesan cheese
- ½   cup seasoned bread crumbs
- 1   large egg, lightly beaten

TOPPING
- 1   cup shredded part-skim mozzarella cheese
- ¼   cup grated Parmesan cheese
     Minced fresh parsley

1. Preheat oven to 350°. Cook noodles according to package directions; drain.
2. Meanwhile, in a large skillet, heat butter over medium heat. Add shrimp and scallops in batches; cook 2-4 minutes or until shrimp turn pink and scallops are firm and opaque. Remove from pan.
3. Add garlic to same pan; cook 1 minute. Add wine and lemon juice, stirring to loosen browned bits from pan. Bring to a boil; cook 1-2 minutes or until liquid is reduced by half. Add crab; heat through. Stir in the shrimp and bay scallops.
4. For the cheese sauce, melt butter over medium heat in a large saucepan. Stir in flour until smooth; gradually whisk in milk. Bring to a boil, stirring constantly; cook and stir until thickened, 1-2 minutes. Remove from heat; stir in the remaining cheese sauce ingredients. In a large bowl, combine the ricotta mixture ingredients; stir in 1 cup cheese sauce.
5. Spread ½ cup cheese sauce into a greased 13x9-in. baking dish. Layer with 3 noodles, half of the ricotta mixture, half of the seafood mixture and ⅔ cup cheese sauce. Repeat layers. Top with remaining noodles and cheese sauce. Sprinkle with remaining mozzarella cheese and Parmesan cheese.
6. Bake, uncovered, 40-50 minutes or until bubbly and top is golden brown. Let stand for 10 minutes before serving. Sprinkle with minced parsley.
1 PIECE: 448 cal., 19g fat (11g sat. fat), 158mg chol., 957mg sod., 29g carb. (5g sugars, 2g fiber), 39g pro.

**WHITE SEAFOOD
LASAGNA**

PARMESAN BAKED COD

This is a goof-proof way to keep baked cod moist and flavorful. My mom shared the recipe with me years ago, and I've been loving it ever since. Add coleslaw, oven fries or your other favorite sides.
—*Mary Jo Hoppe, Pewaukee, WI*

TAKES: 25 min. • **MAKES:** 4 servings

- 4 cod fillets (4 oz. each)
- ⅔ cup mayonnaise
- 4 green onions, chopped
- ¼ cup grated Parmesan cheese
- 1 tsp. Worcestershire sauce

1. Preheat oven to 400°. Place cod in an 8-in. square baking dish coated with cooking spray.
2. Mix the remaining ingredients; spread over cod fillets.
3. Bake, uncovered, until fish just begins to flake easily with a fork, 15-20 minutes.

1 FILLET: 247 cal., 15g fat (2g sat. fat), 57mg chol., 500mg sod., 7g carb. (2g sugars, 0 fiber), 20g pro. **DIABETIC EXCHANGES:** 3 lean meat, 3 fat.

NEW ORLEANS-STYLE SPICY SHRIMP

NEW ORLEANS-STYLE SPICY SHRIMP

We have family members who attended college in New Orleans. This shrimp captures their favorite flavors from The Big Easy, with the right touch of spices and heat.
—*Susan Seymour, Valatie, NY*

PREP: 15 min. • **BAKE:** 20 min.
MAKES: 12 servings

- 3 medium lemons, sliced
- ⅔ cup butter, cubed
- ½ cup ketchup
- ¼ cup Worcestershire sauce
- 2 Tbsp. seafood seasoning
- 2 Tbsp. chili garlic sauce
- 2 Tbsp. Louisiana-style hot sauce
- 1 Tbsp. Italian salad dressing mix
- 4 lbs. uncooked shell-on shrimp (31-40 per lb.)
- 2 bay leaves
  French bread

1. Preheat oven to 350°. Combine first 8 ingredients in a microwave-safe bowl. Microwave, covered, on high 2-3 minutes or until butter is melted; stir until blended.
2. Divide shrimp and bay leaves between 2 ungreased 13x9-in. baking dishes. Add lemon mixture to dishes; toss to combine.
3. Bake, uncovered, 20-25 minutes or until shrimp turn pink, stirring halfway. Remove bay leaves. Serve with bread.

1 CUP: 242 cal., 12g fat (7g sat. fat), 211mg chol., 940mg sod., 7g carb. (4g sugars, 0 fiber), 25g pro.

SEAFOOD-STUFFED SALMON FILLETS

You could get stuffed salmon from a big-box store, but my fillets are loaded with flavor from crab, cream cheese and savory herbs. We love them.
—Mary Cokenour, Monticello, UT

- -

PREP: 25 min. • **BAKE:** 20 min.
MAKES: 12 servings

- 1½ cups cooked long grain rice
- 1 pkg. (8 oz.) imitation crabmeat
- 2 Tbsp. cream cheese, softened
- 2 Tbsp. butter, melted
- 2 garlic cloves, minced
- ½ tsp. each dried basil, marjoram, oregano, thyme and rosemary, crushed
- ½ tsp. celery seed, crushed
- 12 salmon fillets (8 oz. each and 1½ in. thick)
- 3 Tbsp. olive oil
- 2 tsp. dill weed
- 1½ tsp. salt

1. Preheat oven to 400°. In a large bowl, combine rice, crab, cream cheese, butter, garlic, basil, marjoram, oregano, thyme, rosemary and celery seed.

2. Cut a pocket horizontally in each fillet to within ½ in. of opposite side. Fill with stuffing mixture; secure with toothpicks. Place salmon on 2 greased 15x10x1-in. baking pans. Brush with oil; sprinkle with dill and salt.

3. Bake 18-22 minutes or until fish just begins to flake easily with a fork. Discard toothpicks before serving.

1 STUFFED FILLET: 454 cal., 27g fat (6g sat. fat), 123mg chol., 537mg sod., 9g carb. (0 sugars, 0 fiber), 41g pro.

SEAFOOD-STUFFED SALMON FILLETS

CORNMEAL-CRUSTED WALLEYE

These tender fillets are a terrific option when you want a meal that's not too heavy. The corn and roasted pepper side dish goes perfectly with walleye.
—Allen Plungis, Hartland, MI

- -

PREP: 45 min. • **COOK:** 10 min.
MAKES: 4 servings (about 4 cups corn salsa)

- 2 large sweet red peppers
- 4 large ears sweet corn, husks removed
- 3 Tbsp. canola oil, divided
- ½ cup yellow cornmeal
- 1¾ tsp. salt, divided
- ½ tsp. white pepper
  Dash cayenne pepper
- 4 walleye fillets (6 oz. each)
- ½ lb. sliced fresh mushrooms
- 3 Tbsp. butter

1. Broil red peppers 4 in. from the heat until skins blister, about 15 minutes. With tongs, rotate peppers a quarter turn. Broil and rotate until all sides are blistered and blackened. Immediately place the charred peppers in a large bowl; cover and let stand for 15-20 minutes.

2. Meanwhile, brush corn with 1 Tbsp. oil. Transfer to an ungreased 13x9-in. baking dish. Cover and bake at 350° until tender, 30-40 minutes. Peel off and discard charred skin from peppers. Remove stems and seeds. Finely chop peppers. Cut corn from cobs.

3. In a shallow bowl, combine the cornmeal, 1 tsp. salt, pepper and cayenne. Coat walleye in cornmeal mixture.

4. In a large skillet, saute mushrooms in butter until tender. Add peppers, corn and remaining salt; saute 2-3 minutes longer.

5. In another large skillet, fry walleye fillets in remaining oil for 2-3 minutes on each side or until fish flakes easily with a fork. Serve with corn salsa.

1 SERVING: 515 cal., 23g fat (7g sat. fat), 169mg chol., 937mg sod., 42g carb. (11g sugars, 7g fiber), 40g pro.

TUNA MUSHROOM CASSEROLE

2. In a small bowl, combine cornstarch and milk until smooth; gradually add to vegetable mixture. Bring to a boil; cook and stir until thickened, about 2 minutes. Remove from the heat; stir in cheese and mayonnaise until cheese is melted. Fold in noodles and tuna.

3. Pour into a greased 2½-qt. baking dish. In a small skillet, brown bread crumbs in butter; sprinkle over casserole. Bake, uncovered, at 350° until heated through, 25-30 minutes.

1 SERVING: 343 cal., 15g fat (5g sat. fat), 57mg chol., 770mg sod., 27g carb. (7g sugars, 2g fiber), 24g pro.

CRABMEAT BOATS

I've been making this recipe for more than 40 years. You can also spread the filling on small rolls and serve them as an appetizer.
—*June Strang, Grand Blanc, MI*

- -

PREP: 20 min. • **BAKE:** 15 min.
MAKES: 2 servings

  2 kaiser rolls, split
  2 tsp. butter, softened
  1 can (6 oz.) lump crabmeat, drained
  4 oz. Swiss cheese, cubed
  1 celery rib, chopped
  ¼ cup mayonnaise
  1 tsp. minced fresh parsley
  ¼ tsp. seafood seasoning, optional
  ¼ tsp. paprika

Preheat oven to 400°. Carefully hollow out each roll, leaving a ½-in. shell (save removed bread for another use). Spread inside of rolls with butter. In a large bowl, combine the crab, cheese, celery mayonnaise, parsley, seafood seasoning, if desired, and paprika; divide between rolls. Wrap each in foil and place on a baking sheet. Bake until cheese is melted, 15-20 minutes.

1 SANDWICH: 661 cal., 44g fat (16g sat. fat), 148mg chol., 863mg sod., 25g carb. (3g sugars, 2g fiber), 38g pro.

TEST KITCHEN TIP

Celery salt (a blend of celery seed and salt) is the main ingredient in seafood seasoning. Herbaceous, crunchy and slightly bitter, celery seed is a classic addition to seafood dishes. No seafood seasoning? Add a sprinkle of celery seed or celery salt instead.

TUNA MUSHROOM CASSEROLE

The first time I made this dish, my uncle asked for seconds even though tuna casseroles are not usually his favorite. The green beans add nice texture, color and flavor.
—*Jone Furlong, Santa Rosa, CA*

- -

PREP: 30 min. • **BAKE:** 25 min.
MAKES: 6 servings

  ½ cup water
  1 tsp. chicken bouillon granules
  1 pkg. (9 oz.) frozen cut green beans
  1 cup chopped onion
  1 cup sliced fresh mushrooms
  ¼ cup chopped celery
  1 garlic clove, minced
  ½ tsp. dill weed
  ½ tsp. salt
  ⅛ tsp. pepper
  4 tsp. cornstarch
  1½ cups cold whole milk
  ½ cup shredded Swiss cheese
  ¼ cup mayonnaise
  2½ cups egg noodles, cooked and drained
  1 can (12 oz.) light tuna in water, drained and flaked
  ⅓ cup dry bread crumbs
  1 Tbsp. butter

1. In a large saucepan, bring water and bouillon to a boil; stir until bouillon is dissolved. Add the next 8 ingredients; bring to a boil. Reduce heat; cover and simmer until vegetables are tender, about 5 minutes.

CRABMEAT
BOATS

Bonus: Five-Star Desserts ★★★★★

RICH HOT FUDGE SAUCE

RICH HOT FUDGE SAUCE
I've been making this scrumptious topping since the early 1980s. It always turns out smooth and yummy, and satisfies any chocoholic's cravings.
—*Carol Hunihan, Ann Arbor, MI*

TAKES: 30 min. • **MAKES:** 3½ cups

- ¾ cup butter, cubed
- 1 cup heavy whipping cream
- 1⅓ cups packed brown sugar
- ¼ cup sugar
- 1 cup baking cocoa
- ½ cup plus 2 Tbsp. light corn syrup
  Pinch salt
- 2 oz. unsweetened chocolate, chopped
- 1 Tbsp. vanilla extract
- 1 to 2 tsp. rum extract

1. Place the butter and cream in a heavy saucepan; cook and stir over medium-low heat until butter is melted. Add sugars; cook and stir until dissolved, 3-4 minutes.
2. Add cocoa, corn syrup and salt; cook and stir until blended, about 3 minutes. Stir in chocolate until melted. Reduce heat to low; cook and stir until mixture reaches desired thickness, 10-15 minutes.
3. Remove from heat; stir in extracts. Serve warm. Refrigerate leftovers.
2 TBSP. SAUCE: 166 cal., 9g fat (6g sat. fat), 25mg chol., 103mg sod., 21g carb. (18g sugars, 1g fiber), 1g pro.

"This was excellent. Did not have any rum extract so substituted raspberry extract. My daughter is throwing a party later this summer and says I have to make a batch of this sauce for that."
—AQUARELLE, TASTEOFHOME.COM

**POPCORN
COOKIES**

CHOCOLATE CHIP
BANANA CREAM PIE
This rich treat is a hit every time I serve it.
The creamy filling, brimming with bananas,
is refreshing, and the cookie crust provides
a chocolaty crunch.
—*Taylor Carroll, Parkesburg, PA*

- -

PREP: 35 min. + chilling • **MAKES:** 8 servings

  1 **tube (16½ oz.) refrigerated
     chocolate chip cookie dough**
  ⅓ **cup sugar**
  ¼ **cup cornstarch**
  ⅛ **tsp. salt**
2⅓ **cups 2% milk**
  5 **large egg yolks, lightly beaten**
  2 **Tbsp. butter**
  2 **tsp. vanilla extract, divided**
  3 **medium firm bananas**
1½ **cups heavy whipping cream**
  3 **Tbsp. confectioners' sugar**

1. Cut cookie dough in half widthwise. Let
1 portion stand at room temperature for
5-10 minutes to soften (return the other
half to the refrigerator for another use).
2. Press dough onto the bottom and up the
sides of an ungreased 9-in. pie plate. Bake
at 375° for 11-12 minutes or until lightly
browned. Cool on a wire rack.
3. In a large saucepan, combine the sugar,
cornstarch and salt. Stir in milk until smooth.
Cook and stir over medium-high heat until
thickened and bubbly. Reduce heat; cook and
stir 2 minutes longer. Remove from the heat.
Stir a small amount of hot filling into egg
yolks; return all to the pan, stirring constantly.
Bring to a gentle boil; cook and stir 2 minutes
longer. Remove from the heat; stir in butter
and 1 tsp. vanilla.
4. Spread 1 cup filling into prepared crust.
Slice bananas; arrange over filling. Pour the
remaining filling over bananas. Refrigerate
for 2 hours or until set.
5. In a large bowl, beat cream until it begins
to thicken. Add confectioners' sugar and
remaining vanilla; beat until stiff peaks form.
Spread over pie. Refrigerate for 1 hour or
until chilled.
1 PIECE: 481 cal., 30g fat (17g sat. fat),
182mg chol., 205mg sod., 48g carb. (33g
sugars, 2g fiber), 7g pro.

POPCORN COOKIES
It's so much fun to surprise people with
the crushed popcorn in these yummy
cookies. They're definitely a standout
on any dessert tray.
—*Leigh Anne Preston, Palmyra, IN*

- -

PREP: 15 min. • **BAKE:** 15 min./batch + cooling
MAKES: about 2½ dozen

  ½ **cup butter, softened**
  1 **cup sugar**
  1 **large egg, room temperature**
  1 **tsp. vanilla extract**
1¼ **cups all-purpose flour**
  ½ **tsp. baking soda**
     Dash salt
  2 **cups popped popcorn, lightly crushed**
  1 **cup (6 oz.) semisweet
     chocolate chips**
  ½ **cup chopped pecans**

1. Preheat oven to 350°. Cream butter and
sugar until light and fluffy; beat in egg and
vanilla. In a separate bowl, whisk flour, baking
soda and salt; gradually beat into creamed
mixture. Stir in popcorn, chocolate chips
and pecans.
2. Drop by tablespoonfuls 2 in. apart onto
greased baking sheets. Bake until golden
brown, 13-14 minutes. Remove to wire racks
to cool.
1 COOKIE: 119 cal., 7g fat (3g sat. fat), 15mg
chol., 66mg sod., 15g carb. (10g sugars, 1g
fiber), 1g pro.

**ORANGE DREAM
ANGEL FOOD CAKE**

ORANGE DREAM ANGEL FOOD CAKE

A basic angel food cake becomes a heavenly indulgence, thanks to a hint of orange flavor swirled into every bite. The orange color makes slices of the cake look so pretty when arranged on individual dessert plates.
—*Lauren Osborne, Holtwood, PA*

PREP: 25 min. • **BAKE:** 30 min. + cooling
MAKES: 16 servings

<table>
<tr><td>12</td><td>large egg whites</td></tr>
<tr><td>1</td><td>cup all-purpose flour</td></tr>
<tr><td>1¾</td><td>cups sugar, divided</td></tr>
<tr><td>1½</td><td>tsp. cream of tartar</td></tr>
<tr><td>½</td><td>tsp. salt</td></tr>
<tr><td>1</td><td>tsp. almond extract</td></tr>
<tr><td>1</td><td>tsp. vanilla extract</td></tr>
<tr><td>1</td><td>tsp. grated orange zest</td></tr>
<tr><td>1</td><td>tsp. orange extract</td></tr>
<tr><td>6</td><td>drops red food coloring, optional</td></tr>
<tr><td>6</td><td>drops yellow food coloring, optional</td></tr>
</table>

1. Place egg whites in a large bowl; let stand at room temperature for 30 minutes. Sift the flour and ¾ cup sugar together twice; set aside.

2. Add the cream of tartar, salt and almond and vanilla extracts to egg whites; beat on medium speed until soft peaks form. Gradually add remaining sugar, about 2 Tbsp. at a time, beating on high until stiff glossy peaks form and sugar is dissolved. Gradually fold in flour mixture, about ½ cup at a time.

3. Gently spoon half the batter into an ungreased 10-in. tube pan. To the remaining batter, stir in the orange zest, orange extract and, if desired, food colorings. Gently spoon orange batter over white batter. Cut through both layers with a knife to swirl the orange and remove air pockets.

4. Bake on the lowest oven rack at 375° for 30-35 minutes or until lightly browned and entire top appears dry. Immediately invert pan; cool completely, about 1 hour.

5. Run a knife around side and center tube of pan. Remove cake to a serving plate.

1 SLICE: 130 cal., 0 fat (0 sat. fat), 0 chol., 116mg sod., 28g carb. (22g sugars, 0 fiber), 4g pro. **DIABETIC EXCHANGES:** 2 starch.

FUDGE-TOPPED BROWNIES

FUDGE-TOPPED BROWNIES

If you love brownies and fudge, why not combine the two? Mix up a pan of these exquisite brownies for any holiday or special gathering...or just when you want to treat yourself to the ultimate chocolate dessert.
—*Judy Olson, Whitecourt, AB*

PREP: 50 min. + freezing
MAKES: about 10 dozen

<table>
<tr><td>1</td><td>cup butter, cubed</td></tr>
<tr><td>4</td><td>oz. unsweetened chocolate, chopped</td></tr>
<tr><td>2</td><td>cups sugar</td></tr>
<tr><td>2</td><td>tsp. vanilla extract</td></tr>
<tr><td>4</td><td>large eggs, room temperature</td></tr>
<tr><td>1½</td><td>cups all-purpose flour</td></tr>
<tr><td>1</td><td>tsp. baking powder</td></tr>
<tr><td>½</td><td>tsp. salt</td></tr>
<tr><td>1</td><td>cup chopped walnuts</td></tr>
</table>

TOPPING

<table>
<tr><td>4½</td><td>cups sugar</td></tr>
<tr><td>1</td><td>can (12 oz.) evaporated milk</td></tr>
<tr><td>½</td><td>cup butter, cubed</td></tr>
<tr><td>1</td><td>pkg. (12 oz.) semisweet chocolate chips</td></tr>
<tr><td>1</td><td>pkg. (11½ oz.) milk chocolate chips</td></tr>
<tr><td>1</td><td>jar (7 oz.) marshmallow creme</td></tr>
<tr><td>2</td><td>tsp. vanilla extract</td></tr>
<tr><td>2</td><td>cups chopped walnuts</td></tr>
</table>

1. In a heavy saucepan or microwave, melt the butter and chocolate; stir until smooth. Remove from the heat; blend in sugar and vanilla. Add eggs; mix well. Combine flour, baking powder and salt; add to chocolate mixture. Stir in walnuts. Pour into greased 13x9-in. baking pan. Bake at 350° until brownie top springs back when lightly touched, 25-30 minutes. Cool on a wire rack while preparing topping.

2. Combine the sugar, milk and butter in a large heavy saucepan; bring to a boil over medium heat. Reduce heat; simmer, uncovered, 5 minutes, stirring constantly. Remove from the heat. Stir in the chocolate chips, marshmallow creme and vanilla until smooth. Add walnuts. Spread over warm brownies. Freeze for 3 hours or until firm. Cut into 1-in. squares. Store brownies in the refrigerator.

1 PIECE: 128 cal., 6g fat (3g sat. fat), 15mg chol., 46mg sod., 18g carb. (15g sugars, 0 fiber), 2g pro.

CLASSIC TRES LECHES CAKE

CLASSIC TRES LECHES CAKE

Made in Mexican kitchens for generations, this cake gets its name from the three types of milk—evaporated, sweetened condensed, and heavy cream—that help to create an exquisitely moist and tender texture.
—Taste of Home *Test Kitchen*

- -

PREP: 45 min. • **BAKE:** 20 min. + chilling
MAKES: 10 servings

4	large eggs, separated, room temperature
⅔	cup sugar, divided
⅔	cup cake flour
	Dash salt
¾	cup heavy whipping cream
¾	cup evaporated milk
¾	cup sweetened condensed milk
2	tsp. vanilla extract
¼	tsp. rum extract

TOPPING

1¼	cups heavy whipping cream
3	Tbsp. sugar
	Dulce de leche or sliced fresh strawberries, optional

1. Place egg whites in a large bowl. Line bottom of a 9-in. springform pan with parchment; grease the paper.
2. Meanwhile, preheat oven to 350°. In another large bowl, beat egg yolks until slightly thickened. Gradually add ⅓ cup sugar, beating on high speed until thick and lemon-colored. Fold in flour, a third at a time.
3. Add dash of salt to egg whites; with clean beaters, beat on medium until soft peaks form. Gradually add remaining sugar, 1 Tbsp. at a time, beating on high after each addition until sugar is dissolved. Continue beating until soft glossy peaks form. Fold a third of the whites into batter, then fold in remaining whites. Gently spread into prepared pan.

4. Bake until top springs back when lightly touched, 20-25 minutes. Cool 10 minutes before removing from pan to a wire rack to cool completely.
5. Place cake on a rimmed serving plate. Poke holes in top with a skewer. In a small bowl, mix cream, milks and extracts; brush slowly over the cake. Refrigerate, covered, 2 hours.
6. For topping, beat cream until it begins to thicken. Add sugar; beat until peaks form. Spread over top of cake. If desired, top cake with dulce de leche or sliced strawberries just before serving.

1 SLICE: 392 cal., 23g fat (14g sat. fat), 142mg chol., 104mg sod., 40g carb. (33g sugars, 0 fiber), 8g pro.

FROZEN PINEAPPLE-KIWI POPS

Kiwi, pineapple, sugar and water are all you need to make these easy, breezy freezer pops.
—*Colleen Ludovice, Wauwatosa, WI*

- -

PREP: 20 min. + freezing • **MAKES:** 1 dozen

- 3 cups cubed fresh pineapple
- 1 cup water, divided
- 8 tsp. sugar, divided
- 12 paper cups (3 oz. each) and wooden pop sticks
- 2 cups sliced peeled kiwifruit (about 6 medium)

1. Place cubed pineapple, ½ cup water and 4 tsp. sugar in a food processor; pulse until combined. Divide among cups. Top cups with foil and insert sticks through foil. Freeze until firm, about 2 hours.

2. Place kiwi and remaining water and sugar in food processor; pulse until combined. Spoon over pineapple layer. Freeze, covered, until firm.

1 POP: 50 cal., 0 fat (0 sat. fat), 0 chol., 1mg sod., 13g carb. (10g sugars, 1g fiber), 1g pro.
DIABETIC EXCHANGES: 1 fruit.

FROZEN PINEAPPLE-KIWI POPS

RHUBARB-STRAWBERRY PIE

This recipe has become a favorite with us. My husband never liked rhubarb until he tasted this pie...now he asks me to make it often!
—*Sandy Brown, Lake Worth, FL*

- -

PREP: 15 min. + standing
BAKE: 40 min. + cooling • **MAKES:** 8 servings

- ¾ cup sugar
- ¼ cup quick-cooking tapioca
- 3 cups sliced fresh or frozen rhubarb (¼-in. pieces)
- 3 cups sliced fresh or frozen strawberries, thawed
- ⅓ cup orange juice
- 4½ tsp. orange marmalade, optional
- ¼ tsp. grated orange zest
    Pastry for double-crust pie (9 in.)

1. In a large bowl, combine the sugar and tapioca. Add fruit; toss to coat. Gently stir in the juice, marmalade if desired and zest. Let stand for 15 minutes.

2. Line a deep-dish 9-in. pie plate with the bottom crust; trim even with edge. Fill with fruit filling. Roll out the remaining crust; make a lattice crust. Trim, seal and flute edges. Cover edges with foil.

3. Bake at 400° until filling is bubbly and rhubarb is tender, 40-50 minutes. Remove foil. Cool on wire rack. Store in refrigerator.
NOTE: If using frozen rhubarb, measure rhubarb while still frozen, then thaw completely. Drain in a colander, but do not press liquid out.

1 PIECE: 367 cal., 14g fat (6g sat. fat), 10mg chol., 202mg sod., 58g carb. (25g sugars, 2g fiber), 3g pro.

RHUBARB-CHERRY PIE: Omit strawberries, orange juice, orange zest and marmalade. Increase sugar to 1¼ cups. Drain and add 1 can (14½ oz.) pitted tart red cherries. Use a standard 9-in. pie plate.

RHUBARB-RASPBERRY PIE: Omit the strawberries, orange juice, orange zest and marmalade. Increase sugar to 1⅓ cups. Add 1 cup fresh or frozen raspberries (thawed) and ¼ tsp. ground cinnamon. Use a standard 9-in. pie plate; decrease the bake time to 35-40 minutes.

CAKE & BERRY CAMPFIRE COBBLER

This warm cobbler is one of our favorite ways to end a busy day of fishing, hiking, swimming or rafting. It's yummy with ice cream—and so easy to make!
—June Dress, Meridian, ID

PREP: 10 min. • **GRILL:** 30 min.
MAKES: 12 servings

    2 cans (21 oz. each)
       raspberry pie filling
    1 pkg. yellow cake mix (regular size)
 1¼ cups water
  ½ cup canola oil
       Vanilla ice cream, optional

1. Prepare grill or campfire for low heat, using 16-20 charcoal briquettes or large wood chips.
2. Line an ovenproof Dutch oven with heavy-duty aluminum foil; add raspberry pie filling. In a large bowl, combine the cake mix, water and oil. Spread over pie filling.
3. Cover Dutch oven. When briquettes or wood chips are covered with white ash, place Dutch oven directly on top of 8-10 of them. Using long-handled tongs, place remaining briquettes on pan cover.
4. Cook until filling is bubbly and a toothpick inserted in the topping comes out clean, 30-40 minutes. To check for doneness, use the tongs to carefully lift the cover. Serve with ice cream if desired.
NOTE: This recipe does not use eggs.
1 SERVING: 342 cal., 12g fat (2g sat. fat), 0 chol., 322mg sod., 57g carb. (34g sugars, 2g fiber), 1g pro.

"This is a great dessert when camping. I've made it numerous times using different fillings (especially cherry). Also use lemon-lime soda instead of water in my recipe. Get the kids involved and make your own ice cream (tin-can ice cream). Kids roll the can around the campsite, therefore making the ice cream while having fun."
— ANNIMEL, TASTEOFHOME.COM

LEMON TEA COOKIES

LEMON TEA COOKIES

These sandwich cookies taste rich and buttery and have a lovely lemon filling. The recipe has been in our family since the 1950s, when my mother got it from a French friend in her club.
—Phyllis Dietz, Westland, MI

PREP: 25 min. + chilling • **BAKE:** 10 min./batch
MAKES: about 4½ dozen

  ¾ cup butter, softened
  ½ cup sugar
    1 large egg yolk, room temperature
  ½ tsp. vanilla extract
    2 cups all-purpose flour
  ¼ cup finely chopped walnuts
FILLING
    3 Tbsp. butter, softened
 4½ tsp. lemon juice
  ¾ tsp. grated orange zest
 1½ cups confectioners' sugar
    2 drops yellow food coloring, optional

1. In a large bowl, cream butter and sugar until light and fluffy. Beat in the egg yolk and vanilla. Gradually add flour and mix well.
2. Shape into two 14-in. rolls; reshape each roll into a 14x1⅛x1⅛-in. block. Wrap and refrigerate overnight.
3. Unwrap and cut into ¼-in. slices. Place 2 in. apart on ungreased baking sheets. Sprinkle half the cookies with nuts, gently pressing into dough.
4. Bake at 400° for 8-10 minutes or until golden brown around the edges. Remove to wire racks to cool.
5. In a small bowl, cream the butter, lemon juice and orange zest until fluffy. Gradually add confectioners' sugar until smooth. Tint yellow if desired. Spread about 1 tsp. on bottoms of the plain cookies; place nut-topped cookies over filling.
1 COOKIE: 70 cal., 4g fat (2g sat. fat), 12mg chol., 32mg sod., 9g carb. (5g sugars, 0 fiber), 1g pro.

CAKE & BERRY
CAMPFIRE COBBLER

FLAKY BUMBLEBERRY PIE

FLAKY BUMBLEBERRY PIE

This pie recipe makes one of the flakiest crusts ever and is sure to impress! The filling is delicious with the different berries, tart apple and rhubarb.

—Suzanne Alberts, Onalaska, WI

PREP: 20 min. + chilling
BAKE: 1 hour + cooling • **MAKES:** 8 servings

- 1½ cups all-purpose flour
- 1 tsp. salt
- 1 tsp. sugar
- 1 cup cold butter
- ¼ cup cold water

FILLING
- 1 medium tart apple, peeled and diced
- 1 cup diced fresh or frozen rhubarb, thawed
- 1 cup fresh or frozen raspberries, thawed and drained
- 1 cup fresh or frozen blueberries, thawed and drained
- 1 cup sliced fresh or frozen strawberries, thawed and drained
- 1 cup sugar
- ½ cup all-purpose flour
- 1 Tbsp. lemon juice

1. In a small bowl, combine flour, salt and sugar. Cut in butter until mixture ensembles coarse crumbs. Gradually add water, tossing with a fork until a ball forms. Cover and refrigerate 1 hour or until easy to handle.
2. Preheat oven to 400°. On a lightly floured surface, roll out half the dough to fit a 9-in. pie plate. Transfer crust to pie plate. Trim to ½ in. beyond edge of plate.
3. In a large bowl, combine filling ingredients; pour into crust. Roll out remaining dough; cut out decorative shapes with cookie cutters. Place over filling.
4. Bake 20 minutes. Reduce heat to 350°; remove foil. Bake 40-45 minutes or until crust is golden brown and filling is bubbly. Cool on a wire rack.
1 PIECE: 449 cal., 23g fat (14g sat. fat), 61mg chol., 528mg sod., 58g carb. (31g sugars, 3g fiber), 4g pro.

SALTED TOFFEE CASHEW COOKIES

SALTED TOFFEE CASHEW COOKIES

I might be addicted to this sweet and salty flavor combo. Lucky for me, these nutty cookies are also quick to make.

—Crystal Schlueter, Babbitt, MN

PREP: 25 min. • **BAKE:** 10 min./batch
MAKES: about 5 dozen

- 1 cup butter, softened
- 1½ cups packed brown sugar
- 2 large eggs, room temperature
- 1 tsp. vanilla extract
- 2⅔ cups all-purpose flour
- 1 tsp. salt
- 1 tsp. baking soda
- 1½ cups chopped salted cashews
- 1 cup brickle toffee bits
- 1 cup butterscotch chips
  Salted whole cashews

1. Preheat oven to 375°. In a large bowl, cream the butter and brown sugar until light and fluffy. Beat in eggs and vanilla. In another bowl, whisk flour, salt and baking soda; gradually beat into creamed mixture. Stir in chopped cashews, toffee bits and butterscotch chips.
2. Drop dough by rounded tablespoonfuls 2 in. apart onto ungreased baking sheets. Press a whole cashew into each cookie. Bake for 7-9 minutes or until golden brown. Cool on pans 2 minutes. Remove to wire racks to cool.
FREEZE OPTION: Freeze cookies in freezer containers. To use, thaw before serving.
1 COOKIE: 129 cal., 7g fat (4g sat. fat), 16mg chol., 129mg sod., 15g carb. (10g sugars, 0 fiber), 1g pro.

APPLE DUMPLINGS

Mother often prepared this special treat for us, ready to take out of the oven just as we came home from school. I remember so vividly, upon opening the door to the house, the magnificent aroma!
—*Marjorie Thompson, West Sacramento, CA*

- -

PREP: 30 min. • **BAKE:** 45 min.
MAKES: 6 servings

- 1½ cups sugar, divided
- 2 cups water
- 4 Tbsp. butter, divided
- ½ tsp. ground cinnamon, divided
  Pastry for double-crust pie (9 in.)
- 6 small to medium apples, peeled and cored

1. Preheat oven to 375°. For the syrup, place 1 cup sugar, water, 3 Tbsp. butter and ¼ tsp. cinnamon in a saucepan; bring to a boil. Boil 3 minutes; remove from heat.

2. Mix the remaining sugar and cinnamon. On a lightly floured surface, roll dough to a 21x14-in. rectangle; cut into 6 squares. Place an apple on each square. Fill center of each with 4 tsp. sugar mixture and ½ tsp. butter. Moisten edges of crust with water; bring up corners over apples, pinching edges to seal. Place in an ungreased 13x9-in. baking dish.

3. Pour syrup around apples. Bake until golden brown and apples are tender, about 45 minutes. Serve warm.

Pastry for double-crust pie (9 in.):
Combine 2½ cups all-purpose flour and ½ tsp. salt; cut in 1 cup cold butter until crumbly. Gradually add ⅓-⅔ cup ice water, tossing with a fork until dough holds together when pressed. Shape into a 1-in.-thick square; wrap and refrigerate 1 hour or overnight.

1 SERVING: 773 cal., 39g fat (24g sat. fat), 101mg chol., 475mg sod., 104g carb. (62g sugars, 4g fiber), 6g pro.

DAR'S COCONUT CREAM PIE

DAR'S COCONUT CREAM PIE

When I whip up a toasted coconut cream pie, my family goes wild and it vanishes quickly.
—*Darlene Bartos, Shoreview, MN*

- -

PREP: 1 hour + chilling
BAKE: 20 min. + cooling • **MAKES:** 10 servings

  Pastry for single-crust pie (9 in.)
- 4 large egg yolks
- 2 cups coconut milk
- 1½ cups half-and-half cream
- 1 cup sugar
- ⅓ cup cornstarch
- ¼ tsp. salt
- 2 tsp. vanilla extract
- 1½ cups sweetened shredded coconut, toasted, divided
- 2 cups heavy whipping cream
- ¼ cup confectioners' sugar
- ½ tsp. vanilla extract

1. On a lightly floured surface, roll pastry dough to a ⅛-in.-thick circle; transfer to a 9-in. pie plate. Trim the crust ½ in. beyond rim of plate; flute edge. Refrigerate about 30 minutes. Preheat oven to 425°.

2. Line crust with a double thickness of foil. Fill with pie weights, dried beans or uncooked rice. Bake on a lower oven rack 20-25 minutes or until edges are golden brown. Remove foil and weights; bake 3-6 minutes longer or until bottom is golden brown. Cool completely on a wire rack.

3. In a large heavy saucepan, whisk egg yolks, coconut milk, cream, sugar, cornstarch and salt until blended. Bring to a gentle boil over medium heat, whisking constantly. Reduce heat to medium-low; cook 2 minutes longer, whisking vigorously. Remove from heat; stir in vanilla and 1 cup coconut. Immediately transfer to crust.

4. Press plastic wrap onto surface of filling. Refrigerate 2 hours or until cold.

5. In a large bowl, beat cream until it begins to thicken. Add confectioners' sugar and vanilla; beat until soft peaks form. Spread over pie. Sprinkle with remaining coconut.

Pastry for single-crust pie (9 in.): Combine 1¼ cups all-purpose flour and ¼ tsp. salt; cut in ½ cup cold butter until crumbly. Gradually add 3-5 Tbsp. ice water, tossing with a fork until the dough holds together when pressed. Wrap and refrigerate 1 hour.

1 PIECE: 641 cal., 47g fat (33g sat. fat), 182mg chol., 265mg sod., 50g carb. (32g sugars, 1g fiber), 6g pro.

PEACH COBBLER DUMP CAKE

This recipe brings the best of two desserts: sweet, tender cake and beautifully crisp cobbler topping. Add a scoop of vanilla ice cream on the side, and dessert's golden.
—*Keri Sparks, Little Elm, TX*

PREP: 10 min. • **BAKE:** 35 min.
MAKES: 15 servings

- 2 cans (15 oz. each) sliced peaches in extra-light syrup
- 2 Tbsp. brown sugar
- 1 tsp. ground cinnamon
- 1 pkg. yellow cake mix (regular size)
- ¾ cup sliced almonds
- ½ cup cold butter

1. Preheat oven to 350°. Pour 1 can of peaches into a greased 13x9-in. baking dish. Drain remaining can of peaches and add to baking dish; sprinkle with brown sugar and cinnamon. Top with cake mix and almonds.
2. Cut butter into very thin slices; arrange over top, spacing evenly. Bake until golden brown and fruit is bubbly, 35-40 minutes. Serve warm.
1 SERVING: 234 cal., 11g fat (5g sat. fat), 16mg chol., 242mg sod., 34g carb. (22g sugars, 1g fiber), 2g pro.

PINEAPPLE BREAD PUDDING

Pineapple gives a tangy tropical twist to classic bread pudding. Here's a dessert you can make on a moment's notice with simple ingredients from the pantry.
—*Margie Behnke, Neenah, WI*

PREP: 15 min. • **BAKE:** 40 min.
MAKES: 8-10 servings

- 10 slices white bread
- ¾ cup butter, melted
- 5 large eggs, room temperature
- 1 can (20 oz.) crushed pineapple, drained
- ¼ cup dried currants or raisins
- 1 cup sugar
- 1½ tsp. vanilla extract
- ¾ tsp. ground cinnamon
  Whipped cream, optional

1. Place bread on a baking sheet. Bake at 375° for 4 minutes; turn over and bake 4 minutes longer or until very light brown. Cut toasted bread into 1-in. cubes. Toss with melted butter; set aside.
2. In a bowl, beat eggs until thick and lemon-colored. Add pineapple, currants, sugar and vanilla; mix well. Fold in bread cubes.
3. Pour into a greased 2½-qt. baking dish. Sprinkle with cinnamon. Cover and bake at 350° for 30-35 minutes or until bubbly and golden brown. Serve warm with whipped cream if desired.
1 CUP: 348 cal., 17g fat (9g sat. fat), 143mg chol., 306mg sod., 44g carb. (30g sugars, 1g fiber), 6g pro.

PEACH COBBLER DUMP CAKE

GRANDMA'S STRAWBERRY SHORTCAKE

PEAR TART

This pretty pastry looks like it came from a fancy bakery. My sister-in-law brought this fruity dessert to dinner one night, and we all went back for seconds. It is truly scrumptious.
—*Kathryn Rogers, Suisun City, CA*

- -

PREP: 15 min. • **BAKE:** 25 min. + chilling
MAKES: 12 servings

    3   Tbsp. butter, softened
    ½   cup sugar
    ¾   tsp. ground cinnamon
    ¾   cup all-purpose flour
    ⅓   cup finely chopped walnuts
FILLING
    1   pkg. (8 oz.) reduced-fat
        cream cheese
    ¼   cup plus 1 Tbsp. sugar, divided
    1   large egg, room temperature
    1   tsp. vanilla extract
    1   can (15 oz.) reduced-sugar sliced
        pears, drained well and thinly sliced
    ¼   tsp. ground cinnamon

1. Preheat oven to 425°. Beat butter, sugar and cinnamon until crumbly. Beat in flour and walnuts. Press onto bottom and up sides of a 9-in. fluted tart pan with a removable bottom coated with cooking spray.
2. For filling, beat cream cheese and ¼ cup sugar until smooth. Beat in egg and vanilla. Spread into crust. Arrange pears over top. Mix cinnamon and remaining sugar; sprinkle over pears.
3. Bake 10 minutes. Reduce oven setting to 350°; bake until filling is set, 15-20 minutes. Cool 1 hour on a wire rack. Refrigerate at least 2 hours before serving.
1 PIECE: 199 cal., 9g fat (5g sat. fat), 36mg chol., 112mg sod., 25g carb. (18g sugars, 1g fiber), 4g pro. **DIABETIC EXCHANGES:** 2 fat, 1½ starch.

GRANDMA'S STRAWBERRY SHORTCAKE

I can still taste the sweet, juicy berries piled over warm biscuits and topped with a huge dollop of fresh whipped cream. My father liked to add even more indulgence to this strawberry dessert by first buttering his biscuits.
—*Shirley Joan Helfenbein, Lapeer, MI*

- -

PREP: 30 min. • **BAKE:** 20 min. + cooling
MAKES: 8 servings

    2   cups all-purpose flour
    2   Tbsp. sugar
    3   tsp. baking powder
    ½   tsp. salt
    ½   cup cold butter, cubed
    1   large egg, beaten
    ⅔   cup half-and-half cream
    1   cup heavy whipping cream
    2   Tbsp. confectioners' sugar
    ⅛   tsp. vanilla extract
         Additional butter
    1½   cups fresh strawberries, sliced

1. Preheat oven to 450°. Combine flour, sugar, baking powder and salt. Cut in butter until mixture resembles coarse crumbs. In another bowl, whisk egg and half-and-half. Add all at once to crumb mixture; stir just until moistened.
2. Spread batter into a greased 8-in. round baking pan, slightly building up the edges. Bake until golden brown, 16-18 minutes. Remove from pan; cool on a wire rack.
3. Beat heavy cream until it begins to thicken. Add confectioners' sugar and vanilla; beat until stiff peaks form. Split cake in half crosswise; butter bottom layer. Spoon half the strawberries over bottom layer. Spread with some whipped cream. Cover with top cake layer. Top with remaining berries and whipped cream. Cut into wedges.
1 PIECE: 381 cal., 25g fat (16g sat. fat), 98mg chol., 447mg sod., 32g carb. (8g sugars, 1g fiber), 6g pro.

PEAR TART

BLUEBERRY-BLACKBERRY RUSTIC TART

folded pastry with beaten egg; sprinkle with turbinado sugar.

4. Bake 55-60 minutes or until crust is golden brown and filling is bubbly. Using parchment, slide tart onto a wire rack to cool. If desired, serve with whipped cream.

1 SLICE: 464 cal., 17g fat (10g sat. fat), 67mg chol., 134mg sod., 74g carb. (38g sugars, 5g fiber), 7g pro.

APPLE PEAR CAKE

When my sister Catherine made her apple cake for me, I knew I needed the recipe. When I tried it, I added some pears from the trees on our acreage. This cake is so moist and tastes so good. Every time I make it, people want my recipe.
—*Mary Ann Lees, Centreville, AL*

- -

PREP: 25 min. • **BAKE:** 1 hour + cooling
MAKES: 12 servings

- 2 cups shredded peeled tart apples
- 2 cups shredded peeled pears
- 2 cups sugar
- 1¼ cups canola oil
- 1 cup raisins
- 1 cup chopped pecans
- 2 large eggs, room temperature, lightly beaten
- 1 tsp. vanilla extract
- 3 cups all-purpose flour
- 2 tsp. baking soda
- 2 tsp. ground cinnamon
- ½ tsp. ground nutmeg
- ½ tsp. salt

CREAM CHEESE FROSTING

- 3 oz. cream cheese, softened
- 3 cups confectioners' sugar
- ¼ cup butter, softened
- 2 Tbsp. whole milk
- ½ tsp. vanilla extract

1. In a large bowl, combine first 8 ingredients. Combine flour, baking soda, spices and salt; stir into the fruit mixture.

2. Pour into a greased 13x9-in. baking pan. Bake at 325° for 1 hour or until a toothpick inserted in the center comes out clean. Cool on a wire rack.

3. For frosting, in a large bowl, beat the cream cheese, confectioners' sugar and butter until smooth. Beat in the milk and vanilla; frost cake. Store in the refrigerator.

1 PIECE: 613 cal., 30g fat (6g sat. fat), 43mg chol., 306mg sod., 84g carb. (60g sugars, 3g fiber), 5g pro.

BLUEBERRY-BLACKBERRY RUSTIC TART

My dad would stop the car on the side of the road in Maine and say, "I smell blueberries." He had a pail ready. Then Mom would bake the wild berries in a cornmeal crust.
—*Priscilla Gilbert, Indian Harbour Beach, FL*

- -

PREP: 20 min. + chilling • **BAKE:** 55 min.
MAKES: 8 servings

- 2 cups all-purpose flour
- ⅓ cup sugar
- ¼ cup yellow cornmeal
- ⅔ cup cold butter, cubed
- ½ cup buttermilk

FILLING

- 4 cups fresh blueberries
- 2 cups fresh blackberries
- ⅔ cup sugar
- ⅓ cup all-purpose flour
- 2 Tbsp. lemon juice
- 1 large egg, beaten
- 2 Tbsp. turbinado (washed raw) sugar or coarse sugar
  Whipped cream, optional

1. In a large bowl, mix the flour, sugar and cornmeal; cut in butter cubes until crumbly. Gradually add buttermilk, tossing with a fork until dough holds together when pressed. Shape into a disk; wrap and refrigerate for 30 minutes or overnight.

2. Preheat oven to 375°. On a lightly floured surface, roll the dough into a 14-in. circle. Transfer to a parchment-lined baking sheet.

3. In a large bowl, combine berries, sugar, flour and lemon juice; spoon over crust to within 2 in. of edges. Fold pastry edge over filling, leaving center uncovered. Brush the

APPLE PEAR CAKE

CREAMY CANDY BAR PIE

Here's a very rich and creamy pie that tastes terrific. A small sliver is all most folks can handle.
—*Mary Ann Smith, Groton, NY*

PREP: 15 min. + chilling
BAKE: 35 min. + cooling
MAKES: 10 servings

- 5 Snickers candy bars (1.86 oz. each), cut into ¼-in. pieces
- 1 frozen pie crust (9 in.), baked
- 12 oz. cream cheese, softened
- ½ cup sugar
- 2 large eggs, room temperature
- ⅓ cup sour cream
- ⅓ cup peanut butter
- ⅔ cup semisweet chocolate chips
- 2 Tbsp. heavy whipping cream

1. Place candy bar pieces in the pie crust; set aside. In a large bowl, beat cream cheese and sugar until smooth. Add the eggs, sour cream and peanut butter; beat on low speed just until combined.

2. Pour into the crust. Bake at 325° until set, 35-40 minutes. Cool on wire rack.

3. In a large heavy saucepan, melt chocolate chips with cream over low heat; stir until smooth. Spread over filling. Refrigerate for 2 hours or overnight. Cut with a warm knife.

1 PIECE: 427 cal., 30g fat (15g sat. fat), 94mg chol., 255mg sod., 34g carb. (21g sugars, 1g fiber), 8g pro.

"Love it! Made one with the Snickers and the other with Reese's Peanut Butter Cups. We all liked the one with peanut butter cups better, but they were both delicious!"
—SYKES, TASTEOFHOME.COM

BEST LIME TART

BEST LIME TART

This treat is the perfect balance between tart and sweet, and the almonds in the crust are just wonderful. This is one of my husband's favorite desserts. It's sure to get rave reviews from your family, too!
—*Charis O'Connell, Mohnton, PA*

PREP: 35 min. • **BAKE:** 15 min. + chilling
MAKES: 12 servings

- 1¼ cups graham cracker crumbs
- 5 Tbsp. butter, melted
- ¼ cup ground almonds
- 3 Tbsp. sugar

FILLING
- 4 large egg yolks
- 1 can (14 oz.) sweetened condensed milk
- ½ cup lime juice
- 2 tsp. grated lime zest

TOPPING
- ½ cup heavy whipping cream
- 1 Tbsp. sugar
- ½ cup sour cream
- 1 tsp. grated lime zest
  Fresh raspberries and lime wedges

1. Preheat oven to 325°. In a small bowl, combine the graham cracker crumbs, butter, almonds and sugar. Press onto the bottom and up the sides of a greased 9-in. tart pan. Bake 15-18 minutes or until the edges are lightly browned.

2. In a large bowl, whisk egg yolks, milk, lime juice and zest. Pour over crust. Bake until center is almost set, 12-14 minutes. Cool on a wire rack. Refrigerate at least 2 hours.

3. In a large bowl, beat cream until it begins to thicken. Add sugar; beat until stiff peaks form. Fold in sour cream and grated lime zest. Spread over tart. Garnish with fresh raspberries and lime wedges.

1 SLICE: 288 cal., 16g fat (9g sat. fat), 112mg chol., 138mg sod., 31g carb. (26g sugars, 1g fiber), 5g pro.

RHUBARB MANDARIN CRISP

An attractive and unique dessert, this crisp is also a popular breakfast recipe at our house, served with a glass of milk rather than topped with ice cream. Since it calls for lots of rhubarb, it's a use for the bounty you harvest.
—*Rachael Vandendool, Barry's Bay, ON*

- -

PREP: 20 min. + standing • **BAKE:** 40 min.
MAKES: 12 servings

- 6 **cups chopped fresh or frozen rhubarb**
- 1½ **cups sugar**
- 5 **Tbsp. quick-cooking tapioca**
- 1 **can (11 oz.) mandarin oranges, drained**
- 1 **cup packed brown sugar**
- 1 **cup quick-cooking oats**
- ½ **cup all-purpose flour**
- ½ **tsp. salt**
- ½ **cup cold butter, cubed**
  Ice cream, optional

1. In a large bowl, toss the rhubarb, sugar and tapioca; let stand 15 minutes, stirring occasionally. Pour into a greased 13x9-in. baking pan. Top with the oranges.
2. In a large bowl, combine the brown sugar, oats, flour and salt. Cut in the butter until mixture resembles coarse crumbs; sprinkle evenly over oranges.
3. Bake at 350° for 40 minutes or until top is golden brown. Serve crisp with ice cream if desired.
NOTE: If using frozen rhubarb, measure rhubarb while still frozen, then thaw completely. Drain in a colander, but do not press liquid out.
1 SERVING: 323 cal., 8g fat (5g sat. fat), 20mg chol., 187mg sod., 62g carb. (48g sugars, 2g fiber), 2g pro.

BLACKBERRY COBBLER

My grandmother made this cobbler when I was a little girl. I can still remember the fun we had first picking blackberries together in the hills. Blackberries are my favorite filling, but this cobbler can also be made with apples.
—*Trudy Cinquie, Waynesville, NC*

- -

PREP: 20 min. • **BAKE:** 1 hour
MAKES: 8 servings

- 1 **cup butter, divided**
- 1 **cup plus 2 Tbsp. sugar, divided**
- 1 **cup water**
- 1½ **cups self-rising flour**
- ⅓ **cup whole milk, room temperature**
- 2 **cups fresh or frozen blackberries**
- ½ **to 1 tsp. ground cinnamon**

1. In a 10-in. round or oval baking dish, melt ½ cup butter; set aside. In a saucepan, heat 1 cup sugar and water until sugar is dissolved; set aside.
2. Place flour in a bowl; cut in remaining butter until mixture resembles fine crumbs. Add milk, stirring with a fork until dough leaves sides of bowl.
3. Turn out onto a floured surface; knead 3 or 4 times. Roll into an 11x9-in. rectangle. Spread berries over dough; sprinkle with cinnamon. Roll up, jelly-roll style. Cut into 8 slices. Carefully place slices in baking dish. Pour sugar syrup around slices (syrup will be absorbed).
4. Bake at 350° for 45 minutes. Sprinkle with remaining sugar; bake 15 minutes longer. Serve warm or cold.
NOTE: As a substitute for 1½ cups self-rising flour, place 2¼ tsp. baking powder and ¾ tsp. salt in a measuring cup. Add all-purpose flour to measure 1 cup. Combine with an additional ½ cup all-purpose flour.
1 SERVING: 410 cal., 23g fat (14g sat. fat), 63mg chol., 507mg sod., 50g carb. (30g sugars, 2g fiber), 3g pro.

RHUBARB MANDARIN CRISP

**PEACH-BLUEBERRY
CRUMBLE TART**

CHOCOLATE POUND CAKE

An excellent cake with ice cream, it's also delicate enough to serve small slices plain for a tea.
—*Ann Perry, Sierra Vista, AZ*

PREP: 20 min. • **BAKE:** 1½ hours + cooling
MAKES: 12 servings

- 8   milk chocolate bars (1.55 oz. each)
- 2   Tbsp. water
- ½   cup butter, softened
- 2   cups sugar
- 4   large eggs, room temperature
- 2   tsp. vanilla extract
- 2½ cups cake flour, sifted
- ½   tsp. salt
- ¼   tsp. baking soda
- 1   cup buttermilk
- ½   cup chopped pecans, optional
     Confectioners' sugar, optional

1. Preheat oven to 325°. In a saucepan, melt chocolate with water over low heat. Mixture will begin to harden.
2. In a large bowl, cream butter and sugar until light and fluffy. Add 1 egg at a time, beating well after each addition. Beat in the vanilla and chocolate mixture. Combine the flour, salt and soda; add to creamed mixture alternately with buttermilk. Fold in chopped pecans if desired.
3. Pour into a greased and floured 10-in. tube pan or fluted tube pan. Bake for 1½ hours or until a toothpick inserted in the center comes out clean. Let stand for 10 minutes before removing from pan to a wire rack to cool. Sprinkle with confectioners' sugar if desired.
1 SLICE: 353 cal., 11g fat (6g sat. fat), 93mg chol., 248mg sod., 59g carb. (36g sugars, 1g fiber), 5g pro.

PEACH-BLUEBERRY CRUMBLE TART

This easy-to-prepare tart is a family favorite, fresh out of the oven or at room temperature with a scoop of vanilla ice cream.
—*James Schend, Pleasant Prairie, WI*

PREP: 30 min. • **BAKE:** 35 min. + cooling
MAKES: 12 servings

- 1⅓ cups all-purpose flour
- ¼   cup sugar
- ¼   tsp. ground cinnamon
- ½   cup butter, melted
- 2   cups frozen unsweetened blueberries, thawed
- 2   cups frozen unsweetened sliced peaches, thawed
- 1   Tbsp. honey

CRUMB TOPPING
- ¼   cup all-purpose flour
- ¼   cup packed brown sugar
- ¼   cup old-fashioned oats
- ¼   cup chopped pecans
- ⅛   tsp. ground cloves
- 2   Tbsp. butter, melted

1. Preheat oven to 350°. In a small bowl, mix flour, sugar and cinnamon; stir in butter just until blended. Press into a 9-in. fluted tart pan with removable bottom. Bake 15-20 minutes or until lightly browned. Cool on a wire rack.
2. Meanwhile, in a large bowl, combine the blueberries, peaches and honey; toss to coat. In a small bowl, combine the first 5 topping ingredients; stir in butter.
3. Spoon fruit mixture into crust; sprinkle with topping. Bake at 350° 35-40 minutes or until topping is golden brown and filling is bubbly. Cool on a wire rack for at least 15 minutes before serving.
1 SLICE: 229 cal., 12g fat (6g sat. fat), 25mg chol., 70mg sod., 30g carb. (15g sugars, 2g fiber), 3g pro.

TEST KITCHEN TIP

Instead of buying buttermilk, you can place 1 Tbsp. white vinegar or lemon juice in a liquid measuring cup and add enough milk to measure 1 cup. Stir, then let stand for 5 minutes. Or you can substitute 1 cup of plain yogurt for the buttermilk.

CHOCOLATE
POUND CAKE

PINEAPPLE CARROT CAKE

PINEAPPLE CARROT CAKE

This moist cake with cream cheese frosting is the best I've ever eaten. It's simple to prep, too, since you don't have to grate fresh carrots.
—Jeanette McKenna, Vero Beach, FL

PREP: 20 min. • **BAKE:** 35 min. + cooling
MAKES: 12 servings

- 2 cups all-purpose flour
- 2 cups sugar
- 2 tsp. baking soda
- 2 tsp. ground cinnamon
- 1 tsp. salt
- 1½ cups vegetable oil
- 4 large eggs, room temperature
- 3 jars (4 oz. each) carrot baby food
- 1 can (8 oz.) crushed
    pineapple, drained
- ½ cup chopped walnuts
FROSTING
- 1 pkg. (8 oz.) cream cheese, softened
- ½ cup butter, softened
- 1 tsp. vanilla extract
- 3¾ cups confectioners' sugar
    Additional chopped walnuts and
    edible blossoms, optional

1. In a bowl, combine the dry ingredients. Add the oil, eggs and baby food; mix on low speed until well blended. Stir in pineapple and nuts. Pour into 2 greased and floured 9-in. round baking pans. Bake at 350° until a toothpick inserted in the center comes out clean, 35-40 minutes. Cool 10 minutes before removing from pans to wire racks to cool completely.

2. For frosting, in a bowl, beat cream cheese and butter until smooth. Beat in vanilla and confectioners' sugar until mixture reaches spreading consistency. Spread between layers and over top and sides of cake. Garnish with nuts and blossoms if desired. Store in the refrigerator.

1 SLICE: 798 cal., 46g fat (13g sat. fat), 112mg chol., 569mg sod., 92g carb. (70g sugars, 1g fiber), 7g pro.

**BUTTERY
COCONUT BARS**

BUTTERY COCONUT BARS

My coconut bars are an American version of a Filipino coconut cake called *bibingka*. These are a crispier, sweeter take on the Christmas tradition I grew up with.
—Denise Nyland, Panama City, FL

PREP: 20 min. + cooling
BAKE: 40 min. + cooling • **MAKES:** 3 dozen

- 2 cups all-purpose flour
- 1 cup packed brown sugar
- ½ tsp. salt
- 1 cup butter, melted
FILLING
- 3 large eggs, room temperature
- 1 can (14 oz.) sweetened
    condensed milk
- ½ cup all-purpose flour
- ¼ cup packed brown sugar
- ¼ cup butter, melted
- 3 tsp. vanilla extract
- ½ tsp. salt
- 4 cups sweetened shredded
    coconut, divided

1. Preheat oven to 350°. Line a 13x9-in. baking pan with parchment, letting ends extend up sides.

2. In a large bowl, mix flour, brown sugar and salt; stir in 1 cup melted butter. Press onto bottom of prepared pan. Bake until light brown, 12-15 minutes. Cool 10 minutes on a wire rack. Reduce oven setting to 325°.

3. In a large bowl, whisk the first 7 filling ingredients until blended; stir in 3 cups coconut. Pour over crust; sprinkle with remaining coconut. Bake until light golden brown, 25-30 minutes. Cool in pan on a wire rack. Lifting with parchment, remove from pan. Cut into bars.

1 BAR: 211 cal., 12g fat (8g sat. fat), 36mg chol., 166mg sod., 25g carb. (18g sugars, 1g fiber), 3g pro.

PRETTY PINK STRAWBERRY MOUSSE

This pretty pink dessert takes only minutes to prepare. Folks rave about its smooth texture and sweet berry flavor. I like to top servings with whipped cream and strawberries.
—*Jody Cottle, Rigby, ID*

PREP: 20 min. + chilling • **MAKES:** 8 servings

- 2 tsp. unflavored gelatin
- 2 Tbsp. cold water
- ¼ cup boiling water
- 1⅓ cups instant strawberry drink mix
- 2 cups heavy whipping cream
- 2 tsp. vanilla extract

1. In a small bowl, soften gelatin in cold water; let stand for 5 minutes. Stir in boiling water until gelatin is dissolved; cool for 10 minutes.
2. In a bowl, combine the drink mix, whipping cream and gelatin mixture until thickened. Beat in vanilla. Spoon into individual dishes; refrigerate for 1-2 hours or until set.
NOTE: This recipe was tested with Nesquik brand drink mix.
1 SERVING: 262 cal., 22g fat (14g sat. fat), 68mg chol., 111mg sod., 15g carb. (14g sugars, 0 fiber), 2g pro.

PEANUT BUTTER SHEET CAKE

I received the recipe for this cake from a minister's wife and my family loves it.
—*Brenda Jackson, Garden City, KS*

PREP: 15 min. • **BAKE:** 20 min. + cooling
MAKES: 24 servings

- 2 cups all-purpose flour
- 2 cups sugar
- 1 tsp. baking soda
- ½ tsp. salt
- 1 cup water
- ¾ cup butter, cubed
- ½ cup chunky peanut butter
- ¼ cup canola oil
- 2 large eggs, room temperature
- ½ cup buttermilk
- 1 tsp. vanilla extract

GLAZE
- ⅔ cup sugar
- ⅓ cup evaporated milk
- 1 Tbsp. butter
- ⅓ cup chunky peanut butter
- ⅓ cup miniature marshmallows
- ½ tsp. vanilla extract

PEANUT BUTTER SHEET CAKE

1. Preheat oven to 350°. Grease a 15x10x1-in. baking pan.
2. In a large bowl, whisk flour, sugar, baking soda and salt. In a small saucepan, combine water and butter; bring just to a boil. Stir in peanut butter and oil until blended. Stir into flour mixture. In a small bowl, whisk eggs, buttermilk and vanilla until blended; add to flour mixture, whisking constantly.
3. Transfer to prepared pan. Bake until a toothpick inserted in center comes out clean, 20-25 minutes.
4. Meanwhile, for glaze, combine sugar, milk and butter in a saucepan. Bring to a boil, stirring constantly; cook and stir 2 minutes. Remove from heat; stir in peanut butter, marshmallows and vanilla until blended. Spoon over warm cake, spreading evenly. Cool on a wire rack.
1 PIECE: 266 cal., 14g fat (5g sat. fat), 36mg chol., 222mg sod., 33g carb. (23g sugars, 1g fiber), 4g pro.

BANANA SPLIT SUPREME

Transform the classic flavor of a banana split into a whole new recipe! This is a cool, creamy treat with no last-minute fuss since you just pull it from the freezer. It always gets praise from our big family.
—*Marye Franzen, Gothenburg, NE*

PREP: 30 min. + freezing
MAKES: 12 servings

- 2 cups confectioners' sugar
- 1 cup evaporated milk
- ¾ cup semisweet chocolate chips
- ¾ cup butter, divided
- 24 Oreo cookies, crushed
- 3 to 4 medium firm bananas, cut into ½-in. slices
- 2 qt. vanilla ice cream, softened, divided
- 1 can (20 oz.) crushed pineapple, drained
- 1 jar (10 oz.) maraschino cherries, drained and halved
- ¾ cup chopped pecans
  Whipped topping, optional

1. In a large saucepan, combine sugar, milk, chocolate chips and ½ cup butter. Bring to a boil over medium heat; cook and stir for 8 minutes. Remove from the heat and cool completely.

2. Meanwhile, melt the remaining butter; toss with cookie crumbs. Press into a greased 13x9-in. pan. Freeze for 15 minutes. Arrange banana slices over crust; spread with 1 qt. ice cream. Top with 1 cup chocolate sauce. Freeze for 1 hour. Refrigerate remaining chocolate sauce. Spread the remaining ice cream over dessert; top with pineapple, cherries and chopped pecans. Cover and freeze overnight.

3. Remove from the freezer 10 minutes before serving. Reheat the chocolate sauce. Cut dessert into squares; if desired, serve with whipped topping and chocolate sauce.

1 PIECE: 540 cal., 29g fat (14g sat. fat), 61mg chol., 284mg sod., 71g carb. (57g sugars, 2g fiber), 6g pro.

TIGER BUTTER CANDY

This candy is big on peanut butter flavor and fun to make.
—*Pamela Pogue, Mineola, TX*

TAKES: 20 min. • **MAKES:** about 1½ lbs.

- 1 lb. white candy coating, coarsely chopped
- ½ cup chunky peanut butter
- ½ cup semisweet chocolate chips
- 4 tsp. half-and-half cream

1. In a microwave, melt candy coating and peanut butter; stir until smooth. Pour onto a foil-lined baking sheet coated with cooking spray; spread into a thin layer.

2. Repeat with chocolate chips and cream. Pour and swirl over peanut butter layer. Freeze 5 minutes or until set. Break into small pieces.

1½ OZ. CANDY: 225 cal., 14g fat (9g sat. fat), 1mg chol., 40mg sod., 25g carb. (23g sugars, 1g fiber), 2g pro.

BANANA SPLIT SUPREME

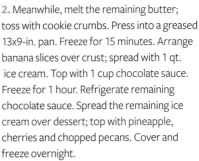

FROSTY WATERMELON ICE

CHERRY GELATIN SUPREME

When I was growing up, this yummy, simple dessert was always on the menu at holiday get-togethers. Years ago, my aunt gave me the recipe. Now when I make it for my family, I think of her.

—Janice Rathgeb, Brighton, IL

PREP: 20 min. + chilling • **MAKES:** 12 servings

    2   cups water, divided
    1   pkg. (3 oz.) cherry gelatin
    1   can (21 oz.) cherry pie filling
    1   pkg. (3 oz.) lemon gelatin
    3   oz. cream cheese, softened
    ⅓   cup mayonnaise
    1   can (8 oz.) crushed
        pineapple, undrained
    1   cup miniature marshmallows
    ½   cup heavy whipping cream, whipped
    2   Tbsp. chopped pecans

1. In a large saucepan, bring 1 cup water to a boil. Stir in cherry gelatin until dissolved. Stir in pie filling. Pour into an 11x7-in. dish. Cover and refrigerate for 2 hours or until set.
2. In a small saucepan, bring remaining water to a boil. Stir in lemon gelatin until dissolved. In a small bowl, beat the cream cheese and mayonnaise until smooth. Beat in lemon gelatin and pineapple. Cover and refrigerate for 45 minutes.
3. Fold in the marshmallows and whipped cream. Spoon over cherry layer; sprinkle with chopped pecans. Cover and refrigerate for 2 hours or until set.
1 PIECE: 248 cal., 12g fat (5g sat. fat), 24mg chol., 101mg sod., 34g carb. (31g sugars, 1g fiber), 2g pro.

"My mom used to make this recipe. It was delicious! I think I'll make it for this holiday weekend."
—DARLENEL, TASTEOFHOME.COM

FROSTY WATERMELON ICE

For a different way to serve watermelon, try this make-ahead frozen dessert. It's so refreshing on a summer day...and you don't have to worry about seeds while you're enjoying it.
—Kaaren Jurack, Manassas, VA

PREP: 20 min. + freezing • **MAKES:** 4 servings

    1   tsp. unflavored gelatin
    2   Tbsp. water
    2   Tbsp. lime juice
    2   Tbsp. honey
    4   cups cubed seedless
        watermelon, divided

1. In a microwave-safe bowl, sprinkle the unflavored gelatin over water; let stand 1 minute. Microwave on high for 40 seconds. Stir and let stand for 1-2 minutes or until gelatin is completely dissolved.
2. Place lime juice, honey and gelatin mixture in a blender. Add 1 cup watermelon; cover and process until blended. Add remaining watermelon, 1 cup at a time, processing after each addition until smooth.
3. Transfer to a shallow dish; freeze until almost firm. In a chilled bowl, beat with an electric mixer until mixture is bright pink. Divide among 4 serving dishes; freeze, covered, until firm. Remove from freezer 15-20 minutes before serving.
¾ CUP: 81 cal., 0 fat (0 sat. fat), 0 chol., 3mg sod., 21g carb. (18g sugars, 1g fiber), 1g pro.
DIABETIC EXCHANGES: 1 fruit, ½ starch.

**CHERRY GELATIN
SUPREME**

Recipe Index